# Advance Praise

Leadership coaching is gaining growing acceptance in India as an important input in preparing senior business leaders for the top jobs. The authors' unique approach of presenting real-life case studies is very effective in providing insights into common issues that leaders deal with, and how they can be handled.

*Roopa Kuduva, Managing Director & Chief Executive Officer, CRISIL*

An engrossing account of real-life cases that highlight the complex situations of leadership development. It is enriched by the fact that it is put together by accomplished professionals who have been on both sides of the table. Told in a narrative that is engaging, the book is a great ally for mentors and aspiring leaders alike.

*Harsh Goenka, Chairman, RPG Enterprises*

This book is the 'Panchatantra' of Executive coaching. The authors, who are pioneers in Executive coaching in India, have developed keen insights into the challenges facing aspirants to the corner office, and have presented real-life case studies to illustrate the core tenets, distilled from their insights. The stories themselves are very absorbing and the underlying truths are even more so.

*R. Seshasayee , Executive Vice Chairman, Ashok Leyland*

These cases are stories of our everyday professional lives. We see, in each one of them, a bit of our own selves, a slice of our context, and shadows of our colleagues. Leaders aspiring for the 'Corner Room' need to be able to style flex, as one dominant style will have limitations.

*Santrupt Misra, CEO, Carbon Black Business and Director,*
*Group Human Resources, Aditya Birla Group*

When it comes to developing global leadership competencies, our 'world view' and what we choose to give attention to, from a contextual intelligence perspective becomes important—how we use language, how we demonstrate nonverbal behaviour, our communication style, our attitudes and values towards groups and community and our time consciousness. All these aspects define and shape our leadership. These cases illustrate how coaches with credibility, senior leadership experience and global exposure are able to help enhance the contextual intelligence of their coachees.

*Anil Sachdeva, Founder & CEO,*
*The School of Inspired Leadership-SOIL*

This book takes us through twenty-five enriching journeys of personal and professional development. The authors distil very valuable, experiential, insightful and practical insights from these narratives, relating them to the Indian context, and presenting them in a creative and very engaging format. A book with immense value, not just for aspiring leaders, but for all professionals looking to make an impact and a difference.

*Anand Nayak, Executive Vice President,*
*Corporate Human Resources and Member,*
*Corporate Management Committee, ITC Limited*

A path-breaking book set in the Indian context that wonderfully blends key coaching insights with reinforcing case studies. The authors' deep understanding of coaching comes alive in this easy-to-read book that distils the essence of typical leadership challenges encountered by persons aiming for the C-Suite. A must-read for coaching practitioners and senior leaders!

*A. Krishna, Senior Vice President (HR), Bosch Ltd*

Most often, development of leaders is left to chance—but this book shows how transformational changes in behaviour can be obtained by focused coaching inputs. A must-read for all CEOs to understand how they can develop their future leaders. Equally, a must-read for all aspiring CEOs to gain insights into the barriers to realizing their leadership potential and how they could overcome them.

*Krish Shankar, Executive Director, Human Resources, Bharti Airtel Ltd*

Behaviour is the 'vehicle' through which we deliver what we know and can do. These behaviours are shaped by our attitudes and beliefs towards many things we encounter. While these attitudes and beliefs are useful aids in our life journey and allow us to 'fit in' and grow, when the world around us or our context changes significantly, these beliefs can become obstacles to effectiveness. The case studies in this book illustrate how leaders' attitudes and beliefs need to be worked with to bring about sustainable behavioural change for greater effectiveness.

*Zahid Gangjee , CEO, Zahid Gangjee & Associates*

While more and more leaders seem to be realizing the need to leverage coaching to improve their effectiveness, the cases in this book raise important questions about some of the conditions that need to be present for such coaching interventions to work. This includes searching questions that the coach and coachee need to ask themselves.

*R. R. Nair, Independent Director, CEO Coach and leadership development facilitator for leading Global and Indian corporations*

Each of the 25 vignettes captures different situations and addresses challenges that CEOs would encounter as they grow and make a difference to their organizations. The stories focus on getting people to bring about change by themselves, which is the true secret of effective coaching. A must-read for all aspiring leaders since it helps anticipate potential challenges in their own evolution as leaders.

*Govind Iyer, Partner, Egon Zehnder*

# Are You Ready for the Corner Office?

Thank you for choosing a SAGE product!
If you have any comment, observation or feedback,
I would like to personally hear from you.
*Please write to me at* **contactceo@sagepub.in**

**Vivek Mehra,** Managing Director and CEO, SAGE India.

## Bulk Sales

SAGE India offers special discounts
for purchase of books in bulk.
We also make available special imprints
and excerpts from our books on demand.

*For orders and enquiries, write to us at*

Marketing Department
SAGE Publications India Pvt Ltd
B1/I-1, Mohan Cooperative Industrial Area
Mathura Road, Post Bag 7
New Delhi 110044, India

*E-mail us at* **marketing@sagepub.in**

## Get to know more about SAGE

Be invited to SAGE events, get on our mailing list.
*Write today to* **marketing@sagepub.in**

This book is also available as an e-book.

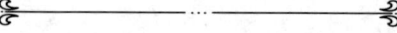

# Are You Ready for the Corner Office?

*Insights from 25 Executive Coaching Experiences*

Pradipta K. Mohapatra

Ganesh Chella

Los Angeles | London | New Delhi
Singapore | Washington DC | Melbourne

*First published in 2014 by*

**SAGE Publications India Pvt Ltd**
B1/I-1 Mohan Cooperative Industrial Area
Mathura Road, New Delhi 110 044, India
*www.sagepub.in*

**SAGE Publications Inc**
2455 Teller Road
Thousand Oaks, California 91320, USA

**SAGE Publications Ltd**
1 Oliver's Yard, 55 City Road
London EC1Y 1SP, United Kingdom

**SAGE Publications Asia-Pacific Pte Ltd**
3 Church Street
#10-04 Samsung Hub
Singapore 049483

Published by Vivek Mehra for SAGE Publications India Pvt Ltd, typeset in 11/13 Minion Pro by RECTO Graphics, Delhi.

**Library of Congress Cataloging-in-Publication Data**

Mohapatra, Pradipta K.
  Are you ready for the corner office? : insights from 25 executive coaching experiences / Pradipta K. Mohapatra, Ganesh Chella.
    pages cm
  1. Executive coaching—India. 2. Executives—India. 3. Career development—India. I. Chella, Ganesh. II. Title.
  HD30.42.I48M64        658.4'07124—dc23        2014        2013050061

**ISBN: 978-81-321-1372-0 (PB)**

**The SAGE Team:** Sachin Sharma, Archa Bhatnagar, Rajib Chatterjee and Dally Verghese

# Contents

## Section C: Shaping Attitudes and Beliefs

*Why Attitudes and Beliefs Affect a Leader's*
*Effectiveness—Zahid Gangjee*

## Section D: Developing New Skills, Styles and Behaviours

*Why Skills, Style and Behaviours Make Such a Huge Difference*
*to a Leader's Effectiveness—Santrupt Misra*

## Section E: Acquiring Global Competencies

*Why Global Competencies Are So Critical Today—Anil Sachdev*

## Section F: Managing Career Transitions

*Why Career Transitions Are Always Challenging—Aroon Joshi*

## Section G: Grappling with Emerging Executive and Entrepreneurial Agendas

*How Do Executives and Entrepreneurs Grapple with
Their Compelling Agendas—R. Ramaraj*

## Section H: Enhancing Coaching Effectiveness

*What Contributes to Coaching Effectiveness—R. R. Nair*

# Acknowledgements

As facilitators in CFI's Post Graduate Program in Executive Coaching, participants would constantly ask us for coaching cases to help them understand on-the-ground coaching issues better. While we did attempt writing a few, we were never quite happy with what we produced and the demand for good-quality cases only kept getting louder. Similarly, when we were in front of prospective sponsors and clients of coaching services, they too would request us for coaching cases and examples. While we would address the need by narrating cases in the old Indian story-telling way, we would always go back wishing we had something more substantial and well researched to offer.

The huge realization that real-life coaching cases are so rare to find in the world is what motivated us to engage in this seminal effort which we believe will help not only coach interns, coachees and their sponsors but also executives holding high offices in loneliness!

If this book has become a reality, we owe it in big measure to all the program participants turned CFI coaches, clients and sponsors for creating in us the creative tension and the burning desire to make it happen. To every one of them we would like to say, '*Thank you so much for asking persistently!*'

Confidentiality and privacy is at the very heart of a coaching relationship. It's a place where coachees are comfortable discovering their unused potential, exploring their fallibilities and uncovering their blind spots. While doing that is by itself a creditable feat, giving their coaches and case contributors the permission to document and publish it in the interest of promoting insights about leader development is truly remarkable. We salute every single coachee for having taken the leap of faith and readily agreeing to be the heroes and central characters in this book. *We do not wish to name you but we will forever remember you!*

The coaches and case contributors are seasoned corporate executives and professionals who are mostly concerned about making a difference to their organizations and clients through their wisdom and expertise. We wanted them to not just tell us their coaching experiences but also become authors, albeit temporarily. This was not easy. They had to listen to our editorial critique and oblige us with multiple iterations in the interest of producing this seminal piece of work.

Dr Anand Kasturi, Kalpana Tatavarti, N. Raghunandan, Oscar Braganza, P. S. Srinivasan, Pradeep Menon, Pradip Shroff, R. R. Nair, Saroja Kannan, Savitha Mathai, Sharada Chandrasekar, R. Sridhar, Srinivas Uppaluri, Sundar Parthasarathy, Suresh Thawani and V. D. Augustine—*this book is entirely thanks to your efforts; you have every reason to be proud of the shape it has taken.*

While the 24 cases threw up interesting insights and perspectives about leader development and by themselves had a teachable point of view, we were keen that we embellish it with further distilled nuggets of wisdom. To perform this onerous task, we called upon CFI's Honorary Fellows. They read a set of cases pertaining to each theme and shared their powerful insights.

Aroon Joshi, Dr Santrupt Misra, R. R. Nair, R. Ramaraj, Anil Sachdev, Dr B. J. Prashantham and Zahid Gangjee—*please accept our most sincere appreciation for your contribution.*

Writing a book is a complex project. Fortunately, we had little to worry on this front because we had the able support of the CFI and totus team including Ashok Jayaram, Saroja Kannan, Charulatha Rajesh, Dr S. Sabesan, Deepak Bhorkhade, Lalitha Arun and Sumathi Mohan. Big thanks to all of them.

Our proposal to publish a book was approved by our publishers in a week's time. Such speed on the part of the Executive Editor, R. Chandra Sekhar, was hugely motivating and inspiring and we remain ever thankful for that. We would like to specifically thank Sachin Sharma for coordinating the entire book project so efficiently on behalf of SAGE.

# Introduction

How will you know if you are ready for the corner office? How will you prepare yourself to get there? How will you succeed, once you are there? How can you learn to enjoy doing all this and stay happy? As a seasoned senior executive, you recognize by now that the wisdom to find answers to these questions does not come from business schools, leader development programs or the World Wide Web.

You realize that you have to find answers to these questions all by yourself, because the answers are unique to you and your situation. You also realize that the journey to find your answers is very personal and intimate. You discover that unless you find the answers by yourself, you are unlikely to be convinced about its truth and to be committed to acting on them. In fact, you abhor the free and unsolicited advice that comes your way about how to get to the top.

The only thing you wish you had was a person you could trust, one who would respect you, listen to you, understand you, ask the right questions to help you gain clarity, challenge you to see your reality differently and support you in finding those answers and finally putting them to use.

We along with a community of accomplished coaches across the country, had the privilege and honour of listening to at least 500 motivated, talented and ambitious leaders who were either aspiring to get to the corner office or had already found a place there or were in the process of getting there. They told us their stories with candour and passion. They leveraged the helping relationship that we extended to them and achieved what they aspired to. While they solved their problems and realized their unused potential, they demonstrated their gratitude by leaving behind some invaluable treasures for us and for many generations to come.

Yes, they left behind at least 500 of their heart-warming, touching and inspiring stories about their journeys towards the corner office, about how they figured if they were ready for it, how they prepared themselves to get there, how they learnt to succeed once they got there, and how they managed to enjoy the journey. Of course the term 'corner office' is really a metaphor for anything significant that these leaders wanted to achieve in their professional careers and personal lives.

This book is nothing but a collection of twenty-five such stories touching upon twenty-three experiential insights. It is meant to inspire, help and educate many, many others who are on a similar quest. The coaches who coached these leaders and the authors who put this narrative together are merely midwives. The real heroes and heroines are the coachees whose journeys were so educative.

This book is also meant to assure them that coaching can in fact be a great source of support in many of the challenges that they face, as is evidenced by the stories that we are about to share with you.

This book will also be of immense value to other coaches and coach aspirants who are excited about the possibility of making a difference through, what we believe, is the noblest profession in the corporate world.

Of course, that is not how the book idea originated. There was certain serendipity involved.

## The Genesis of This Book

In our professional practice as executive coaches we have had the opportunity to meet and interact with hundreds of prospective executive coaches, coach interns, prospective clients and sponsors of executive coaching engagements. In all these interactions we are almost always called upon to explain what Executive Coaching is, how it works, when it does not work, what kind of problems and needs it can address, how these are addressed, when it fails and what contributes to effectiveness and how organizations can embark on this journey and so on. Given the nascent stage of the profession and the amount of myths and misinformation surrounding the subject, our efforts to answer these questions often reach a point where any amount of theoretical definitions and conceptual clarifications just don't help deliver the message. When that does happen we switch to telling them a few real-life coaching stories and their eyes light up and they are all ears. Through these stories they are able to quickly put themselves in the shoes of the coachee or the coach or the sponsor and understand how it all comes together to make a difference.

As some of us sat down and reflected about how other professions address similar issues and enhance effectiveness of their practice, we realized that documented case histories have indeed played a very crucial role. For example, at the heart of education and practice in the legal profession is past judgements. The medical field is no different. Every right and wrong diagnosis and medical procedure contributes immensely to the body of knowledge about that specific field of practice. Same is the case with the field of psychotherapy. Right from the days of Carl Rogers, therapists have relied on the taped transcripts to evaluate the efficacy of their work.

In fact, it appears that it is a professional obligation on the part of those who practice this profession and those who benefit from it, to participate in creating this experience-based body of knowledge that can serve future users well.

As pioneers in the field, we decided to take the first step in this direction by systematically documenting the executive coaching cases that our certified coaches have been involved in so that we are able to throw light on the leader development needs and challenges of those who are leading businesses and functions in organizations large and small. This intimate first person understanding of what leaders need in their journey of development is hitherto not well understood at all.

Through our efforts at documenting coaching cases, we hope to throw some light on what it takes to get to the corner office and stay and succeed there.

That is why this book is addressed to the large number of CEOs and CEO aspirants who can feel reassured that the struggles and challenges that they are experiencing in their journey to the top are not unique to them and that they are very typical in the life-long developmental journey of any leader.

We believe that this book is a definitive step on our part to establish coaching as a credible professional practice that can be subjected to professional review, critique, assessment and measurement of effectiveness.

It will also help us go beyond the placebo effect of coaching (or the feel good factor) and clearly establish how coaching change actually occurs.

This is really the reason and inspiration behind the book.

## The Conceptual Scaffolding of the Book

Over the past seven years, we and the community of coaches that we have been associated with were privy to over 500 coaching cases through a combination of the coaching engagements we have managed and the cases that we have reviewed as a part of our Coach Education Programs.

These 500 coaching cases have helped us gain deep insights into the needs and challenges that organizations and senior executives experience in fulfilling the leadership demands and addressing the resultant developmental imperatives.

Through the insights from these cases and our engagement with clients and sponsors we have begun to recognize that the needs of current and prospective CEOs and other senior leaders fall into three overlapping themes:

1. Developing the competencies to meet the demands of their current roles or prepare themselves for future roles in a national or global context. This of course includes catching up urgently on missed developmental milestones, an issue that will be discussed in detail in the chapter on the human side of leader development. This broad theme includes the following sub-themes:

   (a) Developing one's emotional intelligence
   (b) Developing the right attitudes and beliefs
   (c) Developing the requisite skills, style and behaviours
   (d) Developing competencies that are required to succeed globally

2. Learning to manage the transitions in their careers effectively
3. Addressing the executive and entrepreneurial agendas to promote well-considered decision making

We have observed that all organizations, irrespective of size and scale, seem to be grappling with issues and needs around these three broad themes.

After reviewing insights from these 500 cases across these three themes, we were able to distil at least twenty-three insights covering unique situations, needs and dilemmas, each representing one facet of leader development and leadership effectiveness.

We then went about identifying one outstanding case to showcase each insight. Having selected the case, we invited the coach who handled that coaching engagement to document the case for us. So, the coaches who handled these interesting cases have collectively been able to document and present to us twenty-five cases covering the twenty-three chosen experiential insights under these three broad themes.

Each chapter deals with one insight, illustrated through one or two cases. A brief author preamble precedes each case.

We have also presented three cases which help showcase the challenges in making coaching effective.

We invited five eminent coaches, leaders and, above all, believers of coaching to share with us their commentary about the experiential insights within each theme. Their wisdom has certainly added to the richness of insights in the book.

## The Case Writing Style That Our Case Contributors Have Adopted

It is always a challenge to put into words a coaching relationship that lasts over seven to nine months and has involved several hours of intense human interactions and bound by a non-negotiable commitment of confidentiality. The tools that coaches deploy, the insights that coachees gain, the questions that coaches ask and the actual behavioural changes that coachees demonstrate are too intense and too dynamic to be fully captured within the confines of a few hundred words.

However, unless coaches do this, coaching will always remain a mystery and its efficacy an ever debatable subject. What this really means is that the coaches who present their cases have not presented everything that took place between them and their coachee. It is at best a brief peek into the facet of coaching need that it belongs to, a summary of what transpired between the coach and the coachee and the nature of work that was done, of course highlighting the leader development challenge they helped address.

Since the book is addressed primarily to CEOs and CEO aspirants, the coaches who have handled the cases have written it in the style of a story. This may not necessarily meet research and academic standards. For the same reason, we have kept out coaching-related theories, concepts and models.

All case contributors who are the coaches who actually handled the coaching engagement have attempted to follow a somewhat uniform structure in presenting their coaching-cases starting with a context followed by the broad need and then the new insights, the goals and action plans. While these are mostly presented in a sequential manner, in reality coaching engagements seldom move in such an orderly and predictable manner. There are often delays, contradictions, reluctance and even resistance. It is quite likely that many of these road blocks have not been presented in the interest of preserving privacy and demonstrating respect for the coachee. Readers are therefore well advised to recognize that the reality on the ground was much harsher.

While the contributors have tried very hard to articulate how change actually occurred after goals and action plans were identified, it is quite likely that readers might perceive that change appears to have occurred through some magical process.

Beyond all this it must be recognized that clients who seek coaching, unlike clients who seek therapy, are psychologically well adjusted, highly motivated successful executives. As a result even small doses of strong coaching intervention can provide them with enough insights to make transformational changes. To that extent, the needs that coaches work on are not earth shatteringly complex but surprisingly simple. What was perhaps not realized, until the point they sought help, was their blind spots and how these had prevented them from seeing the reality and the hesitation they had in seeking help. However, once they voluntarily accepted to seek help and were able to define their needs well, half the battle was won.

As you read the cases you will also recognize that every coach has a certain unique style. To that extent the kind of strategies and interventions that they follow are likely to revolve around their unique styles. Their writing styles are also unique and different and we have left it that way. Some have, for instance, written in first person and some in third person!

## Confidentiality

All the cases have been documented and presented in this book with the express permission of the coachees. Their wholehearted support and permission in the interest of furthering education must be lauded. In the interest of confidentiality our case contributors have masked all elements of identity including the coachee's name, organization's name, the industry, the city of residence and so on. To further ensure that the coach–coachee relationship is also anonymous, the identity of the coach who worked with a specific coachee has been masked and pseudo names have been used. We have, of course, presented the names and brief profiles of all case contributors in alphabetical order towards the end of the book.

## How to Read This Book

There is no particular order or sequence to the book. Readers can pick up and read cases one at a time. After all, we have really tried to tell a real life story. So, start where your heart takes you and then keep reading on!

In a chapter titled 'An Introduction to Typical Coaching Processes and Some of the Frequently Used Terms' which you will find towards the end of the book, we have outlined an overview of how coaches typically approach a coaching engagement as well as explained some of key terms in **Coaching**. Readers may refer to this chapter should they have questions about some of the technical aspects of a coaching engagement that find mention in the cases.

# SECTION A

# The Corner Office Seen through the Keyhole of Executive Coaching

# 1

# Executive Coaching in the Indian Context*

The purpose of this book is not to conceptually explain what coaching is, or how it works on the ground, or what the taxonomies in the field are. It is, however, important to take a brief look at executive coaching as it has evolved in the Indian context so that we are able to appreciate the cases better. For this purpose, we present here some excerpts from the research done and documented by Ganesh Chella in his book *Creating a Helping Organisation*.

While executive coaching in a formal sense in India is perhaps less than a decade old, there is already an adequate amount of practitioners' insight to confirm that we are part consciously and part instinctively incorporating certain unique Indian elements into our model of executive coaching. It is important to recognize these unique dimensions when we set up executive coaching processes and frameworks within our organizations so that they are effective in achieving their intended purpose.

*Source: Excerpts from the book *Creating a Helping Organisation—5 Engaging Ways to Promote Employee Performance, Growth and Well-Being* by Ganesh Chella.

## The Three Distinct Elements of Indianness

There are at least three areas where there are very distinct elements of Indianness that are evident in the need for and in the nature and style of coaching engagements in India.

### a. The Current Drivers for Executive Coaching in India

Our country's exciting economic and business context is the most significant driver for executive coaching. Quite simply, every large Indian corporation is looking at a three or four fold growth in revenues within the next four or five years. These projections are based on some very concrete evidence of potential opportunity and there is an extremely high likelihood that it will happen. However as business leaders begin to look at the strategic drivers that will help them achieve their plans they find the leadership void to be the biggest stumbling block. While lack of availability of leaders in enough numbers is one dimension of the void, the absence of contextually appropriate critical competencies among existing leaders is an even more serious dimension of the void. This void is created by several factors.

First and foremost, the sheer size of many of the leadership roles in functional or business domains have expanded very dramatically in the last few years and is expected to expand even more exponentially in the coming years. Be it the Head of Procurement or the Head of Sales or the Head of HR or the Head of Manufacturing or the Head of a business line, the sheer job size in terms of what they are accountable for has become huge. Many leaders have never ever managed roles with this level of accountability.

It is not just the job size that is causing the leadership void. It is the complexity that is adding to the gravity of the situation. Many of the projected revenues for example are expected to come from new markets, often outside the country. A lot of this growth is also requiring leaders to reinvent or innovate existing business models to suit new markets and new customer needs.

Leaders will also have to remain flexible in the face of deeper, faster and more frequent economic cycles, constant technological changes and frequent geopolitical tensions. Finally, leaders of today will need to lead a workforce that has rapidly changing sociocultural values, needs and preferences.

Many of today's Indian leaders are also expected to lead globally. With global markets, a global supply chain and of course a global workforce, Indian leaders are expected to learn and demonstrate skills and competencies that do not come to many of them naturally, given their cultural context.

As a result, the typical coaching needs that one is witnessing among Indian leaders is often somewhat different from the typical coaching needs that one sees among let us say in North American leaders. For example a lot of the coaching data in the US suggests that coaching is often used to correct or modify typical narcissistic or aggressive or alpha-male behaviours which are very characteristic of a highly individualized and achievement, control and power oriented culture. Coaches in India are mostly working on needs that are somewhat different. Recent research undertaken by a leading coaching institution to analyze about 140 coaching cases offers some very interesting insights. Over 40 per cent of coachees or clients seem to need coaching to enhance self-esteem, increase their confidence, become more assertive, learn to say no, delegate more effectively by holding on to one's role boundary, develop a much more formal process based leadership style or present oneself well and display executive presence. Clearly, all of these are indicative of leaders originating from a typical collectivist society learning to operate in a global environment influenced by strong western values.

Ineffective transition is yet another driver for executive coaching. Given the shortage of leaders many were promoted to higher pay grades with the fond hope that they would figure things out and make the real transition from one work level to another. Unfortunately, many did not receive help to even understand what the transition actually meant or given support to actually make the transition. As a result many of the transitions were derailed somewhere along the way. Most transition needs at a leadership level revolve around developing a more effective delegation style, developing the ability to think strategically and see the big picture, developing the ability to respect and lead other functions, giving up one's functional loyalty and developing the ability to engage in developmental relationships to nurture talent.

The leadership void is real for organizations large, medium and small and all of them are actively considering executive coaching as one of the important interventions to fill the void. While some large organizations have managed to integrate executive coaching into their Learning and Talent Development processes and are therefore able to embark on the journey in a well thought through manner, others are reaching out to coaches based on exigency.

We are beginning to witness a keen interest in executive coaching even among entrepreneurial organizations and family businesses with many seeking coaching and mentoring help through formal and informal sources to manage their challenges of growth and succession.

We are also seeing private equity firms reaching out to executive coaches or mentors to help the CEOs of their portfolio companies develop new perspectives, acquire new skills or modify their styles so that they are able to achieve the potential that they saw in them. These are indeed the drivers for Executive coaching in India.

## b. Our Help Seeking Behaviours

In the US or in many of the western cultures, employees have had a long history of seeking help from formal and professional sources like counsellors and therapists. It would be fair to assume that a good number of executives would have had at least one visit or interaction with a counsellor or therapist sometime in their life. As a result I believe that when the western coaching model was built, it was in many ways influenced by the existing counselling and therapy models in terms of engagement processes, ethical considerations including confidentiality, client–therapist relationships, commercial terms and so on. Also, many of the mental health professionals in these countries who have entered the field of executive coaching brought in with them some of the cultural elements of their earlier profession. I would therefore call the classical western coaching model a *'therapy minus model'* set in a business context.

We have examined in great detail the sources from which we in India have tended to seek help. It is evident that a lot of our help currently comes from trusted but informal sources starting of course with the family but also including friends, ex bosses, informal mentors and others in one's social and professional network. Seeking formal help has never been popular. In fact, there continues to be a lot of stigma attached to seeking help from a counsellor or therapist. As a result, even as we build our coaching model, we are in many ways influenced by the trusted informal mentoring models in terms of engagement processes, mentor–protégé relationships and ethical considerations including confidentiality. The average Indian executive wants his coach to be as good as or even better than his informal mentor, guru or guide. He wants to work with a Coach that he can look up to. Given that we are not influenced by the baggage of counselling and therapy, I would like to call the Indian coaching model a *'Mentor plus model'*. While the word **mentor** refers to the warmth, respect and trust in the relationship, the word **plus** refers to the additional dimensions of clear boundaries, rigour of training, ethical considerations, ongoing professional development, supervision and so on that must now be incorporated into the relationship. While the past experience of a mentor has strongly influenced our expectations from our coaches, the onus is on coaches to focus on the plus and ensure quality in the way they set up and engage in their coaching relationships.

## c. Our Expectations from Our Coaches and How We Would Like to Set Up and Manage Our Coaching Relationships

Given our preference for a *'Mentor plus model'*, there are at least two key factors coachees or clients seem to consider in selecting a coach or in defining who would be an ideal helper. First and foremost, coaches are expected to possess sound wisdom and deep business experience and not just be proficient in techniques and models. Coachees also want to work with Coaches who are typically older and 'have been there and done that'.

Second, since most clients are not used to going to a therapist or counsellor they would like to experience a safe, warm and informal setting with a high level of trust and a sound relationship before they can get into the actual coaching process. The whole effort of building chemistry, getting acquainted, knowing each others' background and striking a personal chord is critical for coaches and coachees to feel comfortable to work with one another.

Our cultural context also demands that the coaching relationship and engagement process not be so contractual. First and foremost a coach in India cannot approach the coaching engagement as a session to session relationship with a fee for each session. While some western models tend to promote the practice of establishing Return on Investment (RoI) for each session and a fee for each session, many consider this highly inappropriate in India. It would be important for the coach to see the coachee as a complete and evolving human being engaged in a relationship that has a sense of continuity and not as a client, one session at a time. In that sense, the relationship needs to be a lot more collaborative and holistic with continuity and a lot less contractual. In fact, many clients resist the idea of even signing a contract because they consider it too cold and formal. Second, it is also necessary for coaches to be available to their coachees for a lot of spontaneous support and not strictly go by number of hours or sessions. Third, it is common for coaches to be called upon to act as mentors on some occasion during the relationship by passing on some wisdom, teaching a skill or practice or sharing some relevant information. Coaches in India must therefore learn to skilfully switch roles from coach to mentor in consultation with their clients and fulfil the role of a mentor when appropriate keeping in mind ethical considerations and not flatly turn down the request. Finally, most coaches and coachees prefer face to face discussions and avoid phone based coaching and rightfully so.

## Coaching Is One of the Developmental Experiences

Organizations have been addressing their leader development needs for decades through a range of interventions before the advent of Executive Coaching. So, it is important to clarify if we see coaching replacing other leader developmental interventions or if we see it as being superior to such interventions. The answer is an absolute NO. Neither is executive coaching superior to other interventions nor is it going to replace such interventions.

It is our view that coaching is only one of the leader developmental interventions, albeit a modern one. It very well compliments other developmental interventions like high quality assessment and feedback including assessment and development centres and 360-degree feedback, executive education, experiential and self-awareness promoting leader development programs, challenging job assignments including planned rotations and so on.

The truth is that each of these interventions is able to tackle one aspect of leader development very effectively. For example, executive education exposes leaders to several new perspectives, global best practices, new and powerful conceptual frameworks and deeply educative peer interactions. This cannot be substituted by any other intervention. Similarly, coaching has a few hard to replace advantages. Given its one-to-one nature, the ability to customize, the ability to create a safe space for honest exploration, the ability to support and challenge, the ability to support reflection at one end and concrete actions on the other end, make it extremely useful in addressing uniquely individual development needs in a safe, non-threatening and effective manner. Above all, given the individual nature of the intervention; it is possible to modify 'the dosage of the bitter medicine' depending on the severity of the condition.

Therefore, we strongly advocate appropriate application of coaching and also the skilful integration of coaching with other interventions for best results.

# 2

# The Human Side of Leader Development

The field of leader development has seen rapid advances in the past few decades. There is an ever-growing body of knowledge about things like what constitutes effective leadership, what styles are effective, what it takes to identify potential leaders, what it takes to develop them and so on. The global aspirations of organizations which are so strongly dependent on their ability to find the right leaders has fuelled a thriving leader development industry which is geared to meet the large-scale need for leader development interventions. Unfortunately, some of these standardized interventions run the risk of viewing leader development as a mechanistic rather than as a humanistic process. The role of one's personality, one's preferences and the very personal nature of effort involved in becoming a leader are often ignored.

Given this reality, executive coaching signals a great advancement in the field because it is a very personal, humanistic and deeply impactful developmental experience. The ability of such a one-to-one helping relationship to make a difference to the executive's ability to make significant developmental progress is now well researched and documented.

The gains from executive coaching, of course, go beyond this. Executive coaching engagements are beginning to throw up valuable insights into the unique developmental struggles, challenges and dilemmas of leaders in a manner that was unavailable so far. These insights when captured, analyzed and documented can contribute to radically changing the way we look at leader development in the coming years. This book is our humble effort in that direction. This book also demonstrates our belief that it is important for executive coaches and coach educators to start with the end goal of leader effectiveness in mind rather than get preoccupied with our internal technical intricacies.

## The Three Broad Developmental Contexts and the Twenty-Three Experiential Insights from These Twenty-Five Cases

Based on this view, we began our quest of trying to discern patterns and themes among the hundreds of coaching engagements that we had the opportunity to be involved in. This effort has led us to unearth as of this day twenty three experiential insights into leader development. We call these experiential because they are based on our first-hand coaching experiences. These experiential insights will hopefully open up new vistas for those aspiring to get to the corner office or succeed once they are there.

Each of these twenty-three insights is illustrated through at least one coaching case (in some cases, two). These insights collectively cover the three broad developmental contexts—developing competencies, making transitions and addressing executive and entrepreneurial agendas. These insights are presented in the form of propositions for easy understanding.

We have captured all of this in a mind map (see page 12).

## Developing Competencies

Leaders seem to need help to develop their competencies to meet the demands of their current roles or prepare themselves for future roles in a national or global context. Interestingly the demands of the current role and that of future roles are really on a continuum and not as discrete as they might seem.

Some of these competencies take the form of simple skills while others might call for fundamental shifts in attitudes, styles and belief systems. The deeper the needs the greater the efforts required and the stronger the efficacy of coaching in addressing such needs.

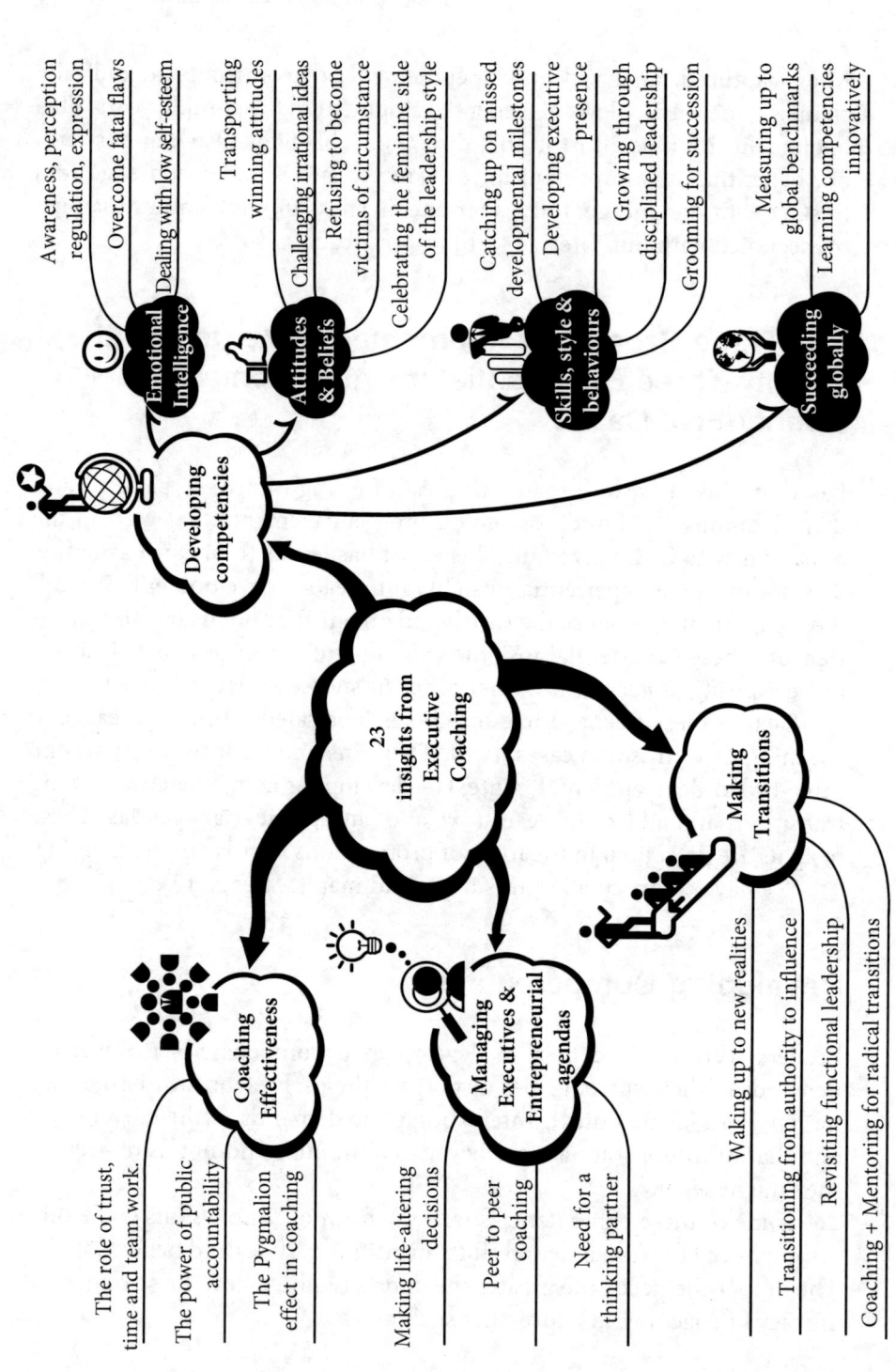

23 insights from Executive Coaching

Developing competencies

Emotional Intelligence
- Awareness, perception regulation, expression
- Overcome fatal flaws
- Dealing with low self-esteem

Attitudes & Beliefs
- Transporting winning attitudes
- Challenging irrational ideas
- Refusing to become victims of circumstance
- Celebrating the feminine side of the leadership style

Skills, style & behaviours
- Catching up on missed developmental milestones
- Developing executive presence
- Growing through disciplined leadership
- Grooming for succession

Succeeding globally
- Measuring up to global benchmarks
- Learning competencies innovatively

Coaching Effectiveness
- The role of trust, time and team work.
- The power of public accountability
- The Pygmalion effect in coaching

Managing Executives & Entrepreneurial agendas
- Making life-altering decisions
- Peer to peer coaching
- Need for a thinking partner

Making Transitions
- Waking up to new realities
- Transitioning from authority to influence
- Revisiting functional leadership
- Coaching + Mentoring for radical transitions

Here are some of the insights that we have gained through our coaching experiences about the various dimensions of competency development including Emotional intelligence, attitudes and beliefs, skills, styles and behaviours, and competencies for succeeding globally.

1. The most successful leaders are the ones who are fully aware of and can read their own emotions, tune into the world of others emotions, regulate their emotions, manage others emotions, express their emotions accurately and leverage their emotions to make good decisions and act with optimism and happiness.

2. All executives have at least a few weaknesses and flaws that can be coped with, but some have one or more flaws that can turn potentially fatal unless they become aware of it and invest in curing it.

3. Despite their many accomplishments and material gains leaders can get into a trough of low self-esteem and then into a regressive cycle that can actually derail their career unless they pull themselves out.

4. Executives often fail to transport their winning attitudes from their experience in one organization to another and end up failing when they need to win the most.

5. What makes executives feel miserable is not the situations that they face but the view that they take to these situations, the thoughts that get triggered in these situations, especially when these are irrational.

6. Executives are often victims of their circumstances including some of their childhood experiences and this ends up impacting their attitudes towards others at work and in their personal lives unless they choose to reframe them.

7. Women executives are often under pressure, often self-inflicted, to suppress their feminine side and overuse the masculine side of their leadership style, leading to several unintended consequences.

8. When executives are rapidly promoted by their managers almost entirely based on their track record, their loyalty and value in a given industry domain without adequate developmental investments or role models, they run the risk of missing several developmental milestones.

9. Organizations are quite adept at developing the technical, managerial and leadership skills and competencies of their executives when they are hard and tangible. When it comes to a competence

like Executive Presence they are confounded by its softness but very concerned about its present day criticality.

10. As entrepreneurs scale their business, they reach a tipping point where they need to learn to go beyond being an entrepreneur and also become a competent manager and leader to ensure disciplined execution of their business plans.

11. When today's promoters decide to hand over the reins of their business to a professional executive, the parameters they apply to choose such a successor go beyond loyalty, commitment and track record. Acceptance by other peer professionals in the leadership team is often very important to them.

12. As more and more Indian businesses get globally integrated and also begin to nurture global dreams and aspirations and more and more global corporations increase their stakes in India, there is huge pressure on Indian executives to scale and measure up to global benchmarks in terms of capabilities, hard and soft.

13. When executives need to learn things that they either don't enjoy or that do not come to them naturally, given their cultural orientation, they need to substitute their passion with innovation to crack the competency code.

## Managing Transitions

Executives very often face and experience significant personal and professional changes. We call these transitions. They might be moving from one organization to another, from one business to another, from functional to business roles, from one culture to another and so on. All of these call for significant adjustment, unlearning and learning.

While organizations emphasize a lot about the role of executives in managing change in organizations, little is understood about what it takes for these executives themselves to manage the changes that they experience.

Here are some of the insights that we have gained through our coaching experiences about the various challenges of managing transitions:

1. Loyal executives who have been a part of the founding teams do not often wake up and smell the coffee—they do not realize that the organization has grown and moved beyond them and that to remain relevant, they have work to do.

2. Not all crucial jobs at a senior level carry position based authority. Many of these positions require executives to rely on their personal authority and personal and professional sources of influence.

3. It is not often that leaders who have spent significant time in business leadership roles return to functional leadership roles. When they do return, it is not the lack of deep functional skills but their inability to appreciate some of the nuances in their functional role that can derail them.

4. When executives are expected to make transitions that are complex and need to do it under acute time pressure, they will need support from multiple sources.

## Addressing the Executive and Entrepreneurial Agendas to Promote Well-Considered Decision-Making

Executives and entrepreneurs are dealing with a lot in their work lives. We call these agendas. There are conflicts to resolve and decisions to make. There are multiple stakeholders to manage and balance. There is also the need to find balance and meaning in all that they do.

It is never easy doing all this alone because there is so much of reflection that is called for. This is one area where executives and entrepreneurs are increasingly looking up to coaches for help.

Here are some of the insights that we gained through our coaching experiences about the various agendas that executives and entrepreneurs grapple with:

1. Young entrepreneurs who are chasing a big dream with passion almost always reach a point where they need to make some very big decisions—decisions that can alter their life and work and these are times when they need help the most.

2. Entrepreneurs can best understand the pain and problems and dilemmas of other entrepreneurs and are in the best position but only if they can get over the concerns of trust and confidentiality and the availability of an able moderator and a sound platform for such helping.

3. Leaders are alone in their journeys and are constantly looking for help in grappling with emerging executive agendas of great

significance, especially when these agendas involve resolving conflicts, achieving clarity or making major decisions, especially with human and emotional implications.

## Making Coaching Effective

The subject of coaching effectiveness has begun to gain a lot of attention. There is a lot that people wish to know about why and when coaching works and why and when it does not. Our own experiences have been quite interesting and seem to validate a lot of research in this area.

Here are some of the insights that we have gained through our coaching experiences about what contributes to coaching effectiveness:

1. When coachees make their intention to make personal change public and through that hold themselves publicly accountable, the probability of such change materialising is very high
2. When a tenured executive is put on a short runway and suddenly expected to make significant change, success depends on whether his/her seniors trust in his/her ability, are prepared to invest a fair amount of their time to work with him/her and be able and willing to provide, when appropriate, referral help, a peer guide and a coach
3. The Pygmalion Effect or the theory of the Self-fulfilling Prophecy works in coaching too. Coachees respond very positively to the appreciation of their supervising managers and make big changes

It must be clarified that the above insights distilled from our twenty five first-hand coaching experiences are by no means exhaustive. Based on our experiences this far, these are the ones that we have found most common and critical. We are sure that in the coming years, as we have the privilege to be a part of more and more coaching engagements, we will be able to expand this body of knowledge and present it to our readers, especially those in the corner office or aspiring to get there!

Now, let us begin to explore each of these experiential insights through the fascinating coaching cases that are to follow.

**The Mystery of Missed Developmental Milestones**

Employees in all organizations move from one job-grade and/or work-level to another in a simple sequential manner. Someone declares that he or she is ready to move and someone else approves this move. Once in the new grade or work level, it is assumed that the person acts and behaves like a person who is expected to behave at that level.

So, what does that mean? Well, we know what it means in the educational system. When a student is promoted from one year to another or from one class to another, it means the student has cleared or passed all the prescribed courses and subjects in the previous class or year and has no arrears or backlog—as simple and straightforwardly verifiable as that.

So, does this simple rule apply in the world of organizations? When a person is promoted from one level to another, does that mean the person has passed all the requirements in the previous grade or work level? Does preparation for the future preclude any backlog of past development needs? Here is where things begin to get somewhat vague and ambiguous. While academic institutions have simple scores and minimum pass marks and cut offs, such simplistic measures are not tenable in the world of business. While organizations do have competency frameworks and potential assessment methods like assessment and development centres, these still do not as yet serve as real-time guides to help the manager check for readiness to move to the next higher role or level.

For a variety of reasons, which include short supply, the person's unique strengths in a few areas and over-emphasis on past performance and under emphasis on the criticality of potential, organizations do end up promoting their executives from one work level to another, even if they are carrying the organizational equivalent of arrears or backlog which are themselves nothing but competence deficits and gaps not just from the previous work level but often from several levels below.

This is what we are beginning to call missed developmental milestones. For example, when a child grows up, there are well established developmental milestones like when they must crawl, when they must walk, when they must discriminate between parents and others and so on. If children miss any of these milestones, they must ring alarm bells for their parents.

*(Box contd.)*

*(Box contd.)*

Similarly, through our coaching experiences, we are beginning to discern certain missed developmental milestones among executives which finally land up as potential coaching agendas.

Let us look at a few examples:

An individual contributor who is in the early days of his or her career would be expected to demonstrate basic life skills which have been defined by WHO as 'abilities for adaptive and positive behaviour that enable individuals to deal effectively with the demands and challenges of everyday life'.

The milestones that would demonstrate such life skills are the ability to communicate and to get along with others, the ability to think critically and take small decisions, and the ability to cope with the everyday pressures and stressors of life and the ability to manage oneself effectively. Unfortunately, ever too often, we find even some in leadership positions who have missed these early developmental milestones.

Now, the first big shift happens when individual contributors become first time managers. They need to learn many managerial skills and develop the values and attitudes of being a manager. The milestones that would signify successful transitions are the ability to get work done through others rather than on their own, the comfort in giving up the tasks and responsibilities that earned them a manager title or the ability to move beyond team relationships to build team and peer relationships. Many coaches are called upon to work with coachees at leadership positions who have missed the developmental milestone of being able to get things done from others.

Similarly, when seasoned managers move to assume functional leadership responsibilities, they are expected to demonstrate real leadership behaviours. The milestones that would signify such a successful transition are the ability to move from valuing one's own function to valuing all functions appropriately, the ability to think and act keeping the big picture or the ability to manage managers differently and not the way one would manage individual contributors.

While the ideal situation is that executive coaching is used to groom executives for the future, it must be conceded that most often executive coaches end up helping their coachees catch up on recently missed developmental milestones or on occasion even milestones pertaining to several stages prior to where the executive is.

*(Box contd.)*

*(Box contd.)*

The good news is that when executives are grappling with few, if not many, developmental milestones, what they need is strong medicine to make rapid change and it appears that coaching is considerably more potent compared to other developmental experiences like training. Coaches are not only able to use very high quality assessment data to enhance their coachee's self-awareness, challenge them about their blind spots and their mistaken ways of seeing things but also support them when they make efforts to change.

# SECTION B

# Enhancing Emotional Intelligence

# The Place of Emotional Intelligence in Leader Effectiveness

## B. J. Prashantham*

The theory of multiple intelligences was proposed by Howard Gardner in his 1983 book *Frames of Mind: The Theory of Multiple Intelligences* as a model of intelligence that differentiates intelligence into specific (primarily sensory) 'modalities', rather than seeing it as dominated by a single general ability. Interpersonal and intrapersonal intelligence, two facets of emotional intelligence were part of the eight intelligences that he proposed. These two, he felt, helped humans live a full life.

The various dimensions of emotional intelligence (EI) have been categorized differently by different groups of thinkers all the way from Salovy, Mayer, Goleman, Thomas International and others along with testing tools to look at several discrete categories and aspects. The research goes on.

High emotional competency is an inevitable part of the human side of the enterprise and long-term leadership effectiveness. These EI competencies are summarized as self-awareness, self-regulation, motivation, empathy and social skills. It will be a gross blunder to view them mechanically or in isolation of other aspects of human behaviour. The strong left brain emphasis of the last several decades needs to be balanced with the use of the right side as well.

Historically and culturally men were less encouraged and expected to express emotions while women seemed to be free to do so. Even

*B. J. Prashantham is Clinical Faculty, Global health, University of Washington and Professor of Counselling Psychology and Director, Institute for Human Relations, Counselling & Psychotherapy Christian Counselling Centre, Vellore, India. He is a Member of the Governing Council of CFI. He is an alumnus of the Texas Medical Centre Houston and Ohio State University.

neurologically, the amygdala, an important part of the brain that is seen as the centre of emotions (though not exclusively), seems to be larger in size in women than in men.

The good news is that people can be helped to develop their EI. The plasticity of the brain allows for reciprocal effect of brain on behaviour and behaviour on brain and opens up many possibilities. The more the practice, the greater the competence, as Malcolm Gladwell, author of the book *Outliers* clearly indicates.

## The Three Cases under Review

All the three real-life coaching stories that are presented here show how a certain set of facilitative skills, moving through general phases of coaching, coachee-centricity, working together with coachee and the sponsors, listening to the story and the story behind the story, the challenging 360 feedback, the goal setting and practical actions, the structuring of the sessions, the skill of the coach, use of several perspectives, the patience, the perseverance, the hope and joy of walking skilfully with the coachee helped in their journey to the next level of excellence of EI through executive coaching.

In the instance of John (recovery of his emotional side), it was reported by the Coach that after the coaching experience, John's approach to work changed remarkably to become more people oriented. His work–life balance improved, evidenced in the joint hobby with his wife. These were the goals identified by the sponsor as also accepted by John. With patient listening and relevant questions, with empathy and gentle challenge, the Coach won the confidence of the coachee and facilitated practical action plans for the coachee to achieve changes. What is most interesting is that the changes were noticed by supervisors, colleagues and family members.

The story of Sunny is another example of the Coachee achieving the goal of 'listening with empathy'. Family relations improve, especially with his daughter. On the work side too there is confirmation that relationships improved. The Coachee felt better prepared to transition into another assignment as COO. The skill of listening and empathy demonstrated by the Coach, the type of open-ended questions that were asked, the exploration of behaviour with the lens of transactional analysis and finally helping him develop action plans resulting in his ability to grow in the realm of relations with his daughter, colleagues and even manage a transition to another job are sought to be shown.

With Rajan as Coachee, the Coach shows how his coaching journey resulted in the Coachee enhancing his EI. Listening to the story, the story behind the story, the identification of the development of the fatal flaw, the openness of the Coachee, the support and toughness of the sponsors, the skill of the Coach, the conceptualizations of the stages of change, the self-limiting belief being replaced, the targets of change, the post-coaching feedback are the effective outcomes of coaching. This was again a great journey of change.

## Emotional Intelligence: A Much-Needed Balancing Dimension for Leaders

In a world which has become impersonal—I-IT instead of I-Thou, it is great to be reminded of the need to be human and humane. The drastic changes in society leading to stress and its concomitants call for a review of the place of emotions and include them in proportion to their importance. Being aware of one's own emotions, being able to manage them, to be aware of other's feelings and be responsive to them can lead to better persons and organizations.

From the three case vignettes it appears that executive coaching among other things may promote development of EI among the coachees—thus generating hope, humanity and dignity in human relations at work and home.

In this connection, the Centre for Creative Leadership (CCL) in collaboration with the Tatas has recently published a book titled *Developing Tomorrow's Leaders Today*. They propose eleven issues facing leaders under three categories of leading self, leading others and leading business. Among the eleven are self-awareness, confidence, managing and motivating subordinates and developing subordinates. EI seems to be connected with these. Pause and reflect, assess and act are the simple processes advocated. Effective Coaching seems to actually help do that.

I congratulate the Coaches for their skill and catalytic assistance and the coachees for their motivation, participation and efforts to achieve success in their lives both at work and at home by intentionally working on developing their emotional competences.

# 3

# The Importance of the Emotional Side of Your Personality

Many executives are able to achieve success in their careers despite not investing in nurturing the emotional side of their personalities. Especially when they are in jobs demanding deep functional expertise, their organizations tend to condone this gap till it reaches a point where it becomes dysfunctional. This is what happened to John and Sunny. John was so duty-bound in his devotion to work that he was never alive and sensitive to the human side at work and at home, and it required his organization to push John to pay urgent attention to it.

Sunny, on the other hand, was choosing to overuse his technical strengths so much that he failed to recognize his emotional flaws until his fragile relationship with his daughter came as a wake-up call. Kavita Gupta and Purab Rai helped John and Sunny, respectively, to value and invest in nurturing the emotional side of their lives, in expressing and demonstrating it at work and at home and enrich their lives and of course made them more complete executives.

## The Case: John's Discovery of His Emotional Side

It was Friday and Govind had promised his wife that he would be home early. He even finished all his work by 6:30 pm. Unfortunately, it was 7.30 pm and he was still in office waiting for his meeting with John. The meeting request had come up unexpectedly. He would have preferred an earlier time but he could not tell John of his predicament. John was the senior vice president in this technology company and one of its long-standing employees, having been there since its inception almost fourteen years ago. He was the head of Delivery and Technology.

Just a fortnight ago I had my pre-coaching meeting with John's manager and the Chairman & Managing Director of the company. He outlined his reasons for offering coaching support to John. John was highly task-oriented and was hardly aware of his own feelings and that of others. Empathy seemed to be missing in his interactions. His work–life balance was also a matter of concern. John's wife had even brought this up in a conversation with the Chairman. He pointed out that during their management committee meetings, John would hardly participate unless prompted and that too would be in the fewest possible words. There was never an occasion when John participated spontaneously. He was a strong results-person who readily accepted all tasks or assignments and kept up his commitments. He would never get into a conflict with the manager and was open to receiving feedback.

Apparently some of the lateral hires in John's team at a senior level did not last and many felt that none of them could work with John and he was, in a sense, responsible for their exit. He was obviously oblivious to it. It did not matter what people thought of him. Work had to be done and there could not be any excuses. Delivery schedules could not be compromised. It was evident that he worked hard. His day would start with a long list and end when all the items in the list were scored off. Meticulous and highly focused, nothing could distract him from his list. His day spent in the office had to be fully justified. Especially during a crisis, he could be fully depended upon to set things right, unmindful of the time he had to spend. He knew the company's activities and so became an integral part of the organization. It was through his sheer attention to detail and commitment to time and promises that John was recognized as an important resource and grew steadily.

Others never understood John and they approached him only if they had no choice. First, his earliest appointment in the day would be at 7:30 in the evening which is when he would have come somewhat closer to the end of his checklist and so would have time for others. People would rather let him complete the list and let him leave early so they could leave early too, which, of course, meant around 9 pm.

It was evident from this meeting that the Chairman genuinely cared for John and genuinely wanted to help him. This meant that John would have the full support in his efforts to transform and become more effective.

After this introductory meeting with the Chairman, I was introduced to John. John acknowledged my presence with a brief nod, a quick glance towards me and a fleeting half smile. Under normal circumstances, I would not have noticed these, but as a coach these were significant data points. He nodded his head when asked whether he would like to go through the opportunity of coaching. His manager, the Chairman, gently and amicably (another data point for me about the organizational culture) told him that he would like John to become more effective as a leader and specifically pay attention to his people skills and also address his work–life balance issues. This, therefore, was the broad coaching agenda.

My first coaching meeting with John was very insightful. John entered the conference room with the fixed 'U'-shaped table. He greeted me and went and sat on the other side of the U table. I rose and suggested we sit on the same side. It was nice of him that before I could walk over to his side he came around and sat a few seats away on my side. He pulled his chair close to the table. Half his body was under the table and he was sitting perpendicular to me. I did most of the talking in this meeting, a bad start for a coach. He hardly looked at me throughout the session and, at the end, I had that uncomfortable question of whether I could ever reach out or be of any help to John.

The organization had recently done a Myers-Briggs Type Indicator (MBTI) profiling for their top management and John emerged an ISTJ (introversion, sensing, thinking, judgement), a type that I could easily relate with having seen him.

I needed more inputs about John and we agreed on a 360-degree assessment. The respondents list given by him had a surprise element—he included his wife as one of the respondents.

The respondents had interesting feedback to offer. Functionally, he was seen as highly task-oriented with no orientation towards vision and strategy. He was good at doing and ensuring timeliness, though not so good at getting things done. He was more hands on. Delegation was an issue. He hardly participated and contributed in senior-level management and peer meetings. He was not seen as supportive of issues taken up by his peer group. While he agreed to certain things, he would finally go and do it his way. He would hardly attend any team celebrations like lunches and even if he did, he would hardly speak.

On the people front, his direct reports did not see him as someone they could go to or confide in, in difficulties. He was seen as highly judgemental and close-minded in his opinions about people. He did not hesitate to ask people to leave if he had concluded that they were not good. Some of them even felt no purpose in giving feedback to John as he had no feelings and did not care about others. He was not seen and experienced as inclusive. John however got along well with people much lower down in the hierarchy. John was also very loyal to the company, high on integrity, committed and hard working.

On the home front, he hardly interacted with his wife and daughter except when needed. Sundays were the days they looked forward to. That's when all of them as family, including John's mother, would attend the morning mass in the church without fail. Another event they looked forward to was their annual holiday drive to any one location, as John loved cars and driving. Every day, after John returned home from work he would switch on the television and enjoy his old film songs. This was the hidden emotional side of John.

John had a sister. His mother stayed with him. John did not talk much about his father even when gently prompted. As a student John was expected to do well in his studies and was not allowed to go out with his friends, lest he gets spoilt. John visited his in laws but hardly spoke to them. John's wife was very understanding and she accepted him as he was. She however expected that he would appreciate some of the dishes she cooked for him. As for his daughter, he hardly met her as she was mostly asleep by the time he returned and left for school in the morning by the time he woke up.

During one of our early coaching conversations, I saw his mobile flashing indicating an incoming call. He looked at it and ignored it. Very soon when we were having coffee, the phone flashed again. I silently invited him to respond. He took the call and curtly responded, 'This is not the time to call' and hung up. I was surprised at his tone but said nothing. Later in the conversation, I asked him who was on the call and 'My mother' was his indifferent response. My eyebrows went up, 'How old is she?' I asked. 'Almost seventy. I tell her not to call me in office. She doesn't listen. I don't take calls from home, when I am in the office' was his response. I soon came to know that he did not even take calls from his eight-year-old daughter, leave alone from his wife. His wife had stopped calling him on the phone. She would rather not go against his instructions.

John agreed to work on demonstrating empathy while dealing with people-sensitive issues. He also agreed to communicate and participate in all forums spontaneously.

In fact, even before the 360-survey was completed John committed to a few immediate actions plans. He would henceforth deliberately and spontaneously participate in all Management meetings. He would schedule all meetings with his direct reports before 7 pm. He would practice more listening and avoid giving instructions. He would leave office by 9 pm as against 11 pm.

Since working on checklists in a disciplined manner was his strength, these new actions were built into his checklist mode because I knew they would get done. Given his style, we also had to promote learning and change by doing rather than through reflection and insights.

In fact even in the session immediately following the one where I shared the 360-survey feedback, there was a breakthrough. Some half way through the session, John's posture changed. He pulled his chair out, turned direction and sat facing me. The frequency of eye contact increased. It was encouraging and I knew that we were moving ahead.

One of the actions that were planned was that John would go home early at least three days in a week and spend half an hour with his wife before he switched on the TV. John did it unfailingly and when we next met, I was eager to hear his experiences. 'How was it?' I asked. 'Good' was his response. 'What happened, what did your wife say?' 'Nothing much— she said she was sleepy and half way through she got up to go to sleep.' 'Oh, so how did you feel?' 'Okay—but I did it every day.' The checklist method was working.

Slowly John started sharing how he started to experience his people differently when he practiced unbiased listening. Slowly I could see that he was beginning to become comfortable with smiling, making eye contact and talking freely. Some of the key direct reports of John started to look forward to having meetings with him.

On the home front John knew his wife was fond of gardening. He therefore decided to take interest in gardening and work towards making it their weekend hobby. He began to spend more time with his daughter and help her with her homework.

His in-laws looked forward to his visits as he started engaging with his father-in-law. His daughter's scores improved and she would wait for her father to return home from work.

Meanwhile, he also reconnected with his childhood friends. These were major shifts as far as he was concerned. On the work front, he was delegating better. He also planned to spend time on finding ways to cut down production costs of his unit while ensuring quality levels are not compromised. He decided to initiate skip level meetings to understand his people and their challenges better. He started working on planning and preparing for addressing his department as a whole. He committed himself to participate spontaneously in all the forums of the company.

He now felt responsible being a management committee member and his participation extended to even finance and HR issues. He would challenge and offer suggestions for doing things differently.

A year later, I spoke to the HR head and asked about John. His words moved me. 'Ma'am, today we showcase John as an example of what coaching can do to an individual.' When I spoke to John, amongst many things he shared, what stood out was that gardening had become a joint hobby for both him and his wife and that is how they spend their time together.

Coaching for John had brought remarkable shifts in him as a person—at work and at home.

I now knew that there was no looking back for John. He has moved on.

## The Case: Sunny Learns to Listen with Empathy

Sunny walked into my office on a pleasant Saturday morning. The rest of our office was enjoying their weekend. We had a brief conversation over phone a couple of days back and had agreed to meet on a Saturday so that we could have some undisturbed time together. A man in his early forties, wearing a pair of jeans and a striped T-shirt with his spectacles well in place hiding his perfect gentleman eyes, knocked on my door. His appearance did not surprise me. Sunny remarked, 'Good office and thanks for the meeting.' Being used to formal meetings with near strangers, it was not hard for both of us to settle down quickly. After a few formal pleasantries and some general comments we were ready to start the conversion. Sunny quickly put his phone on silent mode and displayed an expression of business-like seriousness.

A couple of weeks back, a close friend requested me to talk to one of his senior executives. Beyond this request, I had no idea of the person in front of me. Now, that Sunny was in front of me, my mind was keen to know more of him. Sunny started to speak.

You see, I am heading R&D in my Organisation. The job is challenging, but what next? I want to discuss where I am heading and what needs to be done to move further in my career. I want to see if you can help me.

Sunny had joined the current organization as Senior Vice President (R&D) with a mandate to develop new business opportunities for the Business Unit Heads. With an employee base of over 5,000 and working in the highly competitive telecom domain, the role envisaged strong connect with his Business Unit Heads and customers, engaging with customers with a proactive focus on their problems and offering them new technologies to retain their technology leadership and new solutions to retain their competitive edge.

Sunny had a team of over forty-five associates generating a business of USD 3 million and with a target of USD 50 million in the next three years. As Sunny summed up, 'How to generate strong non-linear revenue for the company? My job is to connect the dots, business and technology, to arrive at new solutions for my customers.' We agreed to work together and defined career progression as the broad coaching agenda.

During the first few meetings, Sunny though open and friendly, came across as a formal and serious person. He had clarity about what he wanted to speak and the message he wanted to convey. The conversation was flowing but measured. He told me that he liked to analyse things with a view to understand them and one could see this as a dominant tendency in his thinking, world view and behaviour. As he spoke, he conveyed a sense of finality in what he said. The continuous wheezing as he spoke did not deter him from projecting a strong, no nonsense, domineering, highly task-oriented achiever image. Work and achievements seemed to have taken centre stage in his life. He was almost preoccupied with it, even at home. In the words of his wife, 'When he is at home, he is just present physically.'

Sunny did not bring up important work-related issues that he was facing during the initial discussions. He was possibly waiting to see if the coach would lead him to disclose. When asked why he was seeking further career progression, his response was,

I want to leave a legacy behind. Want to create an exceptional organization which exploits cutting-edge technology, is highly innovative and successful. As a CEO, it is easier and quicker to realize this dream. But the hurdle is, most associates in today's organization don't measure up to it. That is why one has to drive them to pursue excellence, by raising the bar, and demanding better output.

He said that he is seen by his team as a task master demanding top performance and that he goes out of the way to reward those who meet his expectations. The flip side of the story was that most of them failed to meet his expectations and on the contrary they habitually manifest performance deficit. His goal was to bring them up to his level of expectation and performance. 'The need is to create more clones like me, workaholic and with a drive to achieve superior performance.'

Slowly more of Sunny was emerging from the discussions. We had still not come to defining the actual coaching goal but before that, the questions—why Sunny wants to leave a legacy and why he wants to nurture clones like him had to be answered.

Sunny hailed from a typical middle class family of the pre-liberalization era where the father was a government servant and mother a silent home maker who was adept at ensuring that their economic condition did not affect the happiness of the family. The constant flow of relatives as stay-in visitors further stretched the family resources. Toil and hard work seemed to sum up the purpose and existence of his mother. At times he felt sad for his mother and could not conceal his anger towards his father who left the burden of endless family chores on his mother. As a student he had to solve the toughest of mathematical problems which his father picked up for him. Aspirations hung heavily on Sunny with the parental expectation that he should do well in studies. Being bright was not enough; achievements counted.

Pursuing an engineering degree was a given. He was selected by one of the NITs and decided to major in electronics against the wishes of his father. The euphoria of getting a job immediately upon graduation did not last long. Within three months, Sunny felt choked by the routine confines of an EDP department of a leading manufacturing company and decided to quit the job to the utter dismay of his father. Without a job, he was holed up in his house. Later he had to borrow ₹5,000 from his father to pay as bond for a trainee position in a computer hardware start-up. As Sunny recalls, this was a period of excitement and great learning. He worked day and night, at times even without a break for days together. Computers and the nascent IT world beckoned him. Driven by a new found confidence he made couple of key career moves and had the opportunity to work abroad on the latest of technologies. Two long decades of work experience had shaped Sunny to become a new person. Besides technology, Sunny had imbibed a new work culture—passion, drive for excellence, obsession for results and intolerance for failures. Above all, he developed a strong belief that if you don't achieve, you probably don't matter.

Interestingly, Sunny had a good awareness of how he behaved and believed that it was right and appropriate. On the contrary his predicament was why others were not like him. Here are some of the ways in which Sunny would describe himself. 'I am fully charged by 10 am. Others think that I am stressed at work but I do not agree. I am highly impatient, aggressive and follow up when things are delayed.' 'Whatever I do, including sports and play, I have to come as the best.' 'But I can't take failures—hence I have to do it this way. I can never lose.' 'Always on the run, I need to cover myself, like other bosses.' 'Since I know they will not deliver, I often work in parallel to ensure that tasks are delivered.'

Sunny is a different person at home. His engagement as a family member, other than being a provider is low. Be it shopping, table talk or any other, Sunny is too busy to find time. When at home he is always on his laptop or is taking calls from customers. As he mentioned, he had to be connected to work and customers 24/7. Sunny often found ingenious ways to handle domestic demands. When his son asks for a pencil he simply buys him two dozen of them so that he will not be troubled again. Why not buy a dozen shorts for his son, rather than frequent the shops? He laments. His wife has not stopped goading him to be a more responsible husband and father. In recent times, as a possible compromise, he began to accompany her on her vegetable shopping trips but stays in the car so that he can work on his laptop.

The one big thing that troubled Sunny on the home front was the poor academic performance of his daughter. He says that she does not listen to him. Though he has advised her many times and demanded better performance, he could hardly influence her to mend her ways. He has heard her say many times that he only complained and did not understand her.

His daughter's behaviour had shaken Sunny. She spends hours talking with her friends while she had to be engaged in her studies. How to influence her? Had he gone wrong somewhere was the nagging question in his mind? It was during these discussions that one could see a different Sunny—someone who let down his mask to bare his weakness and his soft emotions and his vulnerabilities.

> You see, I want to understand my daughter and make her feel that she means a lot to me. With this intention I sit with her many times and begin a conversation, but within minutes I am telling her what she should do and find I have lost her. Well, I wonder, these days if the kids are different.

It is during this phase of the discussion that I saw the opportunity to connect Sunny to his emotions, to use his analytical mind to explore another dimension of the world he encounters day in and day out. I invited Sunny to 'connect the dots' at home and at work apart from technology and business.

Sunny sees the point that in spite of all his good intentions and efforts, he does not get the best out of his team. 'If my way is not the best way to lead,' Sunny quips, 'there should be another way and I want to know how to do it that way.' We agreed to keep this as the broad coaching agenda discarding the earlier one.

Having reached a point where Sunny realized that his behaviour did not seem to yield the intended outcome, we decided to undertake a 360-degree-feedback survey for deeper insights. Sunny chose ten participants for the survey and during the interactions with them, it was evident they were a bit surprised that Sunny wanted feedback from them. He included his wife and daughter in the list in addition to his direct reports, peers and his manager. The results reinforced what I had gathered from my interactions and Sunny's self-reporting.

He was perceived to be a very talented person. He was also seen as a highly motivated person. He was highly task-oriented.

At work he was seen as very aggressive and abrasive in his dealing with team members and peers. He complained and criticized openly in the presence of others, leaving them emotionally shattered. He was not consistent in his behaviour. He seemed to realize this and often sat with his team to sort out the issues.

At home, he behaved in a similar style. He did not listen but imposed his views. As his wife said, 'In recent times he understands how he behaves at home but he is not serious about changing. It appears that he does not want to change.'

Sunny admitted that the feedback was on the dot and indicated that he was aware of some aspects and was already working on them. It was evident during the discussion that he was probably thinking deeply about the feedback and was trying to unravel to himself the deep drivers beneath his behaviour pattern. He admitted that though he was normally a rational person, in situations of conflict he did not respond rationally but reacted emotionally. This resulted in behavioural outbursts which others did not anticipate. He had an explanation for his poor listening skills. He said it came from his childhood habit of reading the mind of others or judging others and putting them into quadrants. On his behaviour at home, he admitted that it came from the belief that an earning member was more important than others.

Sunny began to realize that all his rationality was not helping him achieve what he wanted, at home or at work. He had reached the point of no return and was serious about change.

He valued looking at all this through the transactional analysis filter in terms of life positions, beliefs, evaluative and judgemental listening. He concluded that he could drive people but not inspire them. He acknowledged that he was not able to influence his daughter in her decisions and outlook by being a father. If you have to influence someone, relationships do matter no matter how much control you have over them. These reflections let Sunny to ponder how his current ways of functioning would affect his career. With these insights, Sunny expressed that he is ready to define his goals more sharply.

He decided to address the core issue of 'how to listen and respond to others with unconditional acceptance'. He indicated that he was keen to practice this at home also and that he had even discussed this with his family.

We came up with a long list of specific and simple action plans to achieve this goal. This included practice of new behaviours, some disciplined record keeping and a lot of reflection.

At the end of two months, feedback from Sunny indicated that he was consciously trying out the new behaviours with a good degree of success. He was now concerned about finding ways to sustain it. He admitted that he had a tendency to drift into old behaviour when the situation had strong elements of stress. Typically, he classified situations into three groups: normal/neutral (100 per cent success); situations calling for objective based discussions—customers, etc. (50 per cent success); and time critical/stressful situations (0 per cent).

The focus was on the last two types of situations.

At the end of three months, Sunny indicated that he was making good progress in the new ways of listening and responding. Informal feedback from his HR head confirmed this view. He indicated that he intends to persist as he saw good results.

A few months later, Sunny called to inform me that he had taken up a new assignment with another company as COO and indicated that my coaching support had prepared him for the new role.

For me, the biggest gift was that his relationship with his daughter improved considerably and he felt that she was closer to him as she spent more time with him while he was at home. He is now able to just sit and listen to her.

# 4

# When the Flaw Turns Fatal

Most executives have at least a few flaws that fall within the realm of what one might call allowable weaknesses, in the early stages of their careers. This ideally ought to be the right time to fix the flaw and many do end up fixing it in time. In the case of some executives, these flaws remain unattended and tend to turn fatal. By then, everyone except the executive knows about the fatality of the flaw but it is too late. Dr Avinash Banerjee discovers while coaching Rajan that removing fatal flaws can be tough but never too late.

## The Case: Rajan's Victory over His Fatal Flaw

Rajan and the Coach walk across to meet his manager for a three-way meeting to get on to the same page as far as Rajan's coaching agenda is concerned. While Rajan has given the Coach his expectations and wishes, his manager's inputs are vital. As the Coach would soon discover, his manager's views almost sounded like an ultimatum.

### The Sponsor's List

The manager and sponsor explain that there are three aspects identified as critical to Rajan's development as a leader.

Rajan is extremely result oriented. He can fix on a goal and work relentlessly towards achieving it. Culturally however, the organization places very high emphasis on team work and Rajan has challenges here, especially with peers. He needs to learn how to take his agenda forward with his peers on board, on his side.

Rajan seems to be more effective and comfortable when he is in a dominant position in the network, but he finds it a challenge to work within a network of equals—where he cannot dominate through hierarchical power or position.

The second area relates to the organization's values relating to being entrepreneurial on things like escalating issues in time, reporting to his manager on what's going on (for example, if he needs any support), keeping others informed in times of any delays or issues. Rajan needs to do better on these.

The third area (related to the second) relates to the admission of failure, or imminent failure and to accept and leverage constructive feedback. The organization's culture today sees it as a sign of strength to stand up in a meeting and say 'we failed' and then learn from that. Rajan needs to shift his approach in this area also. His level of comfort in admitting failure is low. He leans towards the 'We did OK—the others did not' approach, which is not working for him.

In summary, the sponsor points out that while operational success is going well for Rajan, his career would be stalled if he did not work on the 'people' aspect. While others respect him for his achievement orientation, they are put off with his aggression. He reiterates that unless Rajan works on it, this aspect will be a 'fatal flaw' that will block any development and growth. 'Collaborate—or else!' is the clear and urgent message for Rajan from the sponsor.

Clearly, when the coach meets Rajan first to get his views, Rajan was seeing it somewhat differently and certainly more mildly. The serious purport of the coaching engagement certainly does not come through from Rajan.

## Rajan's List

When the Coach met Rajan earlier, he saw two areas in which the coaching engagement could help.

'How to get people to be aligned along with me … not just because I'm the boss?'

Rajan wants to work through 'consensus'. He believes that being authoritative is important and has its 'plus points', but that it is important to take people along with him. This is his first wish.

'What should I do to be more successful? Have I reached my final position in the pyramid?'

Rajan craves for success. At the same time, he suspects he needs to change his approach going forward, as the parameters for success may differ going up the hierarchy from here.

The coach shares with Rajan a favourite quotation of his on Subtle Influence and asks Rajan to think about the implications for himself in the current context.

Also, he invites Rajan to think through the question, 'What would "success" mean for you?'

## The Coach's List of Questions

Many questions are going on in the mind of the coach after the sponsor's meeting.

How is it possible that Rajan did not see it coming? For such an intelligent and successful person, how did he underestimate the seriousness?

What is the big change in the context that has made these flaws suddenly fatal? After all, he has been with the organization for many years and successful too.

Could it be that Rajan is very low on self-awareness?

What really contributes to individuals who are otherwise successful to end up developing such fatal flaws?

Finding answers to these questions was important for the coach. Fortunately, he did not have to wait for long. The answers begin to flow in.

## Rajan Tells His Story

As Rajan begins to tell his story, the Coach finds a part of the answer to his last question first—what really contributes to individuals who are otherwise successful to end up developing such fatal flaws?

Rajan had an eventful and tough childhood. He lost his father at the age of eight. He and his younger brother were brought up by their mother who took up a job for the first time in her life at that time. As he was growing up, although his mother and others did help and support Rajan, he felt the need for someone to mentor and guide him.

His academic performance was patchy. At one school, he did well with good teachers, and was driven to succeed, compete, and beat others. But at college, Rajan's performance was poor as he became complacent.

Today, looking back, Rajan feels that these tough experiences have made him a stronger and more resilient person—but at that time, life did not look very good.

The unhappy state of affairs continued beyond college. After his degree he does not find a job. After many months of idling at home, he tried his hand at a couple of jobs but was never satisfied. His friends, by comparison were all high-flyers, with 'happening' jobs. Everyone (including Rajan) felt he had 'lost it'. Life was indeed very low.

At this point, Rajan's life changes its trajectory—for the better!

With the help of an uncle, he got his first break—a job with a leading South Indian automobiles company. Rajan learnt many lessons from his boss at this company that are still etched into his personality—especially about being straight ('tell the facts, always') and making decisions quickly. This boss played an important role in Rajan's life—he helped him grow and develop as a corporate citizen.

Rajan joined his current organization in 1996 and soon became a very successful manager. He was posted abroad for a while and then came back to India in 2001 after a personal tragedy (he lost his brother).

Although this event affected him deeply, he focused his attention on his work, and built a reputation as a 'driven' person. Today, Rajan is in a senior functional role with national responsibilities.

## Rajan Is Self-Aware

The coach asks Rajan how he sees himself and he opens up and bares himself.

Rajan sees himself as a very tough person. As a result of all that he has gone through in life, he has developed the ability to withstand a lot of difficulties and come out strong.

He is a very open person—talks straight, says the same thing to everyone.

He is a very performance-oriented person—his growth has been fast, and this is the right way. Rajan cannot digest failures, cannot accept a person who is not performing. His team has to have only high performers. This has some negative aspects, but that's how he is, he says.

He is an introverted person who is not very comfortable in a big, unfamiliar crowd. He trusts only a few people, but trusts them very deeply.

He sees himself as a highly authoritative, dominating person. This he agrees has been the feedback received from many people.

He is also very possessive about his good people and will go all out for them.

His coach is impressed with Rajan's honesty and clarity about himself. He comes across to the coach as a 'straight-talking', 'no-nonsense' person who is willing to talk openly about himself. This bodes well for the coaching engagement.

So, Rajan's difficult past seems to have contributed in some ways to his work values, his style and behaviours. Rajan was also self-aware.

## Old Bottle, New Wine

Rajan explains the organization's current culture as a case of new wine in an old bottle.

While the organization has remained the same in name, the increased efforts to integrate with the parent company and create a global culture had brought about significant cultural changes lately. Executives like Rajan have to now learn to adapt quickly.

For example, Rajan has worked under one manager for fourteen of the fifteen years in this organization. This manager's philosophy has influenced Rajan immensely. He believed strongly in empowering his people to handle things on their own. When he went to him with any problem, Rajan vividly remembers the boss saying things like 'You are paid to manage all that, don't ask me', 'Why are you asking for help? Are you unable to handle it? Are you incompetent?', 'If you want to be successful, remain in control, manage things yourself.'

Of course this helps people like Rajan become more self-reliant but it discourages dialogue or engagement around challenges and failures.

Contrast this with his current manager's expectation. If there is a problem Rajan does not escalate and tries to handle it on his own. His current boss, however, wants to get involved, wants to speak to the people directly, wants to be in the loop right through. Rajan is confused—this is a completely different style and culture, and he does not know how to handle it. 'I don't understand how to escalate and yet remain a winner,' Rajan says.

Similarly, Rajan reflects on the background to his other problem areas.

While Rajan agrees that there is a need for him to take people along and build influence without authority, 'It is still my ship,' he says. He has a strong preference to remain in control. This becomes most evident when there is a conflict of interest – with peers, internal customers.

What is clear now is that Rajan needs to 'unlearn' the culture of the past, and adapt himself to the new realities.

Finally, in the area of taking critical feedback and managing failure, Rajan admits that he is very guarded about himself, his people, his department and he does not like others 'pointing fingers' at him. Maybe it is an 'ego' factor? Rajan feels hurt if someone comments about him, his work, or his team. Although he knows 'feedback is not about the person, it's about the issue'—it is still a problem.

By now the coach finds answers to most of his questions. Based on all that he heard, he is concluding that given his performance and his self-confidence, he was thus far blind to the seriousness of his flaws and was not even contemplating change.

## Preparing to Change

It is said that there are several stages to the process of personal change. Until we got started, Rajan was in the pre-contemplation stage. After his manager made things so abundantly clear and also gave him access to a trust based helping relationship, Rajan was motivated and moved to the contemplation stage. After all the initial deliberations, especially after he was listened to with empathy by his Coach, he was now preparing for change.

The coach and Rajan begin to discuss various dimensions of collaboration, one of the core development needs. The Coach is focusing all along on offering Rajan alternate frames of reference. For example, how does 'win-win' or 'you and I are on the same side' sound as opposed to who is 'right' and who is 'wrong'.

The Coach also invites Rajan to examine ways in which he can make feedback purposeful and forward looking.

These alternate ways of looking at things seem adequate for Rajan to commit to implement two immediate changes:

1.  Focus on the issue, and not on the person
2.  Give real-time feedback to his team members to emphasize improvement (not 'criticism')

The Coach recognizes that these commitments to change are not enough and Rajan will need to do more. He will also need to be challenged with more assessment data. So, he undertakes a 360-assessment.

## Rajan's Stakeholder's List

The 360-degree survey reinforces what the coach discovered thus far. People see him as a committed, competent, assertive, target-driven manager.

They also see him as aggressive, more aligned to his goals than to the organization's goals and not a very collaborative (internal customer oriented) manager, not very open to other points of view or feedback. His peers feel, 'He doesn't co-operate with anybody else's agenda—he does only what his own targets demand.' Another says, 'I need to be careful when dealing with him; I don't know when we will be blind-sided on some issue or other if we're working together.'

Rajan decides to reflect on the feedback before deciding anything. Also he wants to discuss this with a few important stakeholders to gain qualitative insights and land on the critical areas.

## Rajan's Final List

Based on his reflection and his conversations with a number of important stakeholders he decides on three important areas for change:

1.  Internal customer orientation, collaboration
    He believes that he needs to work more collaboratively, build more 'win-win' relationships with his internal customers. Also, he needs to seek and leverage feedback from internal customers in a proactive way

2. Building team harmony

   Rajan says, 'All five fingers of the hand are different'; he believes he needs to work differently with different personalities and build harmony even though each person is different and unique.

   With other teams he sees the need to 'carry them along' and find ways to build meaningful relationships

3. Being more open, reducing 'defensiveness'

   Rajan wants to be more open in his admission of failure, learn from these failures and convert that into strengths

## Strategies and Action Plans

The coach introduces Rajan to various models and frameworks to look at team diversity, customer centricity and collaborative relationships.

Rajan feels especially empowered by the discovery that he needs to adopt a leadership style that is different for different team members.

Rajan makes concrete plans to engage with peers and internal customers.

## Rajan Is Challenged Even More

Having arrived at three concrete goals and several actions, Rajan and his coach are quite pleased and set off to meet with two other sponsors for this engagement—Rajan's immediate manager, and a senior leader in the organization. They expect not just endorsement but also appreciation.

While his immediate manager endorses the goals and even acknowledges early signs of improvement, the senior leader does not miss the opportunity to challenge Rajan further. He stresses that Rajan is very good at completing 'to-do' tasks and may run the risk of viewing coaching as another 'task', a 'to-do' item. He reminds Rajan that he will get the most out of coaching only if he engages in deeper self-explorations. He exhorts Rajan to look at this as a 'personal development' investment and not as an 'improvement project'. He ends by reminding Rajan that his development is his responsibility.

The coach is initially concerned about these comments. *After all, the coach feels, Rajan has shown a keen interest to change and improve and has also demonstrated this as acknowledged by his boss. Why is this sponsor sounding a somewhat discordant note now?*

## Working at the Level of Beliefs

As the Coach and Rajan discuss the comments of the senior sponsor, he admits that there was some truth to what he said—that he had in the past demonstrated a 'tick box' approach towards collaboration.

The coach now perceives the wisdom in the senior leader-sponsor's exhortation for Rajan to introspect and change from the inside, rather than just window-dressing.

Over the next two meetings, the coach helps Rajan explore how he may want to rephrase some of his hard-held beliefs surrounding his goals. Rajan is able to articulate his current beliefs in many of these areas and then painstakingly replace them with more balanced beliefs. For example Rajan considers replacing his belief that 'It is very important not to fail, and never have a "negative mark" with senior management' with a more balanced belief that 'I should be open on issues and potential problems within the organization.'

Similarly, he considers replacing his belief that 'People should be competent enough to do their tasks independently, on their own' with a more balanced belief that 'People may need to be guided on completing their tasks.'

## Making Significant Changes

Rajan's 'goal orientation' coupled with the supportive space for reflection and introspection on one side and the strong wakeup call that the organization delivered leads him to identify and implement many changes in his approach, at a fairly deep level.

He works on being more proactive, more open and more approachable. He takes the initiative to meet with internal customers and engage with them. At meetings, he 'bites his tongue' and yet keeps quiet to listen to others' points of view, though different from his own.

With his own team, he changes his 'tough boss' style to be more supportive and coaching-oriented towards people whose performance is not yet on par, who need his help.

These changes are not easy to make. With people that Rajan knows and has a rapport with it is easier to do. With others, it is more difficult.

But Rajan notices that when it does work well, the stresses and tensions reduce.

## Back to the Start

At this stage, the coach gathers some 'post-coaching' feedback from Rajan's stakeholders. This helps appreciate and further challenge Rajan to stay on course. One stakeholder says, 'After every meeting, he asks for feedback and seems to be keen to reflect and change.'

Another says, 'Not combative, not in a denial mode—earlier as soon as someone says something, he used to immediately jump up to defend, deny, attack.'

However, they also agreed that he is 'visibly and clearly making an attempt, but he still has much distance to go'.

The coach helps Rajan compare where he started—the 'fatal flaw' of poor performance in the 'people' area with where he is today. There are many changes, which are demonstrated and visible to stakeholders. Of course with such deep changes in beliefs and the process of 'unlearning' oneself into a new culture it will take time and continued effort from Rajan. The coach closes the engagement on an optimistic note. He knows that Rajan is committed to and capable of following through on these changes.

As the coach reflects on his journey with Rajan he realizes that Rajan was indeed an 'easy' coachee to work with. He was willing to reflect, confront sensitive issues about himself, be honest and straightforward in his efforts and committed to making change happen. Above all, given his baptism by fire in his early days, he was never afraid of challenging himself.

The sponsors, the coach felt had played a very constructive but tough minded role in his success. They gave him coaching support but did not mince words. In hind sight, the coach is happy that he included them in the process, for without that, the medicine would not have been strong enough.

# 5

# Low Self-Esteem Can Derail a Leader's Career

Low self-esteem is quite pervasive, though not career-derailing amongst many Indian corporate leaders. Many learn to raise the threshold by recognizing and working on their self-efficacy. However, there are many others who are not able to recognize low self-esteem as an inhibitor to their career progression. Executive trappings that come with a good corporate position often work as a shield to low self-esteem. It could lead to careers being derailed. Sarika Cherian through many twists and turns, identifies Sahil's real dilemma and helps him to recognize and accept the need to address the core issue of self-esteem in order to build a sustainable career.

## The Case: Sahil Reclaims His Self-Esteem

'When it rains, it pours,' they say.

For eighteen months Sahil's job-hunt was getting nowhere.

Now, just as Sahil accepted one job offer, the calls for other job opportunities poured in. That was when I happily ended my coaching engagement with Sahil Wasan.

I was introduced to Sahil by another professional friend of mine.

What I heard from the person who made the introduction was that Sahil was going through certain midlife career dilemmas. His immediate challenge was to find another job, a task he had been pursuing for eighteen months.

What struck me about Sahil in our first meeting was his sincerity, earnestness and deep desire to change. Sahil was an engineer, had an MBA and had spent close to eighteen years in the financial services sector. He was an Executive Director in a large global, financial services company which was going through a rough patch. It hadn't made any progress in India over the last couple of years and that wasn't good for Sahil's CV. He was getting rusty and the longer he stayed, the more difficult it would become for him to get a good job. There was also the fear that the company may pack up its operations in the country. Sahil had come to the engagement with a very clear agenda:

1. To seek help and direction to make the right career move.
2. To deal with issues of what he called 'stage fright'—essentially the ability to communicate confidently with large groups of people. In coaching parlance, Sahil needed help with his executive presence.

I could feel Sahil's frustration, but was also encouraged by his determination and sense of purpose.

## Sahil's Story

Sahil's refrain through the first few meetings was that he had to find a new job and soon. His search had been on for over a year but he hadn't made any headway. And he blamed it all on his poor executive presence. He had had a problem with public speaking since childhood but it was now hampering his career. According to him he just didn't come through well in interview situations. He wasn't able to highlight his achievements and sell himself well. This somehow just didn't sound right to me. Sahil was an MBA from a premier B-School in Mumbai and had changed seven jobs during his eighteen-year career. Surely, his ability to face interviews could not be the issue?

I thought Sahil had achieved a lot but for some reason he just didn't seem to think so himself. He regretted having changed so many jobs and felt that the quality of his experience was now weighing him down. In the last so many years he had changed assignments far too frequently and as a result had not got an 'end-to-end' experience on any project.

He was also left with the feeling that had his education been superior, with degrees from better schools and universities, finding a job would have been easier, his confidence and executive presence issues notwithstanding. Sahil seemed to be living in remorse of his past.

He desired financial independence by the age of forty-two which meant that he was no longer needed to work for a living and could pursue other interests. The wonderful human being that he was, he wanted to use his skills acquired through corporate life to make a difference to the lives of the underprivileged; and eventually, to society at large by being in politics. Noble intentions but a bit unreal I thought. 'How many people did he know who were not born into industrialist families or royalty who had achieved such tall ambitions?' I asked. *My hunch at this time was Sahil was creating his own misery by hanging on to the past, not acknowledging his achievements and being overly harsh on himself.* Sahil was for some reason suffering from the 'I am not OK' syndrome.

## In Quest of the Real Story

Sahil was looking at life through a negative lens and I needed to get him to realise this. I thought a couple of psychometric tools, for self-realization would be useful.

**24 VIA Strengths:** I chose this positive psychology tool in the hope that it would help Sahil to shift his focus from what he had not achieved to his gifts.

**360-degree Feedback:** I also felt the need to talk to people close to him. I decided a 360-degree assessment would allow me to open Sahil's eyes to some of his self-limiting beliefs because it would be coming through an objective feedback mechanism rather than me saying it. I spoke to some of the people who were closest to him, his immediate family and others who knew him professionally (business associates, ex-colleagues and subordinates in his current workplace).

## Sahil's Real Story

The workplace feedback that came was that Sahil was a very fine profes-sional—committed, focused and one who certainly knew his onions. He made an extraordinary effort to stay connected and build his networks.

On the personal front, Sahil was very disciplined and lived life by the book. He had to eat the right things at the right time and exercise regu-larly. If he didn't manage to read his three newspapers in a day, he would feel his day had been incomplete.

24 VIA Strengths corroborated what Sahil's family and friends had to say about him. Sahil's top five strengths were:

1. Honesty, authenticity and genuineness
2. Modesty and humility
3. Caution, prudence, discretion
4. Kindness and generosity
5. Self-control and self-regulation

And, not surprisingly, a positive attitude was not one of Sahil's top strengths. *Hope and Optimism featured at rank 17 in Sahil's top 24 strengths.*

The breakthrough insight however came from the 360-degree assess-ment. Sahil had a childhood friend, Akhil who he was very, very close to and whom he constantly benchmarked himself with. Akhil had been far more successful than Sahil. While Sahil may have been as bright as Akhil, if not more, Akhil had just had the good fortune of getting better breaks. He had managed to go to better schools and universities and get better jobs. With the constant comparison Sahil had willed himself to believe that he was just not good enough. *Sahil set very high standards for himself and was never content with what he had achieved because he had grown up suffering from an inferiority complex.*

In his current situation, Sahil's pressure to perform and fear of failure were so high that he was overcome and immobilised by his anxiety. What was a simple job change (something that he had done innumerable times in the past) had become a huge ordeal. He was just setting himself up for failure.

## Getting Leverage

At this stage I decided that for Sahil to find a job was the most pressing task at hand. The longer he took to find a new and challenging assignment, the more damage it would do to his morale and self-esteem. I also realized that finding a job was not really the core issue; we were faced with a far deeper problem of low self-esteem which is what we eventually needed to address.

Sahil and I spent a lot of time brainstorming on how he could go about refining his job hunt. *Could he look at opportunities outside the financial services space? How could he go about identifying such opportunities? Could he leverage some of his networks?*

We then listed out the kind of opportunities that he could explore outside financial services with his kind of experience and qualifications: Corporate Strategy Head, Head of Mergers and Acquisitions (acquiring businesses/integrating businesses, strategic alliances—entering new markets) a B2B role, General Manager in a start-up like solar energy and a CFO role where limited accounting is involved, were some distinct possibilities. Sahil also started to list out the kind of companies he could consider for such jobs.

Sahil and I also discussed some of his interview situations and experiences and what he could do to deal with the bouts of nervousness. I got Sahil to do a lot of reading on how to handle interviews including a self-help book —*How to feel confident—simple tools for instant success*. In all this, my role was to be a thinking partner and to keep his motivation high. He did all the hard work.

## The Leap

And then one fine day, it just happened. Sahil's efforts at job hunting finally paid off and he landed himself an assignment as the MD of a financial services venture backed by one of India's premier business houses. This job was to help Sahil come out of his rut.

The situation however started to get complicated when suddenly a plethora of opportunities started coming Sahil's way. Sahil was once again filled with remorse and self-doubt. *Had he made the wrong choice? If he had waited would he have actually got a better option?* Sahil and I did some objective analysis of all options and finally he felt assured that his choice was indeed the right one.

## Challenging Skills to the Test

*What happened this time round? How did he get a job? It was the same Sahil with the same executive presence issues, the same dismal macroeconomic environment and all of that. So, how did so many opportunities suddenly come his way and how did he actually make it through an interview?* Sahil acknowledged, albeit reluctantly, that the dry phase in his job hunt had very little to do with his own capabilities.

## Goals

Sahil admitted that low self-esteem was something that he suffered from and definitely needed to work on. This was a moment of truth for him. *He realised that another job would have happened anyway. Sahil's real change agenda was to beat his inferiority complex and start believing in himself and his capabilities.*

With one problem solved, Sahil now felt anxious about other things. His new job would require him to do a considerable amount of public speaking. He would have to make a lot of presentations and that was already making him nervous.

We decided that this was a development area that we would focus on. It was a chicken and egg story. *For Sahil to elevate his self-esteem he needed to excel at his new job and for him to excel at his new job, in addition to other things he also needed to become a more confident and impactful presenter.*

Sahil was beginning to recognize the importance of working on his self-esteem.

He was now willing to commit himself to the specific goal of working on his self-esteem and confidence levels so that he would succeed in his job and also carry himself well.

In the next few weeks, we began to evolve several action plans to accomplish this goal.

## To Make New Job a Success

Sahil was clear about how to approach his new job and wrote out a whole action plan on the things he needed to do. The skilled professional that he was, Sahil was completely in control of this part and knew exactly what he needed to do to get off to a flying start in his new job.

1.  Since it was a new industry that he was going to be part of, he would have to do considerable homework to understand it better so he could land running
2.  Capitalize and build on his own network to achieve his professional goals

On the issue of esteem, it was clear that Sahil needed to become a lot more aware and mindful about the things that triggered anxiety and self-defeating beliefs. Sahil began to record these instances in the coming weeks.

Sahil soon realized that yoga could help him at a physical level in dealing with his anxieties and started taking efforts to learn it.

With heightened awareness and sharp focus, Sahil soon realized that he needed expert help. I was delighted when he decided to see a counsellor to deal with his anxiety.

In all this my role was to monitor progress and help him stay on track.

## The Results

Sahil has moved cities and started on his new job. I can see that he is approaching it with a lot of focus, commitment and positive energy. He loves the fact that he is back in action again, doing all the things that he hadn't been doing professionally for the last three years.

As Sahil admitted, what had worked for him was that he had had somebody to help him navigate through the haze and bring clarity on what the heart of the problem was. What he had achieved was awareness and the realization that the so called career crisis was but a mere symptom of his low self-esteem.

Sahil and I both know that the journey is by no means complete. Sahil is on the path to reform and will have arrived only when he exorcises all his deep-rooted self-limiting beliefs. We had started with baby steps but he is now seeking the help of a counsellor. He is also using homeopathic medicine to manage his anxiety. I monitor his progress from time to time and when I spoke to him last he had a far better score to report on his presentations and public speaking experiences.

I recognize that Sahil's work is far from complete.

The good news is that he is approaching it differently this time around.

This time, it is not just one more job change. It is about doing something fundamentally different.

*What made the difference was the relationship of trust that Sahil and I shared.*

# SECTION C

# Shaping Attitudes and Beliefs

# Why Attitudes and Beliefs Affect a Leader's Effectiveness

## Zahid Gangjee[*]

**C**oaching—even if it is focused on enhancing knowledge and skills—has to encompass the Coachee's *behaviour*. Behaviour is the 'vehicle' through which we deliver what we know and what we can do. *How* we speak and act is always as important as *what* we say and do. Many times the 'how' is more important.

*Attitudes* are defined as 'predispositions to behave in a specific way in certain situations'. In other words, human beings are primed in advance to respond in an *already chosen* way when they are put into certain situations. These 'choices' are mostly unconscious (beyond our normal awareness) and based on our beliefs.

*Beliefs* are 'personal truths'. We are all the 'products' of our unique 'histories'—our personal, social, cultural and professional pasts. In the process of growing up we have experiences that leave us with 'codes' of how things are. These are useful aids in the journey of life and allow us to 'fit in' and grow. However, when the world around us changes significantly, or if we are in very different contexts, these beliefs can become obstacles to effectiveness.

It is normal for children to almost blindly follow what they see their parents do. An important 'milestone' in life is Adolescence when teenagers question this 'handed down' wisdom, listen more to peers, seek experiences beyond the known and comfortable boundaries and try to rewrite their identity. It is an important stage as it helps these individuals move

*Zahid H. Gangjee is the Chief Executive, Zahid Gangjee & Associates, Organization and HR Consultancy, Kolkata, which has been helping organizations in India and abroad manage change at the total organization, group and individual levels since 1995. He has directed/consulted to interventions and workshops since 1975. Dr Gangjee has been a Faculty Member in Behavioural Science at the IIM, Calcutta and ASCI, Hyderabad.

from dependency through counter-dependency into inter-dependency—which is very necessary when one is working in organizations. If, for whatever reason, leaders have not been able to make this transition, they are left less than effective in the role.

Leaders in an organization have people reporting to them who are dependent on them for direction, guidance, growth opportunities, etc. The leaders are dependent on them for their contributions and commitment. They are interdependent. Similarly, the leaders—no matter how high up they are in the hierarchy—have people above who provide direction, wisdom and so on and are dependent on them for delivering organizational results. So there is inter-dependency upwards as well.

My experience shows that if, for whatever reason, Leaders have not been able to transition Adolescence well, they may be left in a psychological position of dependency or counter-dependency with negative consequences for the leadership role.

If the stance is Dependency, the Leaders may expect their reportees to check everything with them as this is the 'picture in the mind' they carry. It may also lead to a paternal/maternal style of leadership. This same stance is enacted upward. The Leaders take no major decision without the 'approval' of their seniors; do not use the authority they derive from their role or their personal authority, that is the wisdom derived from one's own experiences. If the stance is counter-dependency, the leaders may seek to be over-controlling downwards (the 'picture in the mind' is 'Rebellion') and do not pay heed to directions or advice from seniors. Unless the coach works at the attitude and beliefs formation levels, the leader's behaviour may not truly change.

Another example of Leadership behaviour arising from past beliefs and related attitudes is competing. This is very common in the sub-continent. There are leaders who compete with everyone—their reportees, seniors, peers, consultants, etc. My experience shows that this arises from our past culture of 'deprivation'. We *did* live in an environment of deprivation—over two decades ago—where there were not enough jobs, not enough food, phone connections, etc. Though the environment has changed, people who grew up in that era (or who were heavily influenced by their parents who carried 'deprivation' in their unconscious) still carry a 'picture in the mind', an underlying assumption, that 'there will not be enough for me/my family and to ensure my share I must be first'. This pushes them to levels and arenas of competing that are very counter-productive.

One can go on with many, many examples. However, the following case studies will give you many incidents to illustrate what I have been trying to highlight: the dynamics of how attitudes and beliefs do affect behaviour and need to be worked with to help bring about sustainable behavioural change.

# 6

# Transporting the Winning Attitude

When executives make career changes, they bring with them to the new roles the skills and attitude that served them well in the past. While the skills are usually portable, attitudes may not be and may need to be in tune with the new environment. Not recognizing this can lead successful executives even with a great track record into a downward performance spiral.

Raghuvir Das found Paddy in such a situation and probably quite late. He had to use a range of intervention to help Paddy regain his lost ground and deliver results which Paddy did.

## The Case: Paddy's Attitude Conundrum

### Call from the Plaintiff

When my mobile phone rang, it showed a Singapore country code. I was quite puzzled because it had been more than six years since I had done any business in that part of the world. 'This is Tan Kok Hin,' said the voice on the other side. I am often confused about how to address people from the Orient—Should I say 'Mr Tan' or should it be 'Mr Kok Hin'? I chose, 'Good morning, Mr Kok Hin—What can I do for you?'

and it seemed to be the right choice. Kok Hin was Director—Asia-Pacific of a European multinational company that was in the infrastructure ancillary business. He had been referred by a mutual friend whom I had met at an airport barely 24 hours ago, and had talked about the difference coaching was making to leaders across the world. If this call had emanated so soon after the reference, the matter was perhaps extremely urgent. Kok Hin needed no invitation to tell his story.

## The Plaint

Kok Hin's organization had recruited a Sales Head from another European company in a similar vertical to be the CEO for its India operations—Padmanabhan (Paddy). The criteria for this selection were Paddy's understanding of the complex matrix reporting structures and his ability to interact with European bosses. Paddy's business connections with the relevant distribution channels, academics (Engineer, MBA) from premier institutions and a good sales track record all weighed in his favour. Two years into his tenure as CEO, Kok Hin felt that the Indian operations were in a mess. Sales were poor, Paddy rarely met his monthly sales commitments, his MIS reports were tardy, and he was ducking phone calls from his Singapore and European bosses. The seniors in Europe were rapidly losing faith in Paddy given his attitude towards delayed MIS reporting and a casual approach to business commitments. Kok Hin's boss was a great believer in life time employment and was convinced that Paddy was a good, competent manager with high integrity, but something was going wrong and had suggested external intervention. I asked Kok Hin for his own assessment of the problem and he suggested that poor performance had resulted in Paddy displaying evasive behaviour. He suggested that I meet with Paddy immediately.

## The Defendant

A fortnight later, I met with Paddy in a quiet corner of Bangalore. Paddy was a quintessential Sales and Distribution manager with a prestigious B-school degree and a track record of over fifteen years in a similar industry. When he was selected as the CEO of the Indian operations of this European company, he had been reporting to Kok Hin's boss—the worldwide sales head sitting at the Headquarters. Now, he was reporting to Kok Hin, the Director for Asia pacific, operating from Singapore. He admitted that the company had given him a carte blanche in budgets, people, marketing, etc., but for reasons that he could not fathom, sales were just not picking up. I unearthed that there was no document on Paddy's Key Result Areas (KRA) and all the reviews with Kok Hin were focussed only on monthly sales versus commitments. Paddy also confessed that it was getting more and more difficult everyday to come up with innovative excuses for non-performance. To a direct question on why he did not resign and attempt to move on, Paddy said, 'The Company has given me so much freedom that I want to prove to them that I can deliver the goods. I never quit when I am down.' That was the positive hook which indicated to me that Paddy would put in his best efforts and work through the problem with his coach. Clearly, he seemed to have exhausted all options to get the sales graph to look upwards and Kok Hin and team were not extending a helping hand.

## Mediating between the Plaintiff and the Defendant

My friends in the legal fraternity have told me that it is 'always better to pay your adversary than it is to pay your advocate'. Sometimes in the Coaching profession, the coachee perceives the coach to be an advocate of the superior's agenda. On the other hand, when the coach's level of empathy with the coachee and coachee-centricity grows, the superior perceives the coach to be a spokesperson for the coachee's issues. I had to tread a very careful path here. Hence I decided to call for a joint session with Kok Hin and Paddy, ostensibly to brain storm the next steps in my engagement. But the real purpose of seeking this mediation session was to ensure that Kok Hin and Paddy jointly arrived at a consensus on what the coaching agenda should be. This coaching agenda needed to have a solid business context as well, so that as Paddy went through a transformation business results would simultaneously improve. Kok Hin himself had to buy in to the coaching process—especially the diagnostic and development methodology, non-prescriptive and non-directive.

While my goal as a coach was to arrive at a coaching agenda, I also wanted to ensure that the Kok Hin and Paddy were on the same page and their perceptions of the problem areas were aligned. More importantly, I did not want to be the judge pronouncing the defendant guilty or otherwise, without giving a fair hearing to both sides. I had, during my individual meetings with both Paddy and Kok Hin, discovered that they rarely had face to face reviews or exchanged strategic and tactical ideas. Very often, geographical distance, cross cultural barriers and the unique nature of the Indian market place, result in powerful intellectual dialogues between a boss and his subordinate getting morphed into a petty diagnosis of mutual faults and finger pointing. I could relate to what Paddy was going through based on my own experience as the Country Head of a Japanese MNC, with a functional Chinese boss sitting in Singapore and an administrative Japanese boss based out of Tokyo, both of them fighting their respective inertia to come down and meet with stakeholders in India.

I therefore decided that it was appropriate that I would pose some key questions to them in a manner that they look beyond the blame game and focus on what needed to be done to produce business results and build Paddy into a competent leader. Paddy was based in Bangalore, Kok Hin in Singapore and I was in Chennai, but through some brilliant scheduling software, we managed to meet in a private hotel room in Delhi. Notwithstanding video conferencing and similar technological breakthroughs, the face-to-face meeting still has its place, and often produces the most amazing effects on the participants if the agenda is set carefully and adhered to in word and spirit.

The mediation session was a major eye opener. What emerged were some honest facts of the case that needed work on all sides:

1.  Both Kok Hin and Paddy were flummoxed by the fact that while they had replicated the sales strategy that worked so well in Paddy's previous company, which was to appoint top distributors in the major metros, everything around him seemed to fail. The distributors were simply not willing to stock and promote the products aggressively. No amount of incentives through higher margins or lowering prices seemed to work. Clearly, their target consumer was not being serviced by the current channel. Paddy volunteered to investigate this.

2.  Paddy felt that while his superiors were constantly asking for results, they were not helping the cause by giving the necessary strategic inputs. Product Managers, Kok Hin and other key functional heads, were fighting shy of visiting India and talking to end users and channel partners.

3.  Kok Hin felt that Paddy's job was demanding more than what he had the competence for. Paddy denied this explaining that in his

previous job he had handled a sales volume that was ten times larger and a team size that was five times as big as it was in his current assignment. Nevertheless, Kok Hin went on the explain that delayed MIS reporting and a poor commitment to sales performance were unacceptable and non-negotiable for a leader of his stature. I butted in at this point to ask him which he considered more important—getting the business graph to over northwards, or getting the MIS reports on time. They both agreed that the former was more critical and if Paddy did figure out a way to get in predictable sales, the other problem of meeting MIS deadlines was very minor.

4. Paddy's operations consisted of a five member team of sales and support personnel spread across the country. Kok Hin felt that Paddy was too soft on his subordinates and was being indecisive in weeding out poor performers. Paddy agreed to this but highlighted that hiring and firing at a rapid pace was not the only solution to the problem. I asked Kok Hin, if he had in his mind a good performing country in Asia-Pacific and describe the churn in sales people in that geography. Kok Hin agreed that Indonesia was performing well and the turnover of sales people was very low. This answer got both of them thinking about how to make their sales people successful as opposed to outsourcing their sales problem to the field force.

As this discussion progressed, it was clear to both Kok Hin and Paddy that there was much to do in terms of:

1. Rediscovering what their approach to the Indian market should be.
2. Doing some comparative analysis on similar Asian markets and studying their sales strategies.
3. Drawing up an effective KRA document for Paddy and his team and institute a review mechanism that was not just focussed on number commitments.

After drawing up a 'To-Do' list with action items and responsibilities with clearly defined time frames, we broke up with the feeling that the problem was not as simple as Kok Hin had imagined it to be. Kok Hin himself had work to do in terms of facilitating Paddy's initiatives and holding his hand while he progressed slowly towards business growth.

## The Hearings with the Defendant, the Emotions and the Case Progression

Using tools such as 360-degree feedback, SOP questionnaire and Strategic Gap Analysis, the coaching goals set were to help Paddy evolve a self sufficient style of creating a strategy and setting goals for himself and his team members. Kok Hin promised to help Paddy draw up a KRA document and also accompany him on selected field visits.

The stage was now set for Paddy to transform—he was now clear that the coach, his own boss and the organization were truly willing to help him give his best shot. In the sessions that followed after the mediation, my cross examination was focussed on how he wanted to go about creating a winning strategy. He thought for a while and said, 'It is not that I have failed completely, I do have some customer and channel successes to build on.' I urged him to elaborate and he revealed that the most consistently performing territory was the state of Kerala and this was because there were a lot of independent houses with sloping roofs that were being built and his distributor was very well connected to the architects who were happy recommending the product. He then decided to make field trips to Kerala and other states where similar market conditions existed.

At the end of the third session and when quite a few field trips had been completed, he called me excitedly and said, 'Coach—I seem to have discovered the secret formula—I should have built my strategy on success stories that really happened around me, rather than on what I believed would work.' I complimented him for this wonderful discovery and did give him a similar example from my own marketing career to ensure that he got the positive stroke that he needed to pursue this new found path. A unique coaching input was for Paddy to do field trips to similar and unrelated businesses to help him think out of the box and not be restricted by his self-limiting beliefs that 'this market works only in this way'.

While it was apparent to Paddy that appointing his old distributors was not yielding results; he had been unwilling to accept that redesigning the channel strategy should be his focus. He revealed that he was resisting this because he had placed all his bets around what had worked well in his previous organization, especially as his bosses there had drummed it into him that this was the only mantra to sales salvation. Finally, based on clinching evidence from the field force and his most successful channel partner, Paddy agreed that a different set of strategies in the market place was the only way forward. He now felt the need to go back to basics, revisit some success stories and redraw the strategy using first principles. Over the next few sessions, which involved a lot of brainstorming along with Kok Hin, Paddy enthusiastically put together a clarified strategy for the India operations.

Paddy's salient conclusions and action points to be implemented were:

1.  The industrial ancillary product that his company made was being appreciated and used well by a growing but insightful customer base. This customer base cared about thermal insulation, sound proofing and being ecologically friendly.
2.  Such products were typically recommended by the architect fraternity. So his company had to use the architects as much as pharmaceutical companies used doctors.
3.  Outbound dealers who had access to both architects as well as this niche customer base were the most successful channel partners. Appointing more such dealers would be the way to go. His current distributors were mostly stockists who expected intermediaries to pick the product through an inbound purchase mechanism. While this inbound approach would work with a mass product, it would fail with a niche offering.
4.  His sales force had to spend more time with architects and getting them to recommend his product, rather than begging the channel to stock it.
5.  Marketing activities had to focus on evangelizing the USPs of the product to the customer base at large to move up the value chain and accept ecological friendliness and the benefits of thermal and sound insulation.

Finally, Paddy pleaded guilty to the fact that he had not applied his mind and used basic principles that he had learnt long ago. He also admitted that since the company had given him the carte blanche to figure this out, he had not committed himself to the fundamental approach and had resorted to taking the short route to growing sales.

## Serving the Sentence

In right earnest, Paddy went about putting together a new channel, a new marketing budget, retraining his sales and support staff and executing what he called a blue print to getting the sales graph look skywards. The help he sought from the coach was a lot of listening and probing. My probing centred on whether every executable task was aligned with his strategy. I was continually seeking his re-assurance on whether he felt that he had the right team in place and how he was evaluating their performance. The overall transformation of the organization took place in the following manner:

1. The flavour of the distribution channel completely metamorphized into a unique set of partners, who were closer to architects. They were mostly located in areas where villas and ashrams were common places
2. A programme to educate architects was launched nationwide with product specialists flying in from Europe and China
3. A KRA document was available in the hands of every staff member and reviews happened relentlessly every month

After a short conference with Kok Hin and Paddy, where they said that the India operation had new found energy and purpose, and that sales were growing, my official role in this case came to an end.

But then, after about ten months, the Singapore number appeared on my cell phone again. I knew it was Kok Hin. His voice was high pitched and excited. The India business had now started giving tenfold sales growth to the company in the months after the end of the coaching engagement. Paddy was sending MIS reports on time, meeting his revenue and cost budgets and the company's world-wide distributor conference was to be held in Kerala. I was being invited to be a speaker. I informed him that I was really happy for Paddy and his company but could not be with them on those dates as I had promised to be on a holiday my family in Ladakh. I could sense the disappointment in Kok Hin's voice as we finished the call.

Obviously, Paddy had served his sentence well and had deliverance bestowed upon him by the market place. What remained etched in my mind was that, as a coach, every time I am briefed by a sponsor on how the behaviour of a leader needs to change, I should spend time checking whether there is a more deep rooted strategic problem within the organization. Otherwise, I would find myself entangled in a conundrum that could suck me into a whirlpool of meetings and sessions with no end in sight.

# 7

# What Makes People Miserable

Albert Ellis, who has done enormous work in the area of understanding irrational beliefs and has come up with Rational Emotive Therapy, says that 'Man is not disturbed by events but by the view he takes of them.' So whenever there is an event that executives face, each of them takes a different view to that event, thereby causing different emotions in themselves and, as a result, they act in different ways.

Coaches who are empathetic and tough-minded in their listening are able to very quickly spot some of the irrational ideas and mistaken beliefs held by their coachees.

As they pick up data from others, they become aware of the unhealthy consequences of such beliefs. Typical unhealthy consequences could include lack of assertiveness, excessive aggressiveness, lack of empowerment, over work, inability to let go, inability to take risks and so on.

Coaches then help their coachees dispute and challenge such ideas and replace it with more balanced ideas or beliefs. This is what Pramodh Bose did with Vicky. Thanks to his efforts, Vicky was able to make behavioural changes that were sustainable.

## The Case: Vicky Flies a Plane with No Hangar Time

Rolling off the runway, the jet plane was moving towards its assigned jetway. As I peered out of my window and caught a glimpse of the hangar area, I recalled what my coachee, Vikram (Vicky) S. K. said in one of our early coaching sessions: *'I often feel like I am flying a plane, with no hangar time.'*

Right after graduating from one of India's premier engineering institutions, Vicky joined a well-known, professionally managed family-owned firm that was into manufacturing, installing and servicing engineered goods, as well as turnkey projects. Vicky worked with this company for over twenty-three years, all of it in one particular business division of the firm. He became an expert in sales and marketing of standard-products, as well as custom-projects. He was reputed in the industry for being an accomplished professional with high technical acumen. Over the years, he gained experience in business development and sales not just within India but also the neighbouring countries. After about twenty years with the company, Vicky was called upon to head the sales, marketing and business development functions for the division, reporting to the chief of the division.

Vicky was looking out for opportunities to move to a general management role and this led to his joining his present employer—the Indian subsidiary of a European-origin multinational company known the world over for innovation and technology in engineered goods and infrastructure projects. The company was looking to establish itself in the Indian-market and found Vicky to be an ideal candidate to lead the newly-formed business division. However, Vicky's was a two-fold challenge—he was transitioning into a general-management role, with a mandate to start a new business and scale it up over time. Further, moving from a professionally run, family-business to a multinational company brought with it some more new challenges.

## Pre-Engagement

After about two years into his present role, Vicky decided to examine the possibility of a coaching engagement. At our pre-engagement meeting, Vicky gave a detailed account of his career and progression, closing it with the present situation, where he often felt he was spinning wheels. He expected that our coaching engagement should help him find the road ahead and gain some traction. I was struck by his determination and initiative to consider executive coaching as an intervention. Our conversation helped him understand that a coaching intervention can give best results when the coachee takes the ownership in terms of bringing the issues to the table—diligently and candidly—as well as working on actions identi-fied with regard to areas for improvement as well as un-availed opportu-nities. Vicky was quickly able to find a comfort level while interacting with me and that got the engagement off to a positive start.

Vicky wanted the coaching engagement to be a professional develop-ment initiative at his sole discretion, with no employer-sponsorship. He was unwilling to involve his superior in the coaching process, because he felt it to be too uncomfortable. However, he was fine with the participa-tion of his colleagues in feedback interviews. Vicky's preference not to involve his boss was the only discordant note.

However, mindful of his proactive approach in seeking out a coach, I decided to stay engaged. I was sure that as the engagement progressed, I will have opportunities to exhort Vicky to engage his boss. In any case, the principle of coachee-centricity served as a beacon to remind me that Vicky had the final call on this matter.

## Vicky, as He Sees Himself

In our initial sessions, Vicky came across as an anxious and harried per-son. Working in a multinational brought for him many first-time expe-riences in terms of work practices, organization structure and culture. Vicky spent a good part of his first year working with colleagues from India and the regional and global head-quarters, to draw up the business strategy and road map. He was also seized of the challenge to bring in talent. Despite the favourable profile of his employer on the job market, it was not easy to attract experienced people into a start-up venture. Well laid out plans and the on-boarding of some good talent notwithstanding, his business unit's performance was off plan, making Vicky anxious. The need to manage the multiple stakeholder expectations in a matrix organi-zation with regional and global docking points was another first-time experience he was coping with.

Vicky assessed his strengths as being values-driven, ability to build trust; ability to lead teams; domain expertise; technical knowledge; com-munication and presentation skills; analytical skills; and results focus. His listing of improvement areas: delegation and assertiveness.

When it comes to delegation, Vicky's emphasis was on 'getting things done right, the first time' and he often stayed engaged with his subordi-nates in a hands-on manner. His propensity to get hands-on was driven by his anxiety that most people on his team were new comers to the company, seized of the challenges of job transition. His disappointment was that despite his 'very supportive' delegation-style, his team was not 'hitting the pedals as they should be'.

Vicky felt there were times when he wished he was assertive in his interactions with peers and superiors, instead of the pole-positions of being aggressive or staying 'passive as a doormat'. He said, 'I sometimes wish that a simple "No" from me worked fine.'

The outputs from his *REBT questionnaire* showed that he was prone to *anxiety about the unknown and uncertain*; he considered it an *absolute necessity to win the approval of peers, friends and family*; and that it *is important to be unfailingly competent, almost to the point of perfection*. His *24 VIA Characters Test* showed that his #1 value in action was *acting with caution, prudence and discretion*.

Virtuous as Vicky understood these beliefs and values to be, I had a hunch that he could be challenged in dealing with the behaviours that are driven by such beliefs and values.

## Vicky, as Seen by Others

The feedback from colleagues confirmed Vicky's own assessment but it also offered some insightful details on the two improvement areas.

Vicky was seen as being unduly focused on risks and mitigations while having delegation conversations. He was prescriptive in delegating. He expected only exception-reporting in follow-ups/reviews—and reportees were not expected to bring recommendations/solutions. It appeared that his reportees felt stifled to show ownership, creativity and to be pro-active in learning by doing. On his need for assertiveness, the consistent feedback was that he is sometimes docile while dealing with superiors or with people who are experts in fields that are outside his area of expertise (like finance, for example).

## Making Meaning and Arriving at Goals

In conversations that followed, as we explored Vicky's beliefs and values, he connected the dots between what his challenges were (that is, areas where he was ineffective) and the reasons for why the things were the way they were (that is, why he was ineffective). Vicky could identify some childhood experiences to be the genesis of most of his beliefs and values. These centred around a strong focus on academic achievement, and ensuring that nothing would ever be done that could potentially come in the way of this overriding objective. However, our conversations also helped in Vicky acknowledging alternate realities, beliefs and other values that he could strongly relate to from his experiences both as an adult as well as a professional, especially when he recalled occasions on which he did not succeed in the manner that he would have liked to, but was nevertheless seen to be sincere, hard working and a good learner, and therefore provided opportunities to correct himself and come out a winner on subsequent attempts.

As our conversations progressed, Vicky was also able to appreciate that his belief to be seen as being unfailingly competent was making him adopt a prescriptive style while delegating work. His penchant for caution and prudence influenced his approach to delegation, and the choice of words that he made while having delegation and review conversations with his subordinates, not realising the resulting overemphasis on risks and failures. He was able to see that not only was his team's performance hindered by his ineffective approach to delegation but was compounded by his low emphasis on solution-orientation in follow up reviews. His comfort with sales functions made him spend disproportionate amount of time with issues in that function (which some felt as *micromanaging*) and less time on other aspects of business. More importantly, our conversation helped him reflect on his own career progression and acknowledge that he had worked with bosses who were not anxious but were empowering at delegation, leaving him with the room to take initiative. They were tolerant of failure by seeing it as a necessity for one's professional progress— and for the continuous building of competence. This represented the potential to become a huge breakthrough moment, demonstrating to him how the very attributes that he was unable to subscribe to in his dealings with others were the ones that had helped him in his career when they were subscribed to by his superiors in their dealings with him.

Our conversations about his belief on the importance of having the approval of others helped him understand his lack of assertiveness and his motivation for, in his words, 'Saying yes when I should really be saying no.' On the other hand, he considered the possibility that his aggressive behaviour was a manifestation of his displeasure at his *unfailing competence being questioned*. He appreciated that as a business unit leader, he must be able to 'better manage the pressures from the eco-system' without being pliant or unduly aggressive—both of which caused 'emotional drain' on him.

Our conversations helped him see how beliefs about his fear for the unknown and the need to be unfailingly competent, can feed into each other and thereby reinforce risk-averse behaviours and approaches. Vicky appreciated the importance of risk-taking for the scaling up of a start-up venture and more importantly, the conversation helped him acknowledge how some professionals that he personally knew, succeeded because they had risk-taking ability. He recounted some of his experiences of moving out of home to go study in a college that was very far away and the journey thereafter that had many accomplishments to his credit. He said, 'I have done many things that no one in my family has even thought of! Now, doesn't that take some risk-taking ability?'

Our conversations helped Vicky see the mutually reinforcing linkage between his beliefs and behaviours. Vicky also appreciated that beliefs can spawn strengths that may have been relevant in the past but may now be unduly over-emphasised in the present context and past success can trap a professional into a comfort zone. Delegation for performance; becoming more assertive and improving risk-taking ability became Vicky's final coaching goals, and he said, 'It is now starting to make sense. I like this clarity.'

## Moving to Actions

Vicky showed increasing confidence as we progressed in our engagement. His demeanour was far from the tentative one that I saw in the early stages. Despite my repeated suggestions, Vicky remained firm about not involving his boss. However, at our first session for action-planning, he told me that at a recent one-to-one meeting with his boss, he made a disclosure about his coaching engagement and shared his goals. Vicky's boss was supportive of his proactive move to seek coaching and added that the goals were relevant from his perspective as well. Pinned to his soft-board next to his desk, was a print of the power-point slide that I gave him at one of our early sessions, listing the key attributes of a 'Fully Functioning Person'. As I held my gaze on that slide, he quipped, 'It's about being in touch with oneself and moving from existing to living.'

Vicky chose his first goal as 'Improving Delegation'. Our conversations helped him arrive at the specific behaviours that he will aim to cultivate and consistently deploy: 'By focusing on my approach to delegating tasks—without being prescriptive—and on reviewing performance by seeking a solutions-bias on part of my reportees.' He decided to espouse an alternate belief that failure is a part of the learning process that leads to enhanced competence. Vicky decided to have delegation-conversations that drive better ownership on part of his subordinates. He planned to achieve this by avoiding over-specification/being prescriptive, but instead drawing his reportee out to think and talk about his/her understanding of the task and how it will be achieved. He decided to make conscious effort to curb his tendency to over-emphasise on 'what-can-go-wrong', and conduct conversations that help his reportees think about the same and help them identify steps for avoidance/mitigation. Finally, he will set the expectation for his reportees to come into his follow-up reviews not with a mere status-report, but with a presentation on analyses of exceptions, on causes and recommended remedies (that is, solution-bias). So as to deal with his propensity to spend too much time with sales department, he decided to have monthly business review meetings where all his direct reports will participate and a review calendar was set up for the next twelve months.

On his goal to improve assertiveness, Vicky identified actions that will help him to '... be able to say "No" or say a "Yes" that is OK with me'. He chose to cultivate the habit of being able to be 'in touch with myself', while in crucial conversations, by recognizing his emotional state and keeping a check on his belief that 'approval and harmony is vital'. Vicky identified the need to engage in an inquiring conversation to better understand what is being suggested/expected, keeping a check on emotions—and regulating behaviour. He substituted an alternate belief that the need for approval/harmony affects his ability to engage in authentic conversations. This will give him the objectivity and steadfastness to say, 'No', but with well articulated reasons. And if not, to find middle ground for convergence that leads to a 'Yes' that is acceptable. He also now believed that he can explore the opportunity for an offline conversation to be had later, rather than be hasty in the present. Finally, he found it useful to apply discretion in determining which conversations to engage in.

To improve risk-taking ability, he identified actions '... to be less risk-averse and more entrepreneurial'. He chose to keep a constant reminder on the value of having an action bias. He said, 'It was about choosing between the failures likely due to actions versus failures resulting from inaction.' He decided to deal with the anxiety by building a balanced-picture (that is, favourable factors and risks; positive outcomes and negative fall outs; the-prize-of-action and cost-of-inaction) and by being proactive in identifying risk mitigation measures. Vicky decided to lever-age the diversity—within his team and in the extended organization—in helping him generate clarity; create alternatives; and deploy specific strengths to enhance risk-taking ability.

Vicky also decided to maintain a personal journal on his actions that he aimed to review weekly. With the goals and action plans in place, our engagement moved to the next phase—implementation of the agreed action plans. Vicky turned out to be a model coachee in the next few weeks. He meticulously worked on the actions that had been agreed with his coach, maintained a log of what he had done, the experiences that he had gone through as a result, and the emotions he felt when some things went according to the script while others threw up surprises. In the next couple of meetings the coach encouraged him to look at alternatives to whatever didn't work, and to persist with even greater vigour on the new approaches that sat well with him and seemed to produce the responses that he had hoped to get from his team members. Soon it became evident to Vicky that he was developing a modified style that combined the areas that had worked well for him in the past with a new set of approaches that addressed the areas of concern that had been identified at the com-mencement of the engagement. The coach suggested an abridged closing 360-degree feedback exercise with a select group of colleagues, and Vicky readily agreed. The results were predictable, and most gratifying. Almost every respondent confirmed having noticed changes in several aspects of Vicky's managerial style, and these corresponded to very areas that Vicky had worked on in the preceding months.

## Vicky, Still Flying

Vicky's goals, especially the first two, were so fundamental in nature and yet, the inadequacies of these skills were felt only after he moved to his new job. It is quite possible that owing to his deep functional expertise and the company culture at his previous place of employment, these inad-equacies remained subdued, only to get significantly magnified when he moved to a general management role in a multinational company. Vicky's case tells us that a back-to-the-basics approach may well be the outcome of a coaching conversation—and it need not always be about new skills, but about dusting-off and embellishing some basic skills. Simple as it may sound, this going back-to-the-basics involves the diligent examination of one's beliefs and behaviours as a coachee, and the non-judgemental space that a coaching-engagement provides is much needed for the coachee to succeed. But above all, I consider Vicky to be a copy-book example of a 'coaching ready' executive, which he amply and consistently demonstrated this by his courage to introspect; proactive action-bias; and diligence in actions.

A year later, I ran into Vicky at a management seminar. He had just returned from an in-company, global leadership retreat. Vicky was one among the very few participants from India, and was acknowledged by many for his active participation and perspective-sharing. I asked him about his plane and he said that his business unit was at the top of the table for performance-bonuses paid out recently and added, 'I still fly that plane that has no hangar time … and it is fun!'

# 8

# Executives Succeed When They Refuse to Become Victims of Their Circumstances

Executives are often victims of their circumstances, including some of their seriously unfortunate childhood experiences, and this ends up impacting their ability to trust and therefore their attitudes towards others in their work and personal lives. Liberating oneself from the shackles of this is very tough, but possible. This is what Sandhya did, thanks to the timely support of her insightful and empathetic coach, Gowri Mithra.

## The Case: Sandhya Learns to Trust

I caught myself staring at the vast expanse of the city, from the window of my office, lost in thoughts, while the bustling city was going about its business on this mid-autumn afternoon.

I had received Sandhya's call sometime back giving me the news of her having got the coveted role of Global Lead for her business competency, a role that was keenly fought and contested by many, but finally won by her, fair and square. 'Ma'am, I did it, I got the role! Thank you for everything.' Her voice sounded triumphant, excited and full of self-confidence.

I put the phone down with a satisfied smile. It had been quite a journey for the two of us and I couldn't help wind back in time and reflect on the events that had led to today and the distance she had travelled in the last eighteen months.

## How It All Began

Sandhya had just finished her annual appraisal session with her boss, Renuka and the entire experience had left her completely unsettled. The usual platitudes about her commitment to work, professional attitude, willingness to adapt to change and being reliable and trustworthy, etc., notwithstanding, the appraisal seemed to suggest that there were serious questions on her suitability for the role of Associate Vice President and Delivery Head that she was currently performing.

Sandhya had received less than expected ratings on certain key behavioural parameters from all her peers and superiors and was perceived as biased and closed to suggestions, brash and abrasive, and non-collaborative. Her communication style and inability to connect with people and carry them along were seen as major barriers to success given the high degree of relationship building and networking, across teams and geographies, required in this role. Also, this was the stepping stone for all future leadership roles in the organization and it was critical that she make a success of it.

Sandhya came back deeply perturbed and reflected long and hard on what had led to her being adjudged thus, especially since she had a track record of being a highly awarded and exceptional performer in her earlier role as Operations Head.

She grudgingly acknowledged to herself that working with people and teams did not come easily to her as she found it difficult to trust others and let go, but did not seem to think it was so bad that it could affect her performance ratings.

Renuka, on her part, was well aware of how critical it was that Sandhya succeed in this role given that her future career was at stake here. She was also familiar with some of Sandhya's personal challenges and was truly keen to help her work things out and move ahead in life.

She suggested that they look at executive coaching as a possible intervention to help her with her issues.

Sandhya agreed but was not sure what to expect. She did not know what executive coaching was and whether this meant that she was marked as a non/poor performer. It was in this frame of mind that she met me, her coach, and in the very first meeting her emotions came out with a rush and intensity that took me by surprise.

## Sandhya's Story

We met at a coffee shop since she was keen that I meet her outside of her workplace and home. At first sight, she struck me as a pleasant and warm though slightly diffident person and there was nothing to suggest that she was out of the ordinary.

She spoke candidly about her appraisal and feedback and the 'issues' as she called them and asked me if coaching could help address these. I needed to hear more to be able to answer that question honestly.

Sandhya was promoted last year, within just three years of working with her current company, from a limited visibility and highly operational role in the company's middle management to a more strategic senior management position with an involved matrix reporting structure and working multiple domestic and international teams.

Her new role, a management level position, demanded extensive interaction and collaboration with her peers from other business units, reliance on teams from other geographies and quick turnarounds on deliveries despite several dependencies that were not in her control.

Initially excited about the challenges of this new role, she soon realised that she was unable to make much headway or get much support from her peers and even team members. She described herself as a perfectionist and task oriented and expected others to keep up to her high standards of work. She did not think much of their competence and felt she needed to closely oversee the work produced by her team and most of the time step in to save the day as 'at the end of the day the job had to be done and done well!'

However despite all this, she believed that she was facing discrimination, by peers and superiors due to the way she had been positioned , as non-collaborative and brusque in her dealings and her inability to communicate effectively.

Her somewhat cynical assessment of her situation was that she was losing out on account of seemingly extraneous issues such as communication and people skills, despite being a workaholic and a perfectionist and that people with lesser merit/abilities were moving ahead on account of their abilities to build effective people relationships.

## Early Life's Unkindly Cuts

As Sandhya was speaking I could sense that while she tried to sound objective and matter-of-fact her eyes and body language were narrating a story of their own. Especially in her references to how people around her behaved with her I perceived some deep rooted biases. I made a mental note of this and decided not to pursue this or challenge her at this stage of our relationship.

We changed tacks and I asked her to share her early years' experiences, especially her growing up years.

Sandhya mentioned to me that she came from a very conservative family background where girl children were educated only up-to high school/early college level and then expected to get married. She was the middle child among her three siblings and was raised very affectionately, especially by her father, who was a reasonably successful businessman in a small town in South India. She was permitted to attend college and pursue a degree but with the clear understanding that after graduation she would get married and not pursue a career.

At the age of nineteen, when Sandhya was in the final year of college, she lost the use of her right arm due to an accident. Her father was so shattered by this that he died of a heart attack within a week of the accident. This double blow completely unsettled her and she even contemplated ending her life.

Sandhya's elder sister was already married by then, but her younger brother was still studying so she had to pull herself together and take charge of the house and its affairs. She worked on her left hand extensively and trained herself to manage and do everything with one hand.

Her education being incomplete she was not likely to get a good job. So she decided to pursue a diploma course that got her a reasonably good placement. She settled down well in her job, met her future husband (who wanted to marry her despite her disability) and looked forward to a comfortable future, but that was not to be.

Her husband lost a lot of money in failed business ventures and so she had to get back to work again to support her family which by now included her in-laws and two children. She did not get any emotional support from her spouse; if anything she had to bear the brunt of his insecurities and failures. Her personal life was stress-filled and a far cry from everything that she had hoped for and its day to day demands, in the absence of a caring home environment, had left her bitter and cynical.

She invested all her energies into her professional life and rose rapidly at work. Her job involved back end operational work, that required a high degree of technical skills but limited people skills, and she managed to do it very well. This led to her being promoted to her current role.

However, in this role, she had to handle people/teams and interact with other departments for successful completion of projects, especially in an MNC environment and her poor communication skills, both business and interpersonal as well as behavioural issues including brusque and unfriendly demeanour, nit-picking and fault finding, inability to take people along cropped up.

## A Coach's Hunch

Listening to Sandhya's story I was struck by her resilience, her apparent passion and her total commitment to making her professional life as successful as she could possible do no matter what curve balls life threw at her.

As a coach, one is trained to not just listen to the coachee but also be in touch with one's instincts and hunches about the unspoken and the unsaid.

Life had not been very kind to her and nothing had come easy. This and the feeling of constant, un-ending struggle had left a deep sense of disappointment in her. She appeared wary, did not trust easily and found it difficult to believe that people could like her or find her interesting.

It seemed to me that her profession/work was both her sustenance and a means to escape from the grim realities of her day to day life. She was very invested in her work as she had nothing much to look forward to in her personal life.

I shared my observations with my guide and also decided to do a 360-assessment to verify some of these hunches.

## Sandhya, as Seen by the Eyes of Others

Over ten respondents, both from professional and personal domains, formed the basis of my detailed 360-assessment. The nature of assessment was conversational, forward looking and focussed on her positives and strengths and opportunity areas for improvement. I got tremendous insights and rich data from all the respondents and that helped me clear a lot of my early hypothesis about her struggles.

What stood out across all, as her dominant positives, was her passion for her work, her complete ownership of whatever she takes on, her desire for perfection and total commitment to her work and team.

All of them were equally unanimous in articulating her developmental needs: her inability to work collaboratively with peers, delegate effectively to her team members, communicate effectively with her counterparts in other geographies and network purposefully with clients. Her people skills were abysmal and almost 'dysfunctional' as described by her superior.

It became apparent to me that while each of the respondents knew some part of her past or her personal struggles, no one knew the full extent of what she had gone through.

It clearly came through that she did not have many friends at the work place, hardly socialised at work and made no attempt to network/form a relationship of any kind at work.

Given that almost all her issues were rooted in the domain of interpersonal relationships and stemmed from a deep mistrust of other people, I decided to administer the tool FIRO-B. Her 'expressed' and 'wanted' scores on the 'inclusion' and 'affection' parameters further reinforced this fact.

## Moment of Truth

Through all these data points: her story, others' observations and comments, my own hunches and psychometric assessments, a picture began to emerge slowly but surely.

It appeared that her early life experiences of losing her arm and her father in quick succession, her struggles to get back on feet and provide for her mother and brother, her inability to get any financial and emotional support from her spouse and having taken on all the responsibilities of life single-handedly, had all made her extremely insecure about trusting others. Even when she found someone to be competent and helpful she was very suspicious of their motives, given how many times life had seemingly let her down. (This came out explicitly in her 360, especially in the interviews with her sister and nephew.)

She was constantly viewing everything and everyone through the prism of her past experiences and was unable to move forward without her past baggage.

She needed to realise how it was affecting her especially her work life for her to be able to make any headway going forward.

When I shared the composite feedback with her, it took her a while to come to terms with the data and the implications contained therein. It was one thing to get this feedback from a formal appraisal but another thing to get it from the very people she had nominated for the 360 and whom she saw as her trusted associates and friends.

While she agreed that she wasted little time in getting to know people well and forming a relationship of trust with them, that her actions could be seen as brash, abrasive and most importantly 'dysfunctional' was hard for her to take. There was deep hurt and denial about how people saw her and interpreted her seemingly 'appropriate and business like demeanour'.

I gave her a while to absorb this and asked her to reflect on the possible thought that her people issues and deep mistrust were a possible manifestation of her early years' bitter experiences. I pointed out my observations including a few comments and verbatim utterances of hers wherein her response was totally out of sync with the situation.

She was a bit taken aback. It had not occurred to her that she was perhaps viewing everyone in her life through the lens of her unfortunate past experiences. Could it be that her wariness of trusting others resulted from fear of losing control and letting go, the consequences of which could again be unpleasant? Is the cloak of brusqueness a means to protect herself from further getting hurt?

She left that meeting with me even more deeply disturbed than when she had come to see me the first time.

## And Then the Penny Fell

I let her be for a while and beyond generally checking about her welfare, I controlled my urge to broach this again till she had time to resolve this within herself.

We continued for a session or two but did not make much headway as she had retreated into a shell. I was wondering if I had gone too far and if this whole thing had been too much for her to take and was contemplating raising this with my guide when one day, out of the blue, she called me and said she needed to meet me urgently.

Not sure what to expect but somewhat hopeful, I went to meet her. She greeted me with a big smile and a hug and excitedly launched into how, a seemingly innocuous interaction with her teenage son, and his gentle but stinging response to one of her comments to him had completely jolted her. He had apparently accused her of the exact same things and asked her pointedly as to how she could ever trust any outsider if she couldn't trust her own son!

If it had come from anyone other than her own flesh and blood she may not have taken it so seriously. But this incident lead her to examine some of her recent interactions with her peers and team members and she could clearly see the pattern of repetitive mistrust that was emerging in her dealings with people around her. She conceded that her actions, however un-intentioned, could have been interpreted as that of arrogance and brashness.

When the possible explanation for her deep and somewhat misplaced mistrust of people became clear to her it was as if a cloud had lifted and she had finally found an answer to what was bothering her all this while.

## Moving Forward: One Step at a Time

We had now reached the stage where Sandhya was comfortable working out her change agenda and goals for the future. She chose to focus on two key areas that would help work on her people skills and build a relationship of trust with them. Together we crafted these into actionable goals with well laid out action plans, putting progress metrics in place.

*Her first goal was* 'to improve her listening skills both at workplace and home'. She decided that no matter what the situation and the provocation was she would commit herself to conscious and active listening and getting more facts before commenting or reacting to the situation and take her time to provide a considered response instead of jumping in with a solution or comment.

*Her second goal was* 'to consciously get out of her shell and network with peers and team members'. She decided to take time to interact with at least one team member every week over informal coffee and lunch breaks and make an effort to get to know them. She realised that this goal would take a lot of effort on her part and also on the part of others as they needed to be sure of her intentions and motives.

She detailed out a plan on how she proposed to do this, including keeping a log book of how many times she spoke in a meeting before others did, her reactions to her own listening efforts and others' comments about her behaviour.

She also co-opted Renuka and another peer to help her with this. They gladly agreed and, on their part, went onto sensitize others in the organizations to her sincere efforts and resolve in this direction. They also kept a keen eye on her and took every opportunity to remind her of her goals and ensure that she was working towards them.

## Sandhya's Journey from Here on

Sandhya and I met regularly, every month and she recounted incidents from her well-maintained log book of how many times she had attended meetings and just patiently listened to what others had to say. She was candid in confessing that initially it was extremely trying for her to do so, especially when people expected her to cut in and respond in her usual style. She smilingly recounted how one of her subordinates commented on her silence and asked her if she was unwell or had a bad throat!

Given her passion for seeing things to their logical conclusion, I knew that she would find a way to see herself through this and she sure seemed to be doing so.

In parallel, she had also started work on her communication skills by joining the Toast Masters club. This gave her a lot of confidence in dealing with people, in her professional space.

Slowly but surely, by working on her first goal and the active support of her co-opted boss and peer, she was able to reach out to and build bridges with at least some of her peers and that helped her with her second goal of networking. She has started by first going out with people she is somewhat comfortable with and eventually plans to enlarge that group.

However, the most satisfactory though somewhat unexpected outcome was that her personal life had also slowly begun to fall into place. Her ability to see her son's point of view, her controlled temper and active listening had begun to have a salutary effect on the home front.

Coincidentally, though unrelated to this, things improved on the financial front as well as her husband's business began to pick up and he was gainfully employed and consequently upbeat about life.

In our last meeting, I noticed that she appeared noticeably calmer and more cheerful than before. She mentioned that she was continuing to practice listening intently and purposefully and had also taken up yoga and meditation lessons.

Most importantly, she had managed to make the time and effort to take a break and go on a vacation with her family. There was a fair amount of evidence of her consciously acting on her behavioural change agenda and the impact it was having on her.

Her phone call last month, informing me that she had clinched the global role, a role that required a high degree of inter-personal skills, was a ringing testimony of her new found confidence in herself and her having overcome the ghosts of her past.

She has embarked on this journey, into a new phase of her life, with positivity and hope.

## My Journey Down This Road

This was a particularly challenging though immensely satisfying coaching engagement for me. Initially I was somewhat overwhelmed with the enormity of the issues Sandhya was facing and the various misfortunes which had befallen her.

Her early experiences had deeply impacted her and her self-esteem and image had taken a terrible beating. I had to continuously check myself from becoming too involved or excessively sympathetic as that would have impacted her progress substantially.

I was unsure if I would be able to help her at all and whether she was right to have placed so much trust in me. It would not be an exaggeration to say that I started out on this journey with some self-doubts.

By keeping the discussions future focussed and goal centric rather than dwelling on the futility of the unavoidable, I managed to slowly get the confidence that, no matter what the final outcome, I will be able to help Sandhya in her journey of self-discovery just by being there for her and taking it one step at a time.

Most significantly, I realised how our value systems, early experiences, previous relationships and our own expectations from life form the prism through which we view ourselves and others. Our ability to take these in our stride, not let the negative experiences define us and not hesitate to reach out and seek help, determines how successful we are at maintaining and nurturing interpersonal relationships at work or at home.

To me Sandhya is a symbol of hope, positivity and courage and I remain deeply inspired by her.

# 9

# Celebrating the Feminine Side of a Woman's Leadership Style

As more and more women begin to surely but steadily reach higher positions in the corporate ladder, they are confronted not just with external challenges and constraints, but internal dilemmas too. One of the biggest internal dilemmas is whether women should disown their feminine side because it is likely to be a sign of weakness and act in more masculine ways because it might be a sign of strength. As a coach, Preethi Ganguly demonstrated not just deep understanding of this psychological dilemma, but great skill in helping Revathy confront this dilemma and actually celebrate the communal or feminine side of her leadership style.

## The Case: Revathy Moves from Agentic to Androgynous Style

'Guess what? I am in the running to head the Pune centre!' I could hear the triumph and excitement in Revathy's voice when she called me on a late Tuesday evening, 'I am just coming out of a meeting with Vidharbh,' she continued, 'and I am on the fast track for being groomed to take on the role in two years!'

Revathy was a seasoned IT professional with Aprett, a networking leader headquartered at California with software development centres in Bangalore and Pune and Sales centres across the country. Founded in the late 1980s, the company grew aggressively, with current annual revenues of USD 30 billion and 40,000+ employees worldwide. India was a special area of focus in terms of both increased head count and sales revenues.

'I am calling you because the learning and development (L&D) team has drafted a development plan for me which includes Coaching; I have suggested I would like to work with you. They will probably contact you soon.'

I had first met Revathy at a Leadership Development Intervention I was facilitating for Aprett's high-potential leaders, and had been struck by her incisive intelligence and forceful personality. She had later reached out to me to discuss career choices and challenges at work on several occasions; I was delighted to hear the latest development and wished her good luck.

I was a little pensive after the call, though, as I considered what I knew about Revathy. With eighteen years' experience in software systems and operations, across domains, Revathy had joined Aprett eight years ago after a Project and People Management role in a start-up (seven years) and previously as an individual contributor with a Multinational (three years). Currently heading the healthcare domain, she led three teams, comprising 500 engineers and ten Project Managers spread across Bangalore and Pune.

Revathy was known for her 'driving' skills as she called them; her results orientation and problem-solving skills ensured that she was a top performer. Direct and focused, she was not one to shy away from conflict or confrontations. Though these were the reasons for her growth, I knew that they had also presented some challenges for her earlier. It would be an interesting journey, I thought to myself, as I wound up for the day.

I was therefore not surprised to receive a call from the L&D team the next day, informing me that both Vidharbh and Revathy had chosen me to be her coach for the developmental journey, after the coach–coachee fitment process.

'I am supporting her on this,' said Vidharbh, Director, who had been her reporting manager at a previous organization, and currently her manager's manager 'but I know there is some work to be done to enable her step in smoothly into that role. Do you agree, Revathy?' he asked when the three of us met together for a chat at the office cafe. I knew Vidharbh too and had suggested this informal meeting among the three of us before the formal coaching sessions began.

'Yes of course there is a lot to learn, Vidharbh, but I'd rather focus on and hone my strengths, than look at this as a "set-Revathy-right" exercise,' remarked Revathy, being her usual direct self.

'Sometimes, a strength carried too far can become a weakness, Revathy. And developing an effective leadership style means knowing the difference. Think about it, as you work with your coach.' Vidharbh left us with those prophetic words as Revathy and I dug into the sandwiches we ordered.

After a reflective silence, Revathy said wryly, 'Perhaps that should be our agenda: to develop an effective leadership style. Vidharbh has this ability of hitting the nail on the head.' We agreed that would be the broad objective and we would crystallize the goals through some diagnostics.

I suggested we might benefit from a 360-degree that I would do and in addition, we could delve into some of her performance appraisals together. We also discussed the logistics and schedules of our future sessions; we agreed to meet once a month, initially for six months and take stock at the end of that.

The 360-degree confirmed Revathy's strengths.

'Very dynamic and result-oriented'

'Extremely hard working, driven and committed'

'One of our top performers'

'Provides clear and specific direction'

It also threw light on our coaching agenda.

'She can be very cutting with her feedback.'

'I have often noticed that she steps on people's toes and becomes abrasive when handling conflict.'

'She is so focused on what needs to be achieved that rarely have I heard her praise/celebrate achievement or effort.'

'I don't feel I have any space; she is too directive and monitors so closely that I feel claustrophobic. Buy-in is not important for her.'

The performance appraisals revealed similar trends; we spent our first session discussing the developmental feedback in detail. Interestingly, Revathy did not seem perturbed with the feedback.

'I have worked hard to be the person I am today; it did not come naturally to me, you know. I believe this kind of toughness is required if one has to deliver results. People don't take you seriously if you are soft and understanding. Why should I pussyfoot around? I am not here to be popular; I am here to do what it takes to deliver results.'

As we worked together, I would come to respect this single-minded determination of Revathy's to achieve any goal. However, my antennae went up as I heard her speak about pussyfooting around and popularity.

I asked her to list, for the next session, what behaviours she would term as 'tough' and 'soft' which might help us in our understanding of effective leadership styles.

In the meanwhile, HR had shared some feedback from exit interviews as well as metrics on attrition levels in her team for the past two years. The feedback from the exit interviews was very similar to the 360-degree; though the attrition metrics was something that required introspection, Revathy agreed.

'I have been thinking about the attrition levels and wondering ... On one level, I would like to lose a certain kind of people; I cannot tolerate complacence and inefficiency. But on another level, I am concerned that I am losing those that I want to retain ... the performers. How can I make this better? This is definitely on my agenda.'

Our second meeting was a turning point in our journey. In hindsight, I believe the change process began here. Revathy came with a list of behaviours she termed as 'tough' and 'soft' as below:

Tough: Self-confident, forceful, driving, demanding, impatient, assertive bordering on aggressive, ambitious, competitive, clear, directive, dominant, independent, courageous, highly energetic, action-oriented.

'It is to me an admirable thing ... this toughness; something I have seen top leadership wield very effectively. In every situation I make sure there is no ambiguity or slack. That is my endeavour. I aspire to be the above person.'

We shared some common experiences that made these behaviours effective. I talked to her about my experience as sales head leading a team of aggressive successful salesmen in the automatic identifications systems industry. She talked about the times when her team looked to her for direction and clarity. I could hear the note of satisfaction and passion in her voice.

I drew her attention to two elements: 'impatient', 'assertive, bordering on aggressive'. How does she see these playing out? In others and in herself?

'I have seen how TG (their CEO) is, okay? In meetings, for example, I see how he cuts to the chase when people are meandering along.

Impatience is key for bringing direction and clarity. Even Vidharbh, people only notice his easy going style, but he is so aggressive with clients and management when he disagrees with them, or when he wants to push for what he wants.'

'What about Sulekha? Your Legal Head? She is on the board, isn't she?'

'Sulekha is one of the toughest people I have met. She is a good friend. In fact, I would say she embodies all the above tough behaviours I have outlined.'

We looked at her list again. I was curious to see what she included in the 'soft' list, though I had a fair inclination.

Soft: affectionate, helpful, kind, sympathetic, nurturing, gentle, compassionate, encouraging, praising.

'Give me some examples,' I nudged her.

'Jyothi. See the way she is with her team. They are always running to her with their problems ... all the time she is trying to accommodate them; they all love her! Even when they do what is expected of them, she makes it out like they have moved mountains. But look at the team's performance. The recent project they took up was a disaster. What is the point in having a team that loves you if you can't generate performance out of them?'

'Or Nivedita. She is so soft and gentle, in the last review meeting, she could not even stand up for her team.'

'It irritates me that people expect me to be their mother. To molly cuddle them and constantly praise them. We are talking about adults here, aren't we? What is this constant need to be praised? And sympathize with them. Can't people manage their disappointments and struggles? I do it all the time. I get very annoyed when people come to me wanting to cry on my shoulder.'

I noticed that her breathing became faster and her face started flushing as she spoke; there were some things we needed to work on here.

I considered whether I should back track or lead her on the same road. I decided to use one of her own tactics:

'Why are you breathing so hard, Revathy?' I asked her directly.

She paused for a moment and looked at me. 'I am irritated.'

'What is it about the "soft" behaviours that is irritating you?'

'I don't think they are effective. In my opinion, that is the reason many women lose out. I have seen how women fall into that trap ... be this soft gentle nurturing person ... and before you know it, you are out of the game.'

'Let us first deal with what is irritating you and then perhaps we can discuss whether they are effective or not.'

'What is irritating you? Just stay with this irritation. What is behind it? What is the deeper issue here?'

We spent some time exploring her agitation.

I was intrigued that she had associated the 'soft' behaviours with only women and those that were 'not successful'. It was also interesting that she had not mentioned the 'soft' behaviours for TG, Vidharbh and Sulekha. Was she seeing only what she wanted to see?

I brought her attention to this; I knew Revathy was primarily driven by her intellect and it was necessary for her to understand things before we worked on them. That was the action plan till we met next:

1.   Watch TG, Vidharbh and Sulekha if they are deploying any of the 'soft' behaviours.
2.   Watch herself when she found herself getting 'irritated'.

She was to use a weekly journal for this.

We closed the meeting with that; it had been an exhausting session for both of us.

As I sat down with trying to capture all this on my Sony VAIO, many thoughts were jostling in my head:

Three things had emerged during the session:

1.   Revathy's association of the 'soft' behaviours with women and implicitly, the association of 'tough' behaviours with men.
2.   Revathy viewed the tough–soft as dichotomous rather than a continuum.
3.   There was some resistance to deploying the 'soft' behaviours.

The journey was now clear to me. Explore the resistance, realign the tough–soft dichotomy and enable effortless deployment of 'soft' behaviours.

I know that many women wrestled with this same issue, due to my work with other women leaders. In an effort to fit into the majority, and the perceived leadership 'tough' paradigms, Revathy's leadership style was in danger of becoming skewed. The most effective leaders, irrespective of gender, develop a holistic leadership style that is an integration of both masculine and feminine behaviours. (I call it the 'yin-yang' leadership style.)

For Revathy to be an effective leader, she would need to more consciously and overtly integrative of both the behaviours into her repertoire.

I sent her some case studies on successful female leaders: Indra Nooyi, Hema Hattangady and Chanda Kocchar.

I recalled that on her MBTI, she scored high on Thinking, on the 'Thinking–Feeling' dichotomy. I would use this to help her practise behaviours from the feeling spectrum and include it in her repertoire of leadership behaviours.

At the next meeting we discussed the case studies and Revathy's journal observations on the three leaders in her organization (TG, Vidharbh and Sulekha).

We had a good collection of leadership styles and I encouraged her to dwell on their behaviours—what they were doing and saying so she could imbibe them.

With this, my purpose was to address Revathy's tendency to dichotomize leadership styles. As we studied the behaviours, I brought her attention to how Vidharbh, TG and Sulekha leaven the 'tough' behaviours with deployment of 'soft' behaviours and vice versa. For example, she conceded how Vidharbh pushed people to perform and, at the same time, made it a point to give praise when it was required. We noted how Sulekha's aggression was used in consonance with her relationship skills.

Once we addressed her need for data (remember, she had a preference for 'Thinking'), we looked at her journal. What was behind her 'irritation'?

I have found the technique of watching and journaling our emotions very effective in working through negative emotions such as anger, anxiety, etc. This draws from the principle of awareness as propounded by sages from time immemorial. It is a simple technique of bringing our awareness to our breathing, without rejecting or fighting the feeling. I had trained Revathy in this technique in our last session and now asked her what had emerged for her.

'It is quite a struggle. I don't seem to be able to get it.' I made her practise it once again. I also asked her if she could spare fifteen minutes a day for a short meditation session, which would help in this. She agreed and I put her in touch with someone who could train her on this. Her journaling, of both leader behaviours and her own emotions, was to continue till we met next after a month.

The third session onward, I decided it was time to bring in some behavioural work.

I believe change can happen both from the inside-out and outside-in. What leadership behaviours of Revathy's would she say were required to change to develop a more holistic leadership style? What behaviours would she need to develop?

I then read out some feedback from the 360 in front of me.

Her current manager, Sunil, when I asked him to describe what he meant by his description of Revathy as 'impatient' said: 'she cuts other people's sentences short or fills in; generally tries to take charge of meetings, even when we are all warming up with some jokes, etc., she is trying to push us to the agenda. You know … almost like a hostel warden?'

One of her high-performers in an exit interview: 'somewhere I felt not guided, but pushed; I enjoyed the pressure, of course, she is very driving. But at the end of the day I never felt it is my achievement, if you know what I mean? As though I am a cog in the wheel … a little empty ….'

I paused and waited for her to reflect and come back with what might be that one behavioural change that she would like to begin work on immediately.

'Listening?' Revathy offered. I couldn't agree more. 'Listening to others' was an area that she needed to focus and get to work on.

We then broke this into elements that she could deploy in everyday activities. We role-played and practised them with feedback. She committed to start using these in identified situations. She would 'live' with this one behaviour change for the next month.

I asked her how the second point in her journal was progressing.

'Slowly,' she said, 'I learnt the meditation technique though and am practising it about five days in a week.'

We practised the breathing and attention focus technique again.

Listening turned out to be a powerful experience for Revathy and it opened the doors to other related behaviours in the spectrum.

'As I just stopped my internal thinking, which is sort of 'go-go-go', I was able to really get into the heads and hearts of others. This changed something deep inside me. It made me relaxed and less tight.'

'Like the other day, when we were estimating the time for a new project, Nitin (one of her team members) was saying how we won't be able to complete it in three months. My first instinct was to push; I held myself back and asked him to explain. I could see the surprise in his face.' She laughed.

'I also think I am now able to hear the unsaid; you know, like I am kind of in tune with others … It's like how I am with my sisters (she came from a family of three sisters) and my children. Not something new for me as a person, but new in the workplace.'

'You know that question you keep asking me about what is irritating me about the soft behaviours? What is behind the irritation? I think it is that I really want to succeed. I am afraid I won't; especially if I am seen as "soft". I have seen so many women who fail because of that; or so I thought, till we did that exercise of observing successful leaders use the soft behaviours …'

Our practice sessions continued for almost six months after that. We chose the following supportive and nurturing behaviours to work on that we agreed were critical for a holistic leadership style.

## Expressing Praise When Required

### Conveying empathy and understanding

The practice sessions constituted identifying situations where the behaviours could be deployed, role playing them with feedback and reviewing the results post deployment in real life situations. We supplemented this with training programs she attended that were part of the leadership development curriculum of the organization. I also sent her several articles and referred books that could help.

I did one brief 360 degree five months into our coaching. There were very few, but perceptible changes in behaviour by the environment. It was a slightly uphill journey, but Revathy's tenacity helped.

In all we did about twelve sessions together, which were spread over a year and one month. Some of the later sessions, were spaced longer apart to enable more time and scope for application.

I did a final 360-degree at the end of the twelve sessions; there was more perceptible change as reported by her team, Sunil and Vidharbh.

'I think the most significant difference I see in her is that she is more interpersonally savvy … more sensitive. Another important change is her relationship with her team: Though she always stood up for them, it is now a less conflicted relationship' was how Vidharbh put it.

Sunil, her reporting manager, was more specific:

'For starters, I haven't had any of her team members leaving, which is a relief. I also see her delegating more; a big kudos to her for the way she is developing her team. I especially like the creative methods she has developed for building acknowledgement and praise into the team review process.'

One and a half year after our sessions began, the engagement survey revealed higher satisfaction scores from Revathy's team.

About six months ago, I received a call from a jubilant Revathy:

'Guess what? I am taking over as Pune head next month!'

# SECTION D

# Developing New Skills, Styles and Behaviours

# Why Skills, Style and Behaviours Make Such a Huge Difference to a Leader's Effectiveness

Santrupt Misra*

I feel personally connected to the four cases in this part of the book as these are stories of our everyday professional life. We see, in each one of them, a bit of our own selves; a slice of our context and shadows of our colleagues. Leadership is a difficult task in all circumstances. It is even more difficult in business organizations as the external environment gets more complex and volatile. At the end of the day, only that leadership matters which delivers the results. While results come through a complex set of interactions between the organization and the environment, the organization's ability to direct, influence, adapt to the environment is determined by the energy, culture and capability of the organization—the tone and foundation of which is set by the leaders through their leadership. Whether an organization has only leaders or has abundant leadership is shaped and influenced by the styles, behaviours and skills of the leaders.

The styles, behaviour and skills also follow a complex pattern of shaping and influencing each other. We experience styles of leaders through their behaviour and these styles are embedded as patterns through repeat behaviours. When a particular behaviour becomes acceptable to a context, it rapidly settles down as a definitive style. In such a situation, even if the

*Santrupt Misra is CEO, Carbon Black Business and Director, Group Human Resources of the Aditya Birla Group. He is a Director on the Aditya Birla Management Corporation Private Limited Board, the apex decision making body of the USD 40 billion, Aditya Birla Group.

external context helped the organization to achieve the results, often the style is credited with the results, giving it a further enduring character. Only when the external context changes or internal acceptance levels for the behaviour lowers does the style come under strain. Initial challenges to the style of the leader are often ignored or resisted as an aberration. This friction leads to undermining results or relationships in the immediate period and certainly leads to suboptimal results in the long run. Skills can help one to accentuate or soften the impact of behaviours and styles. Particularly when one's business or functional skills deliver results, at least for some time, the style and behaviour issues are tolerated or ignored at the most. It becomes hard to isolate and differentiate the impact of the skills from style and behaviour. It is at least difficult to separate them for those who are not the most savvy and sensitive to the finer aspects of the two.

Leaders, on the other hand, are so absorbed in the day to day that they have hardly any time to step back and look at their own impact on the organization. They often mistake good results as an indicator of the positive impact they create. The current results may have been achieved in spite of the impact the leader creates (often unknown to the leader) and in the process, an opportunity is missed to obtain even better results. The older you are in an organization, the more senior you are, the more powerful you are and the closer you are to the power centre, the less likely is one to receive signals of feedback that is contrary to the self-perception of your impact. That is what changes when new people come in or the demographics of an organization changes with younger employees coming in as we experience now a days. The natural response of an incumbent leader is to rationalize the effectiveness of his current style and behaviour as being effective and attributes the negative feedback to the inability of others to appreciate it. Some reminiscence about old times and their strong association with the organization and hesitate to change. Raghavan's story is a case in point.

All leaders and more particularly, those aspiring for the 'Corner Room' need to understand that we need to be able to style flex and that is an important capability. With M&A, JVs, client partnerships growing, one dominant style will have limitations. Changes to our context of working, consequentially alters the quality of the skills and the style that is expected from us. When we engage more with the external world such as regulators, customers, media, credit rating agencies, lenders and others, we need to have a style that is welcoming, warm and influencing. The skills required are to be able to influence, persuade rather than instruct or direct. Our messaging has to be subtle yet clear depending on the situation. Others make an assessment of us based on our skills, style and behaviour as those are the only direct data points they have about us—the rest is hear say. Ambassadorship is one of the key tasks that come with one's growth in career. One cannot play that role effectively without appropriate styles, behaviour and skills.

While external engagements can be rather short and transient, our styles, behaviours and skills have a profound impact on the motivation, output and the ability of others in the organization to deliver the best. If the leader has a high sense of self-importance or a low self-image— both impact the style and behaviour and we see that in both Naren and Sridhar's case. Complexity demands creative solutions and that comes from being able to involve and include people in brain-storming, decision making and effective execution. These are style issues and some people are more comfortable and some are less in dealing with the style issues. Delegation is perhaps the most basic of the style issues that most struggle with and not just Ashwin—our hero in the first case.

So we have a few clear lessons from the cases. First, as we grow in our careers, our learning needs to keep pace with our growth. Any misalignment between the two is likely to show up at this most difficult moment in our professional career. Second, while on-the job learning is a very powerful tool, it is useful to do some purposeful preparatory learning to be effective in our future roles. Such preparation can be done in many ways and executive coaching can be one of the most effective ones. In the case studies, the coaching intervention appears more remedial, that is, that we need to fix problems with people through coaching. However, coaching can be equally effective in helping us leverage our strengths in terms of our styles, behaviour and skills. With prudent investment of time, discipline and taking small yet well planned steps we all can benefit from executive coaching. All the cases point out that coaching was successful where the coachee was highly motivated to seek and implement beneficial change. These are no small lessons for us to imbibe.

# 10

# Catching Up on Missed Managerial Learning Milestones

Professionals in large, well-structured organizations have the opportunity to transition from individual contributor to first-time manager to seasoned-manager positions successfully through stage-appropriate experiences, structured training interventions and seasoned managerial oversight. Unfortunately, those in smaller organizations without the benefit of such managerial oversight and other developmental inputs may be given higher responsibilities but continue to perform as individual contributors leading to suboptimal results. Sameer Datta was able to coach Ashwin, one such manager, to quickly catch up on missed managerial learning milestones.

## The Case: What Ashwin Missed while Growing Up

The founder of Beta Pharmaceuticals, Dinesh Shah is now eighty years old. It is understandable that he wants to give up executive responsibilities in the company that he founded thirty years ago when he was fifty. Having built a successful ₹3 billion business, Shah's wish is to transition into retirement and spend time only in mentoring and guiding his executive team.

Shah however realized that his transition into retirement was not going to be that easy. His son, Jayen was part of the business, but his first love was music and spent considerable time pursuing this interest. With his son not in a position to give his full-time attention to Beta Pharmaceuticals, Shah was obviously worried about the future.

He would now have to rely on his two home grown Executive Directors to play a larger role and take the company forward.

As Shah was thinking about all this, suddenly a bell rang in his mind and he made a connection. He recalled his discussions with me just a week back. Having known Shah for the last fifteen years, I had mentioned to him that I was now not only a retired Managing Director but also an accredited Executive coach. Maybe I can request Sameer to provide executive coaching support to my two Executive Directors so they can run the day to day even as Jayen continues to provide strategic leadership to Beta Pharmaceuticals, he thought.

The very next day, Shah asked for a meeting. He spent time to understand the nuances of Executive Coaching and how it would work. He also requested me to share these inputs with his team.

After some discussions, Shah decided that I should start by working with Ashwin, his Senior Executive Director, Sales and Marketing.

Typical of an entrepreneur, Shah gave me a rather simple engagement brief.

'Ashwin is our blue eyed boy. He has been with our company for fifteen years. He works very hard. Perhaps he is the last person to go home in the evening. I want to improve his executive effectiveness. He is busy with so many things that some of our more important projects do get delayed.'

With these preliminary observations, Shah invited Ashwin to join the meeting. Ashwin heard me out and immediately and enthusiastically said yes to the idea. Ashwin was very happy that he would be the first in the company to receive executive coaching. He knew that Shah had his best interest in mind and trusted him fully.

## The Story of Ashwin's Rapid Ascend

Ashwin completed his Bachelors in Pharmacy in the year 1990. He then joined a multinational pharmaceutical company as a Medical

Representative. He loved working in the field and that showed. He was soon promoted as a Supervisor. After working for over two years, he completed a diploma course in marketing. He then joined another multinational pharmaceutical company as a Product executive. 'I learnt a lot about getting maximum value from my limited sales promotion budget,' he said. After six years of sales and product experience, Ashwin joined Beta Pharmaceuticals in 1996 as a Product Manager. He did very well in his job and over a period of time, he was promoted as Marketing Manager and then as Marketing Director. He is now the Senior Executive Director responsible for Sales and Marketing. In about fifteen years, Ashwin had moved from Manager to Senior Executive Director. His growth came on the back of strong results, a basis that is adopted by many organizations despite their intent to pay attention to potential. Ashwin was compensating for the lack of formal grooming and planned development inputs with sheer hard work and long hours. He was among the last to leave work which was typically around 8.30 pm. Ashwin's view was that this was the best time to reach all his sales team members over phone.

As Ashwin narrated his story and his work day and I tried to put myself in his shoes, the first thing I got in touch with was the state of his family life. Almost spontaneously I asked him, 'How would your family feel if you did go home early?' 'My wife has been telling me that for quite some time. I need to find a way to make that happen.'

As home work to be done before the next session I asked Ashwin to write down his responsibilities and Key Result Areas (KRA) as Senior Executive Director.

I quickly invested time to understand Ashwin as a leader through the eyes of his team.

My 360-degree interviews helped me immensely.

Ashwin's 360-degree feedback confirmed that he was well respected by his subordinates for his concern for people, knowledge about the industry and products. The most frequent area for development that surfaced was around Ashwin's availability to discuss issues with his team and delays in decision making. Interestingly everyone was sympathetic and seemed to accept these delays because they could see that he was overloaded and working hard to cope with his job. I also discovered that while everyone filled up their self-appraisal form, one to one formal feedback meetings were rare.

## Awareness, Insight and Preparation to Change

Ashwin was very happy to receive his 360-degree feedback report. The first thing that he noticed was the feedback from the marketing team: 'Boss we need more time from you.'

Ashwin was quick to land on the core issue: 'My goal is clear. I need to organize and delegate work so that I can give adequate time to all functions in the office. When I do this it will be nice if I can keep my family happy by going home early. This is a big task and I will need to do a thorough job so that my business does not suffer.'

As he reflected further on his day to day work, he realised that for effective delegation to happen he would need to strengthen his function and adopt a better system of managing performance.

I asked Ashwin to identify for himself a simple measure of success in his coaching journey. Ashwin chose a rather simple one! He said it would be the time of his departure from the office! Since this appealed to him, I went with it. Little did I realize that it would soon become the cornerstone of the engagement!

Given Ashwin's strong action orientation on one side and need for simplicity on the other side, I realized that the strategies that we employ needed to be grounded, easy to execute and quick to deliver results. I had to stay away from intellectual deliberations about delegation or focus on underlying belief and attitudes and focus instead on hard actions. I also realized that I could rely on my long years of experience to suggest to him a few simple ideas and techniques.

As a first step Ashwin agreed to do the following and report the results in the next session:

1. Keep a detailed daily record of all activities performed.
2. Prepare a simple 'to do' list for the next day, every day in the evening before leaving the office. 'This will help improve my productivity in the morning,' he said.
3. To come to work half an hour early and save on travel time and also leave office by 7.30 pm. 'This way I will reduce about half an hour in the office everyday,' he said.
4. Use my evening travel time to catch up with anyone over phone.

In the next session Ashwin shared the analysis of his diary. We began to discuss the time he spent on various activities against his KRAs.

He quickly marked off the things that he could simplify and or delegate. He then shortlisted two activities that took the highest time.

1. Ashwin has a sales team of almost 1000. Even a modest 15 % attrition meant fresh recruitment of twelve to fifteen sales persons every month for which he needed to interview at least twenty-five candidates. Ashwin's calendar showed that he spent extended time interviewing.
2. The company was adopting an anniversary based approach to compensation review (which means each employee's pay gets reviewed on the date of his joining). As a result, his calendar reflected that on average Ashwin was reviewing compensation and promotion plans for about 100 employees every month!

'It is now clear to me that I can give proper attention to all my functions if I reduce my time on final interviews for territory manager positions and reduce my own involvement in compensation reviews.'

For the next phase Ashwin wrote down the following action plans:

1. To reduce time for final interviews I will empower my zonal managers.

   (a) I will request the zonal manager—South who had an excellent track record in selection and training of territory managers to share his process of interviewing with other zonal mangers.
   (b) I will arrange for formal training in interviewing skills for all my zonal managers.
   (c) I will include Recruitment, Selection, Training and Retention as part of the zonal managers' KRAs.

   The measurement criteria will be the retention rates in the Zone he said.
2. To reduce the time taken for annual compensation and promotion review by improving the system

   (a) I will modify the existing appraisal system for territory managers to ensure that the performance assessment and measurement parameters are as objective as possible.

    (b) I will develop a policy guideline and evolve a formula that can link up performance appraisal outcomes to compensation review.

    (c) I will review compensation only by exception for the cases brought to me by HR.

3. To give time to the Marketing function

    I will schedule a meeting every Friday morning with the marketing team to review and take necessary decisions on various product management plans.

4. I will use my drivers' log book to verify the time I spend in the office.

As post-session homework, I asked Ashwin to prepare a wish list of activities that he would love to do in the evening and weekends.

## Change Begins to Happen

The first thing that Ashwin reported was that he was able to carry out all his work and go home at 7.30 pm without too much disruption.

In the subsequent sessions, Ashwin reported significant progress on actions taken.

1. He decided to promote the zonal manager—South as AGM Sales. This helped him completely and effectively delegate all the activities of recruitment and training to him.
2. He had a meeting with all zonal managers and discussed his plan to delegate recruitment, and training of the sales team to zonal managers. He also explained their modified KRAs and measurement.
3. He developed a modified appraisal system with inputs from Shah, Jayen and HR and conducted a training session for the zonal managers for its implementation.
4. He had started planned weekly meetings with the marketing team.

Ashwin was now able to leave office by 7.00 pm and even felt that once every one took up their increased responsibilities, he would be able to leave office by 6.30 pm.

I could clearly see in Ashwin a shift from 'Knowing to Doing'.

## Making It Sustainable

The next phase in the coaching engagement was to help Ashwin retain his work and family balance so that he could really shift from 'Knowing to Doing to Sustaining' the change.

In our next session I asked Ashwin if he had given thought to his wish list of activities for the evening and weekends.

'I used to play tennis in school days. I enjoy that game and I want to now play regularly and perfect my game. It will help me remain physically and mentally fit. I will join the MIG Club and start paying tennis. I would also like to hire a coach to perfect my game.'

'I also discussed this with my wife. My daughter is in class ten and she will be happy to learn English and Mathematics from me. This will also give me an opportunity to spend quality time with my family.'

I was very excited about the possibility that these two activities would keep Ashwin bonded emotionally and in fact pull him out of the office every day in the evening.

Over the next several weeks, Ashwin was implementing his plans with gusto.

I decided to do a follow up 360-degree assessment after about sixth sessions to confirm progress.

1. The GM and AGM sales were happy that they had more authority in recruitment and selection of their sales team.
2. The GM Sales was very happy that there was now a more transparent appraisal system which was linked to the individual's compensation.
3. The marketing team was very happy as they could see faster implementation and more involvement and guidance coming from Ashwin.
4. Ashwin was now leaving office by 6.30 pm.

In the closing session, Ashwin said, 'I am extremely thankful to you for helping me. Having moved up from the position of a Medical representative, I was too attached to selling in the field and working directly with the sale team. I am now a Senior Executive Director responsible for developing and leading Sales and Marketing strategies. I now balance my time between sales and marketing function. I believed that leaving office by 6.30 pm was something that I could never achieve. Now I am keen to finish my day's schedule as my game of tennis and my daughter would be waiting for me.'

Ashwin handed over to me an invitation from his wife Sujata for a dinner over the weekend.

Shah too acknowledged improvements in Ashwin's performance as well as in the function. 'Sameer, what you have accomplished in eight months is something that I have been trying for last three years,' he said.

Ashwin was a very motivated and willing coachee. He loved action in the field and was enjoying but burning himself out trying to do everything. Unfortunately he never had the benefit of receiving well-structured stage appropriate developmental inputs. He was doing what he knew. With some help he was so quick to understand what needed to be done differently.

It was necessary for me to go back and start from the very basics. For me as a Coach, doing what would help him was more important that doing what would be considered 'cool'.

# 11

## Developing This Mysterious Thing Called Executive Presence

> Most organizations are well-honed in developing their key executives in conventional, technical and managerial skills. These are typically hard skills which the incumbent develops either through training or job rotations. Executive presence is one of the softer skills which remain beyond formal development process. These are easy to spot, but difficult to develop as is realized by Prathap Chawla the coach in Naren's case.

## The Case: Naren's Journey to the Unexplored

Naren has been a one-company man for all the twenty two years since his graduation in Electronics and Communication Engineering. His employer, a global software services company is known to nurture young talent and has a history of retaining people much better than its peers. During early years Naren moved from one technical desk to the other and acquired rich and specialized experience as a software developer. Somewhere along time came for him to lead smaller groups as a supervisor and larger groups thereafter as a department manager. He has handled his job rotations as first line manager rather well; though learning people management skills was through process of observation and experience rather than any formal training on those subjects. 'Push the guy to the deep end and he will learn to swim' has been the training philosophy of his employer; as is common to many other peer corporates.

It is not as if Naren has had no difficulty in getting on top of the job at hand! Some years ago when the software industry was going through a slum; his employers decided that it is time to look for outside customers rather than remaining an in-sourcing company. Naren with considerable experience in various domains was given the job as one of the business development managers. For the first time in his career Naren found it hard to learn on the job. 'The first year was a disaster' as Naren reminisces. He was called into the corner office and given a gentle knock on his knees by the President of the company. Fortunately Naren is given to learning new skills quickly and to his good luck, the tide in the market changed. Naren began to first breathe easy and then sit on the top of the job later. He however continued to have a strange sense of discomfort to be elegant in his communication with senior managers in his client companies. Being reflective enough Naren also knows that his discomfort in getting engaged with senior people is a problem he always had even within his own company. However, till he got into his new job it has been bit of a non-issue. More of it later.

All and all Naren is happy with his lot. Married to a fellow software engineer who chose to be a home maker after their two daughters came into school going age. Coming from a middle-class family Naren thinks 'God has been kind to us after all,' even though Naren often describes himself as an atheist; God does turn up in the conversation every now and then. In the deep recess of his mind Naren sometimes compares his achievements with his fellow batch mates in the engineering college. Some have done better than him but a vast majority have not done as well as Naren. That puts Naren's mind to rest albeit temporarily. It's in the office that he finds too many fast trackers over taking an ever so often some of them don't have the length of experience of Naren. Naren now realizes that performance alone gets into a point but there is something else that makes you the Vice President. Sadly, months of reflection and several rounds of conversations with the Vice President Human Resources never got Naren the answer to his dilemma.

Till the coach an acquaintance of VP-HR arrived in his office one day. In a three way face to face meeting Naren was rather amused by the concept of executive coaching; which he had never heard of earlier.

While unsure of the process and outcome, he was instinctively motivated to try it out. So the coach and Naren started their journey as coach and his new coachee!

## A Difficult Journey Begins

The coach was quite enthused to coach Naren. He knows from experience that to find a coachee as motivated as Naren is half the battle won! The coach thought that Naren's strong ability to reflect and keen desire to learn also comes as a bonus. Directionally the coach knew that the coaching agenda would broadly be Naren's inability to get deeply engaged and strike a rapport with his boss and other important seniors in the organization (also significant seniors in client organizations). The coach's real search therefore was to hear from Naren as to what is the reason for the lack of engagement? What indeed is the story behind the story? From experience, the coach began to build several hypotheses in his mind. Could the reason be lack of exposure in the past? Could it be in some way fear of authority leading into inelegant communication? Could it be that the process of engagement with seniors is too transactional and therefore devoid of any strategic conversations? Or are there issues still deeper than these?

Many incisive coachees have a deep sense of the cause. In this instance however, the coach realized to his disappointment that while Naren knew the questions, he was rather clueless to the answers namely the reasons leading into the situation. The conversations were powerful enough but threw up limited insights. The coach's 360-degree conversations with significant others around Naren led to some perceptions but not complete enough. The feedback respondents did identify Naren's development areas namely social sensitivity, networking, influencing others, connections up the hierarchy and finally communication with seniors. The good news was that the feedback was completely aligned to Naren's own perception of his developmental agenda. Nobody however was in a position to assist the coach on how to build an action agenda for change. The coach realized that in the absence of a tangible action plan, it would be appropriate to elicit more data points by using some psychometric tools. The coach decided to use Character Strength Finder, the Sources of Pressure and Belief Inventory as three psychometric tools to understand Naren somewhat better. Tangible clues began to flow in. The coach realized that managing the organization (particularly people-related situation), is a significant source of pressure on Naren. He is generally challenged in social intelligence and expression of emotions. The tools threw up a set of very strong positive attributes of Naren namely fairness equity and justice, honesty, authenticity and genuineness and open mindedness.

Armed with this psychometric data, the coach started a deeper level of conversation with Naren. By now there was reasonable clarity that higher order of engagement with the boss and other seniors is emerging as the most important goal. Naren was asked to describe some typical situations of interactions that take place between him and his boss and other seniors. Naren was asked to describe not only the process and outcome of such meetings but also to describe his feelings. 'Aha!' moments were to arrive soon enough.

Naren only gets into a conversation with his boss when there is a need to transact something specific. These meetings have short, to the point and ends as abruptly as they start. Very transactional and nothing other than transactional information sharing and a decision probably emerges out of the meeting. There is seldom an opportunity to discuss anything that is strategic or long term in nature and never a moment where anything other than work gets shared. Naren does not feel encouraged to have social meetings to let the hair down and discuss anything other than work. The second insight was that Naren's formal communications are rather clumsy. In his desire to pack in as much data as possible every slide in the presentation is very crowded. His presentation lasts far beyond time slotted for him and often ends abruptly. Brevity in presentation is not his forte. He fears that brevity might lead into missing an opportunity to have database discussed and lack of data-based discussion might lead into questioning credibility of the presentation. The coach was now ready to motivate Naren to create an action agenda.

## Tangible Actions

The coach would like to describe the first action agenda as rather mechanical namely, seek and find more opportunities to be with the boss. In tangible terms Naren is to find at least two opportunities a week to meet the boss. The second item in the agenda is to find opportunity to spend time beyond the transactional issue at hand. Third action agenda is to exchange information about each other in the early days and get into a conversation of appreciative enquiry as time elapses (in short this means keeping window open for a more informal personal conversation outside work). Finally, the coach realised that over some years Naren has developed an incredible tool called 'Strategic Decision Tool' all on his own. He often uses this tool in teaching his subordinates on how to appreciate this decision making process by using a structured thinking. The coach asked as to whether his boss is aware of this tool? Hearing the reply negative another aha moment appeared. Can this proprietarily tool of Naren be used to take the conversation between the boss and Naren to a significantly higher plane?

The coach began to breathe easily. He knew that once a tangible action plan has been drawn up, Naren is likely to be motivated enough to implement with all the rigor needed. Naren would hereafter report weekly progress made to the coach. Certain mechanical details to be logged were the extent of time Naren spent with the boss and what percent of the conversation was non-transactional in nature. Naren began to make serious progress in this area much to his own surprise and delight of the Vice-President HR.

As the assignment was coming to an end the coach was immensely pleased that the VP-HR has given a rather new but appropriate name to what Naren ended up achieving. In his communication to the coach VP-HR said 'We have seen, we have witnessed significant enhancement in level of Executive presence of Naren. He is now seen as an executive who is displaying gravitas that is transforming him from his current role to be ready a more strategic role.' While the coach hadn't labelled Naren's goal as 'Executive Presence' he is now happy with the appropriateness of the label. Finally, the icing on the cake arrived some twelve months after the coaching assignment was over. The call was from a resort hotel in Kerala where Naren has taken a two weeks family break. The purpose of the call is to inform the coach of Naren's elevation to the level of Vice President few weeks ago. A great sense of achievement for both Naren and the coach!

# 12

# Growing a Business through Disciplined Leadership

The early stages of business are characterized by a typical start-up culture where everyone knows everybody and everyone does everything. During this stage the entrepreneur is often filling in for many of the functional gaps in the organization. As the business grows larger, the entrepreneur ends up hiring people but continues to work in the same start-up style of being involved in everything. This can demotivate his leadership team, defocus the entrepreneur and even derail the growth of the business. The lucky ones like Sridhar realize their blind spots and get to work with seasoned coaches like Rahul Dayal who can quickly instil some managerial and leadership wisdom into them.

## The Case: Sridhar Learns to Delegate

I went to meet my coachee Sridhar after some gap. We had concluded our engagement two months ago and the purpose of my visit was to check how he was sustaining the momentum of the changes beyond the coaching period.

Sridhar was punctual as usual. He updated me that the markets had been tough and yet his company was successfully growing. The company was also beginning to see improved results in the international markets. He said that he continues to track his time and ensures that the spread is maintained as planned.

*As I left his office, I could not help smiling, feeling very proud of the commitment my coachee had demonstrated and the giant strides he had taken in last few months in changing his approach to managing his company and guiding it to the next level.*

## Background

Sridhar, the Founder and CEO of a successful professional services company, was introduced to me by my golfing partner. We met one Friday late in the evening in his office and my first impression was that he was very sincere and highly energetic. I wanted to understand why he may need coaching and if he would be comfortable working with me.

Sridhar had an impressive track record of leading his company to be one of the best in its category in the country. He has ambitions of leading it to next level including being counted as a significant player in the Asia-Pacific region in the next few years. He realized that he needs to lead this ambitious growth plan from the front, but was struggling to take his time out as he was bogged down by day to day operations. He stated that he was a self-taught leader and that this was the right stage for him to enhance his leadership skills to guide his firm to the next level.

We seemed to have developed mutual respect for each other from the first instance and I felt more confident when Sridhar stated that he was looking forward to leveraging my wide experience and was excited about working with me.

*Sridhar wanted the coaching to focus on helping him to improve and grow as an effective leader, who could guide his organization to the next level. Specifically, he wanted to evaluate and understand improvements in his leadership style, essential for enabling the growth of his organization.*

Sridhar felt that there was great potential in the market and yet he was feeling somewhat, restricted. He had been working on creating the launch pad for growth, having rebranded the company, relocating to world class facilities, and working on new positioning in the market over the last one year. He had been working on developing improved platforms for providing his professional services, proactively added new solutions to address changing market needs and introduced new range of services to be one stop shop for his customers.

He was growing anxious, that the growth was not gathering speed and he seemed to be caught in day to day running of the organization, with limited time to focus on expansion.

I probed into the working of his organization, his team, and how he spends time. We structured the discussion by each business unit and department.

Sridhar had built this organization with a lot of hands-on approach, having worked closely with his team in delivering predictable solutions to their clients. He imbibed a strong sense of customer orientation and domain skills within the team. This was specifically true for the business units which were focussed on the Traditional Offering of the company. The entire team, including the leadership and the critical middle management were groomed by him and had grown with the company. He was very confident about their abilities and domain strength. There was a high degree of institutionalizing and predictability in its operations.

As they expanded their offerings in the market, Sridhar had to create newer business units to service these offerings. These units were largely staffed by lateral hires. Sridhar had handpicked the leadership for these units. They were highly experienced and very skilled. The middle management was also comprised of lateral hires but Sridhar in particular was uncomfortable with these people. He did not trust their commitment and their approach to customer issues. He felt that they were being indifferent to customer issues and attributed such attitudes to cultures of their previous company. He felt that extent of standardization and institutionalization was low. He was reluctant to let them run on their own and preferred being involved hands on in their operations. This really took up his time and he ended up spending almost 30 per cent of his time.

*It appeared to me that Sridhar was out of his comfort zone with the middle to senior lateral hires. This was a critical area and it was clear that the organization would not grow without embracing the lateral hires and his being able to effectively work with them. It would be imperative that Sridhar enhances his comfort levels with lateral hires and ensures that they successfully transcend into his organization.*

Sales and Marketing was another area where he was spending substantial time. He was quite uncomfortable about how the team was performing. He was also very unhappy about the consultants they had hired for the job and called it a wasted effort. Overall he felt that the team lacked domain knowledge and therefore did not have ability to engage with the customer. Their preferred style of selling was menu-driven and feature-based, which was okay only for small sales. They were not effectively engaging the larger clients. He felt that there was a lack of processes and their approach to selling was more feature driven. This approach was contrary to the positioning he desired in the market. He was involved in all the key transactions and this took almost 30 per cent of his time as well.

*In Sales and Marketing as well it appeared to me that Sridhar would rather instruct each step, than hold the team for end result.*

From the beginning Sridhar was involved in the development of the platform and tools that provided their services. He had a clear vision of the product evolution and was personally leading the development of the new version. He was looking for a leader in this area, but felt necessary to drive the building of the new version himself, at least for the next one year. He was spending nearly 30 per cent of his time in product development.

I was not surprised when Sridhar updated me that planning and reviews were unstructured and random.

We summarized his time distribution and this is how it turned out. He was spending about 30 per cent of his time in each of the areas of sales, new business units and platform and tools development and around 5 per cent in traditional business units.

Having understood the story from Sridhar's perspective, it was critical I saw it from others' eyes as well. We agreed to do a 360-degree assessment exercise that included all his senior leadership and few customers.

## Sridhar Story—Others' Perspective

The respondents unanimously gave credit to Sridhar's vision and extraordinary energy and passion. In their view he had a vision for a large business even from the early days. He was seen as being extremely passionate about his business and as someone who sets high standards for others to follow. 'Highly energetic and can put in great amount of work' was a common observation.

Sridhar was seen by the market and his colleagues as a domain expert and somebody who is constantly working to stay ahead and striving to add value. The other great quality was openness to feedback and willingness to learn. In one of the respondent's words, 'Very frank, and open to feedback and takes inputs and actually implements them.'

Sridhar was highly customer centric and was seen as stretching to any limit to meet customer commitments. In the words of one of the respondents, 'For a client he is always approachable; can call any time, whatever the size and nature of issue, he is always available.' Sridhar was seen as a calculated risk taker willing to make mistakes. He was also seen as a very fast learner, quickly implementing his new learnings.

The management team of the company, however, saw him as being very informal and unstructured. Reviews were random and there was no review calendar in place. There was lack of clarity on plans and performance measures, feedback was largely transactional and no formal appraisals were held for senior management team. All Administrative approvals were only through him.

There were a few complaints as well. He was seen as someone who prefers only people with domain knowledge and does not encourage other skills.

People also observed that delegation was minimal. Many of his senior leadership felt that he was under-leveraging their potential and was not giving enough room for them to take responsibility and deliver. Sridhar was seen as taking decisions for everyone. In their view, he got involved in everything and participated hands-on.

It seemed that almost everyone in the organization looked to him to play the role of subject matter specialist, constantly involve him in the solution development and would leave all decision-making to him, thereby not owning the decisions and the problems.

I prepared diligently for providing this feedback to Sridhar and was a bit nervous about how he would take it.

One of Sridhar's strengths is that he is a keen learner and is all ears to understand how others perceive him and therefore showed keenness throughout the session. It was quite smooth. I paused after each important feedback, letting him internalize it all.

He requested time to study this more closely and said he would come prepared for the next session to discuss and take necessary steps.

## Introspection

The next session was very critical. Having internalized the perspectives, we discussed various aspects and where the focus needs to be.

'I wonder,' Sridhar said, 'if this is the right time to make transition to a formal management? The only reason I closely get involved with tight controls over operations is to ensure that the business delivers at all costs. As an entrepreneur I have to ensure that the culture of the organization has imbibed the true spirit of the business. I have no hesitation to let go of all controls and run the business through systems and processes, but can I adapt similar approach to the newer units?'

'So what are the alternatives?' I asked. 'Will the predictability improve if you continue to participate hands-on or will they continue to let you drive everything, feeling comfortable that you are taking the accountability for these units to perform?'

Sridhar thought for a while and said, 'I have no desire to work hands-on, but just wanted to ensure that the business runs. I have handpicked the leadership to the new units, it is perhaps time for them to take ownership of bringing about this change.'

'You will have to facilitate making this change happen,' I said. 'They should have clarity about what you expect and how will you measure. I think there is an urgent need to introduce structured and formal management.'

Sridhar was quick to accept the lack of structured management and need for increased delegation. He felt that his ability to free time would depend upon the confidence he developed in his team's ability to become customer centric and more accountable. He felt that newer business units, with more lateral hires would need to get more structured and standardize their operations and so as to improve the overall predictability.

Sridhar further added that he should perhaps give more room for the teams to work, measuring them on impact rather than supervising them on every action. He also agreed that he should allow solutions to emerge at various levels. Organizationally, he also felt they should be more tolerant of mistakes.

The organization's inherent domain strength had been the key to their success. However, he agreed that strong customer relationships must co-exist along with domain specialization. He also noted that he needed to engage and communicate with the larger organization, specifically the lateral hires on the importance of these aspects. He felt this was essential for lateral hires to successfully make a transition into the company.

*He essentially agreed that it was time for a more formal management system and that he should create a structured environment.*

He identified the key goal to be *to improve delegation so that he can release his time to focus on growing the organization to the next level.*

We parted, deciding that in the next session we would spend time working on action plans of how he will effectively delegate and what his time projections will be once he effectively delegates.

One of the pleasures of working with Sridhar was the preparation he did between sessions, internalizing our discussions, piloting some actions and compiling data of issues for our deliberations. The sessions therefore became much more focused and extremely productive.

He came up a with a projected time-spend:

1.  Profit and Loss (P&L) responsibilities to business units with clear revenue target and expense budgets and managed by the units
2.  P&L responsibility supported by standardization of policies—people structures and pays, travel policies, etc.
3.  Setting up review mechanisms—publishing a review calendar
4.  Enabling senior management appraisal

I shared best practices from other companies including annual calendars for reviews, etc. and Sridhar liked the idea very much. He agreed to publish a calendar of reviews for his company.

As a next step, we discussed the strategies to achieve the desired goals. The key action plans that emerged to ensure effective delegation included to hand over P&L responsibilities to business units with clear revenue target and expense budgets managed by the units, supported by standardization of policies—people structures and pays, travel policies, etc.

He recognized that he should oversee Institutional strengthening, standardizing and improving predictability as key requirements for business units to take up P&L responsibilities. He also felt that this would help him to spend more time in developing markets.

## Sridhar's Progress with Delegation and Related Action Plans

The balance sessions focussed on the progress of delegation and how well he was able to put in place the action plans and free his time to focus on growth as he aspired.

Sridhar is a highly motivated individual. It was very pleasing to see that the actions plans committed were promptly completed by the next meeting.

He started with delegating the P&L responsibilities to various units, together with setting up clear measurement mechanisms. He also ensured that transparency was established with specific goals of a unit being visible to all levels within that group.

Some initial pilots included, enabling the business units to finalize the annual pay raises, unlike previous years, where it was directly done by him. Obviously, he provided the budgets and framework for this exercise and reviewed it with rigor and compliance.

Next, he ensured policies across various areas were standardized to enable decision-making at ground level.

He set up formal review calendars for various areas and saw that structured review processes came into place.

After enabling delegation at a senior management level, Sridhar worked on cascading it to the next level, with a specific goal that they provide oversight and troubleshoot. He also ensured that they take accountability for the customer end results, and do not hide behind transactions.

In case of business units, second and third layers structuring and delegation was set up as:

1. Top Managers—Customer Relationship Management.
2. Next layers only monitor and guide and strictly no processing.

Another change Sridhar had worked on was to be very firm and clear about his expectations with every group. Once communicated and accepted, he decided to be sure on expecting results.

Sridhar feels that he has been able to successfully delegate. Most of the groups have successfully adapted to this change. Some functions, however, were still lagging behind a little on this. With some streamlining of processes and mentoring systems in place, in his view, he would be able to bring about improvement in this team as well.

Sridhar has been maintaining time sheets and calendars and closely monitoring his time. He is confident that he can continuously fine tune the action plans so as to ensure that the organization delivers the results he expects.

He believes the benefits will be more visible in the long run as the organization matures.

## Results That Were Achieved

Sridhar has successfully improved his delegation and has implemented related action plans. From the perspective of the coaching journey, Sridhar believes he has experienced changes as:

1. His approach has become more structured and streamlined.
2. He is prioritizing well and is very planned in his activities (calendar-driven).
3. Much more firm about the outcome-focus and not being lenient about diversions and delays.
4. His shift from crisis management to more structured reviews.

He does not foresee any major challenges and is expected to continue to divide his time optimally, as per plan.

He continues to fine tune the action plans and has been able to successfully improve the predictability in his new business units.

I thanked my golf buddy for introducing me to Sridhar. I have really enjoyed working with someone who is so dedicated. Whether its golf, life or business the lessons are the same. To quote golfer Gary Player who said, 'The more I practice, the luckier I get.' The toughest part in case of Sridhar was letting go of his need to control. He always had the commitment but is now working, in a structured manner, towards being involved but at the same time being detached. I wish him well.

# 13

# Helping the Chosen One Claim His Succession Space

Loyalty and functional expertise are very important ingredients when it comes to being considered for succession especially in a promoter-led organization. However, in today's competitive and complex business environment these are necessary but not sufficient conditions especially when it comes to leading a business. The loyalists may fail to demonstrate leadership competencies that are now necessary for success. Unfortunately, promoters find it difficult to be honest about these deficiencies with their loyalists who are potential successors. The potential successors also find it difficult to understand these new demands. When one such promoter invited Gagan Rao to work with her loyal executive and potential successor, the measure of success was very clear in her mind—Raghavan should make himself acceptable to his peers and claim his space.

## The Case: Raghavan Learns to Claim His Space

### Light at the End of the Tunnel

It was around 5:30 pm, October 2012. My phone rang. The call was from Raghavan. While my engagement with Raghavan had ended in March 2012, I knew that there were some developments at his end. So, I was not surprised to receive his call.

Raghavan said that he was happy to report some good news. He was coming out of a meeting where it was formally announced that Mr Ramkumar who had been appointed recently as an advisor would be taking over as President of the company and Raghavan would succeed him in twelve to eighteen months' time. The announcement was also to be made to rest of the organization. I asked Raghavan how he felt about it. He said that he was very happy because finally a public announcement was made about his becoming President and a clear date was also visible to him. He told me he was looking forward to working with and learning from Ramkumar in the coming months.

Only two weeks ago Ramkumar who is a good friend of mine called me and told me that he had joined Radiant Industries as an advisor and one of his main tasks was to groom Raghavan to take over as President. He asked for my views and insights because I had worked with Raghavan in a coaching relationship recently. After obtaining the MD, Ms Janaki's permission I shared some of the three way meeting summaries with Ramkumar. Clearly, Ramkumar was taking over from where I left and that made so much sense.

Having started my coaching engagement with Raghavan in March 2011, it was very gratifying that eighteen months later Raghavan could see light at the end of the tunnel with the public announcement about his progression. Raghavan had come a long way.

While I was happy for Raghavan, I was full of appreciation for his MD, Ms Janaki. She was fairness and firmness personified. I have not met many sponsors who are so deeply committed to grooming their leaders from within and are yet not willing to drop their expectations and standards in terms of what it will take to get the top job.

I was introduced to Ms Janaki who is the promoter and MD of Radiant Industries part of the GKS Group by another member of the GKS family. In my first meeting with her she outlined her immediate concern around succession in Radiant Industries. She had been running Radiant Industries for many years. A few years ago, she hired a person from outside as President to take over from her and run the company. Unfortunately this did not go well and the person left. The one person who had always been in contention for the job is Raghavan who was among the first employees to join the company when it was formed. Obviously, Raghavan felt he was passed over when the person was hired from outside.

When he left, Raghavan thought the job was his but Ms. Janaki was convinced that he was not yet ready.

She clarified to me that she has been telling Raghavan that he had the potential to get that job but had to work towards it. She had done her bit by sending him to several training programs and having him assessed and profiled by various consultants. Unfortunately, none of this had helped, she said with a sense of remorse. In fact, Raghavan was not even as effective as he used to be, she said.

In the very first meeting, it became clear to me that things were not going well at all with Raghavan and she seemed frustrated. Good thing was that she did not want to give up. Her expectation was that I should help Raghavan make the transition from functional head to business leader and become capable of heading the organization. I agreed to work with Raghavan.

As a part of my familiarization efforts I made a visit to the factory in Coimbatore and met Raghavan and all his colleagues. The visit helped me understand the organization, business and culture. It also helped me meet Raghavan, establish chemistry and explain Coaching to him.

## Raghavan Tells His Story

A few days after my visit, Raghavan called me and confirmed his willingness to take things forward and asked for a meeting. He came down to my office on the appointed day.

Raghavan was in his late 40s. He was married and had one daughter who was now in high school. It was very easy for Raghavan to establish rapport and start the conversation. He was also quick to narrate his story to me.

It appeared very important for Raghavan to let me know how his connection with the Group ran very deep. He had studied in the school run by the group. His father had worked in the group and his brother was currently working in the group.

Having completed his Engineering, he joined Radiant Industries as a Trainee in 1985, the year the company was founded. In the early years he grew primarily in the technical function. Over time, Engineering and Manufacturing was also added to his responsibility. In 2001 he was made Plant Coordinator with responsibility for all functions except Finance and Marketing. He also became the youngest General Manager. In 2005, he was made responsible for setting up a new facility in the North which unfortunately did not go well. In 2006 he was made responsible for strategic planning and development, strategic sourcing and R&D. Raghavan spoke eloquently about his strengths like results orientation, his ability to learn quickly and of course his loyalty. He acknowledged that he was somewhat rigid and also low on his social relationships.

He admitted that it was important for him to be accepted by his other peers in his team when he does become the President. He clarified that he was very keen on coaching and he was happy to work with me.

I asked Raghavan his permission to speak to his peers and team members for a 360-degree feedback process. Raghavan readily agreed to it and set up these meetings.

## The strange 360-degree experience

I visited Coimbatore and gathered feedback from all of them. Since I had not had the opportunity to have a formal three way meeting between Raghavan, his MD and myself, I also asked for the same to be arranged. I thought I would also use the opportunity to meet her one-on-one and obtain her 360-degree feedback. What actually happened in that meeting was interesting, challenging and even intriguing.

The MD decided to combine our three-way meeting with the 360-degree feedback session. Yes, she shared her feedback about Raghavan to me in front of Raghavan. At one level it was indicative of the comfort and depth of their relationship and at another level it appeared that my presence perhaps served as an opportunity for Ms Janaki to choose to be rather candid with Raghavan about her expectations and her disappointments. While I tried as well as I could to maintain a sense of balance in the meeting it appeared that Raghavan was beginning to feel extremely defensive.

Ms Janaki shared her perception of Raghavan's strengths but also her concerns around his interpersonal relationships and peer interactions. She said she was beginning to have doubts about his acceptance among peers. She also shared her expectation that Raghavan should be willing to give up his functional responsibility and focus his energy on larger organizational agendas. Raghavan agreed to think about the feedback so we could meet again and take things forward.

When the three-way meeting ended, Raghavan clearly looked somewhat disturbed but as a true loyalist he smiled and said that it was all being done for his good and he would learn to see it that way.

Raghavan's strong loyalty on one side, his MD's commitment to his development on another side and her sense of disappointment on the third side gave me the impression that the task at hand was much harder that it appeared initially. There were some missing pieces, I thought. Fortunately, I did not have to wait too long for my answers.

## The penny drops

Raghavan and I met very soon for our next meeting—the one where the breakthrough came.

I asked Raghavan how he felt about the last two weeks, especially since the last three way meeting. Raghavan told me that his last meeting with the MD had not gone too well. When the MD followed up with him about his giving away his principal responsibilities and taking on certain organizational roles, he had expressed his reservation. He felt that in the recent years many of the roles were assigned to him and then taken away without any justification.

Raghavan pointed out that he was now thoroughly frustrated because talks about his becoming President have been on for over five years. He implied that he was now seeing Coaching as one more process step and that was frustrating him. The manner in which functions close to him were being taken away made him a lot more anxious he said. He felt that as a result, his image in the eyes of the others was also impacted. Ever since 2006, things have not been going well, he said.

Raghavan was perhaps for the first time ventilating his anger and frustration with intensity and I was happy for him. I encouraged him to say more. If Raghavan could ventilate as much as he could, it might help him to start thinking more clearly, I felt. I asked Raghavan to tell me more about 2006. It appeared that 2006 was the time when the organization had begun to hire people from outside and Raghavan was beginning to feel somewhat anxious about this and the changes it meant for him. 2005 was when the new project led by him failed and 2006 was the time when he was moved away from many of the line responsibilities and given special assignments. Raghavan felt that after waiting for five years the coaching assignment was now creating a new goal post for him. In some ways he was blaming his MD for not giving him the job.

As the conversation progressed I invited Raghavan to talk about his contribution to the situation he was in. Raghavan struggled for a while to answer this question. I then asked him whether he had ever looked at the situation from his MD's point of view. To drive home the point, I role played with Raghavan, playing the role of his MD. Raghavan slowly began to reflect. The 360-degree feedback that he received from his peers and his MD combined with the catharsis a short while ago helped Raghavan begin to see things somewhat differently.

He began to realize the paradox of the situation—*he wanted to be appointed as President, so that he could act as one. On the other hand his MD wanted him to act like a President before she could appoint him as one.* Raghavan conceded that to behave like a President he did not require any approval. Raghavan agreed that he would think deeply about making effort to act like a President, because that was the only way he could win back his MD's confidence. *'To act like a President'*, therefore, became Raghavan's goal and mission statement!

Before closing the meeting he told me that he had been invited by the MD to be on the Board of the Group's School Trust, a privilege given to very few outside the family. When asked what it meant to him, he confessed that this was a symbol of the MD's trust in him and he had to now take the next step.

It was almost as if a ghost has been exorcized at the end of the meeting. His body language, his tone, his enthusiasm was suddenly limitless and exciting.

## Committed to change

Over the next few weeks Raghavan's Manager and MD was more in touch with me than Raghavan. She was keen to push Raghavan in his journey of moving from functional leadership to business leadership and in her view if Raghavan had to succeed he had to give up direct responsibility of the functions he was handling and focus on organizational issues.

The interactions with the MD helped me understand Raghavan's story even better. From a time when Raghavan was the centre of the universe, the organization had now moved on. Many functional leaders had now come on board and settled down. Many of the ad hoc responsibilities assigned to Raghavan were taken away and handed over to these full time specialists. During this period Raghavan was expected to scale up and learn to play a larger role. Unfortunately, he had not managed to. Given this situation, the MD felt that time was running out and she was becoming increasingly impatient. Why is Raghavan not doing enough to take charge? Why is it so hard for him to trust us, she seemed to be asking. On the other hand, Raghavan was wondering how he could show leadership without being given the job?

She also sounded me out on some of the organizational changes she was contemplating which impacted Raghavan. While I was keen to be of assistance as a sounding board, I was careful not to cross my boundary of being a Coach. I did not also want to internalize her anxiety about Raghavan. In fact, in one of these meetings, I told her that the process would take a lot of time and she will need to be patient. I could see that she was genuinely trying to push him in a certain direction but clearly Raghavan was too anxious to take the lead for fear of failing. I suddenly remembered Raghavan telling me about the new factory project which he was responsible for and how its failure was difficult for him to get over.

While this was happening, Raghavan was coming to terms with the reality of his situation. Acting like a leader, the President was up to him. His MD's firmness in wanting him to make a personal change before granting him the job also helped him accept that reality. That he now had a Coach to support him was comforting. His commitment to the goals and change was now quite high.

Over the next two months I helped Raghavan evolve several concrete steps to give shape to the goal of acting like a President. His own action orientation fuelled him to start acting.

Reflection was right on top of the action plans for Raghavan. Raghavan had to become a lot more self-aware if he had to know how his behaviour was affecting his peer relationships on a daily basis. Self-awareness from the 360 was just a starting point. Self-awareness had to become an integral part of his journey to progress. Raghavan agreed to read all the assessment reports to aid this self-awareness. He also agreed to make notes about how he carried himself in meetings and interactions.

He also agreed to start seeing things from others point of view because the lack of empathy was a big part of his challenge. He had to start putting himself in the shoes of his MD, his peers and his team members.

He had to demonstrate far greater sensitivity in his peer interactions.

He also had to show the courage to give up some of the functions and take on new responsibilities.

Above all, he had to get back to being his natural self. Being a cricket player, I offered Raghavan a cricketing metaphor. As he was nearing his century, there was an understandable anxiety. But should he keep looking at the score board or play his natural style. Raghavan agreed that it was time to play his natural game, like he used to before 2006.

While Raghavan agreed to several action plans and strategies, the focus of his change efforts had to centre around his peers because that is where he had to make most immediate and lasting impact. He had to get into meetings and avoid being partisan, avoid emotional outbursts, play a facilitative role, be approachable to people and carry them along. He had to be seen as the first among equals, someone others would come to for solutions and support.

Given his natural style preference, it was not very easy to get Raghavan to be disciplined in maintaining records, sending mail updates and responding to my session summaries. This frustrated me for a few weeks. I then decided to make some spontaneous follow-up phone calls and that worked. He was also not too much of a reflective person. He often preferred to pose certain questions to me and seek my guidance. This included specific questions about team management and other nuances in dealing with his peers. I had to rely on my judgement and honour his requests when I felt they were genuine. It was often necessary for me to set aside time for some mentoring inputs at the end of my coaching sessions.

Over these two months, we stayed focused on making progress in the areas of improving his peer relationships. It was also important for Raghavan to remain convinced that it was up to him to pursue his dream by taking definitive steps. Raghavan reported good progress in these areas. What helped was the fact that he was a lot more at peace with himself and a lot more comfortable relating to me. A strong foundation of trust had indeed been established. I could now leverage this trust to challenge him when required.

While I was convinced about the progress with his peers, I continued to be concerned on two counts—his lack of structure and discipline as a manager (as experienced by me) was concerning me. I was also not hearing enough about his progress in his relationship with his MD. In fact, Raghavan mentioned that he received a very cold response to one of his recent formal communications to the MD. I decided to explore this with him.

For a relationship that was well over two decades old and strong, there was some fragility in the relationship, I realized. Raghavan did on occasion give me the impression that he was anxious about her perceptions and her approval.

As I explored this issue with him, it became clear that Raghavan had not invested in building a formal relationship with the MD—a relationship that any President of a company would be expected to have with the promoter and MD. He was not seeking her time for structured and planned meetings, engaging in structured reviews, structured briefing sessions and so on. Even when there was a meeting that he was invited to attend, he would take it on the fly and go rather unprepared. It was clear that the MD was becoming extremely uncomfortable with this style.

All new hires had a formal relationship with her. They were structured in their interactions with her, they had a clear agenda, they followed the structure, they made formal presentations, sent her summaries and meeting notes. Raghavan on the other hand remained stuck in his old style—a style that worked when they were a start-up. On the other hand, he was reading between the lines and worrying about his relationship with her instead of using formal communication skills and managerial abilities to achieve alignment on key issues.

On more than one occasion, I invited Raghavan to look at his style from the MD's point of view. I asked him to explore the implications of this style on his becoming President. He slowly realized that he was almost taking her for granted. To drive home the point, I asked him how a President hired from outside would deal with the MD and Raghavan smiled and said he understood.

I shared several examples of the styles of great CEOs I knew and this helped Raghavan. He agreed to pay greater attention to this area.

Raghavan and I came up with a few action plans to practice a more formal style. This included spending a lot more time in formal, structured face to face meetings. He must get on to her calendar more often. He also agreed to constantly ensure align of expectations. He also agreed to prepare a lot better for his interactions. He also agreed to hire a secretary for himself and take that person's help to get discipline in managing his calendar among other things.

Unfortunately, I did not see enough progress on this front.

## Time for Validation

As Raghavan was reporting genuine progress I felt it was opportune to do a follow up 360 to obtain external validation of progress made by Raghavan. Raghavan was quite excited with the idea.

The 360-degree feedback results were quite heartening. Everyone including his team members, peers and his MD reported great progress. They all uniformly reported that the old Raghavan was back—his natural self—confident, cheerful, self-assured and enthusiastic.

Their experience of him in meetings had improved dramatically. He was listening, encouraging others and facilitating them towards a good decision. He was also sharing his knowledge with others and building on others ideas.

In that past month, there was a very volatile employee relations situation in the factory involving the workmen and the local community. Raghavan apparently went out and led the conciliatory efforts from the front despite potential dangers, much to the relief of all. He was clearly beginning to act like a President.

Interestingly all this coincided with a religious ceremony in his house for which he invited all his colleagues at work. The manner in which all of them turned up, stayed on and joined him in celebration really enthused him. He was now convinced that they liked him.

Of course they all had suggestions for further improvements and sustenance. While the MD was pleased, she made it clear that there was a lot more to do. She shared with me the next gradient he had to scale. It was little surprise that Raghavan was craving for her appreciation.

The biggest expectation his MD had from him was in the area that I had already flagged off—developing a formal work style that would help him cope with the many pressures of a President's job.

She also shared with me her thoughts about making Raghavan the head of a large scale business process improvement project they were embarking on with the help of a leading global consulting firm. She was keen that Raghavan makes a success of it and uses it as his launch pad for the President's job. She was reciprocating his efforts and that was great.

Raghavan was delighted that this was happening. He was now ready to give up all his functional responsibilities and take on this role. No anxiety but a huge leap of faith, I thought.

One other expectation emerged from his peers. They still saw Raghavan struggling to deal with conflicts, especially inter-functional conflicts. Rising above his old functional identity was still hard for him.

Raghavan was happy to address this area. I asked Raghavan to take the Thomas–Kilmann Conflict Mode Instrument. The results clearly pointed out that his natural and strongest preference was *competing* and his least preferred was *accommodating* and *collaborating*. Raghavan found the framework very useful. He was especially able to see the relevance of this in the context of his relationship with his Head of Operations with whom he had the most conflicts. He agreed to work on this specific relationship immediately through certain collaborative efforts.

In the coming weeks, Raghavan made good progress in building his relationship with the Operations Head. Clearly, on the people front, he was now in flow state.

Raghavan also used me as a sounding board to brainstorm on what it will take to lead the consulting project. He could see that there was a managerial dimension, a persuasion dimension and a people dimension. On the people and persuasion dimensions, Raghavan had made sustainable changes with little risk of relapse.

On the managerial side, it was still a long road given his natural style preference. It was clear to me that Raghavan will have to do a lot more work in this area.

Meanwhile, the MD made an organizational announcement that Raghavan would lead the prestigious project for the company that was aimed at saving crores of rupees.

## Time to Close

This seemed to be the right time for us to start winding down the engagement. I asked Raghavan to decide if he felt self-sufficient and if we could close the engagement and he said yes.

We had a closing meeting with the sponsor, the MD. The MD once again acknowledged that Raghavan had made significant shifts. She also acknowledged that his first few weeks in the project were going well. She however decided to use the closing meeting to keep the momentum and pressure on Raghavan. The MD wanted Raghavan to demonstrate a much more formal work style and be a lot more managerially effective.

Going by her recent announcement, she was demonstrating her sustained commitment to his development by appointing Ramkumar as an interim President and mentor for Raghavan.

On his part, Raghavan was convinced that his progress was in his hands. He was also beginning to see the rest of the team accepting him as the first among equals. The fact that he was being groomed formally through coaching and the fact that he was heading this mission critical consulting project were messages enough to say that he was the chosen one and to their credit his peers were not protesting. Raghavan was now showing so much of leadership, flexibility and acceptance and strengthening his case.

I am certainly happy for Raghavan and am waiting for the next call from him announcing his elevation as President. I am sure this will happen.

As I think back, I must confess that if Raghavan succeeds, a big part of the credit must go to his MD.

# SECTION E

# Acquiring Global Competencies

# Why Global Competencies Are So Critical Today

## Anil Sachdev*

Our 'world view' as leaders is the lens through which we view reality. This is deeply influenced by our mental models caused by our past experiences. What we choose to give attention to—our contextual intelligence is important. Many forces are shaping our planet. What we notice and consider as important shapes is the way we think and act.

Our cultural competence in terms of how we use language, how we demonstrate nonverbal behaviour, our communication style, our attitudes and values towards groups and community and our time consciousness are all aspects that define shape our leadership.

Our comfort with working in virtual teams and the use of technology to enhance relationships enables us to be effective as leaders.

Our self-awareness which helps us to pay attention to what we do well and what impact we have on others and what we need to do differently is at the heart of the global mind-set.

Our ability to establish rapport by genuinely enjoying diversity through interaction with people and learning to appreciate their uniqueness is also an important dimension.

Our authenticity and openness enables us to deal with many difficult and often ambiguous situations.

Our capacity to learn through feedback and through introspection and reflection help us to learn from mistakes.

*Anil Sachdev is the Founder and CEO of the School of Inspired Leadership (SOIL). He was also the Founder of Grow Talent Company Limited.

I enjoyed reading all the cases presented to me.

In the case of Vikram, it is clear that after some initial struggle to define his goals for coaching, he was able to realize how crucial it was for him to develop his emotional quotient. The coach enabled him to leverage his strengths of focus and task orientation to bear on his need to become more skilful in dealing with people. He began to appreciate the cross cultural nuances and seems to have introspected about the feedback given by multiple sources including the 360-degree process.

The coach seems to have shown him the mirror, made him accountable for his own development and maintained regular and deep contact with him to monitor progress.

Ramila is another fascinating case of a leader who has been enabled to get out of her comfort zone to learn by taking risks and trying new behaviours. The coach created a safe environment for her to express her issues and anxieties and to explore what mattered most to her and how she intended to take responsibility for the goals that she was defining for herself. It was very moving to read about how she was helped to read some classics to enrich her world view and how she adopted a strategy to become a great conversationalist and a presenter with the help of her coach.

In all the cases, they understood the context of their coaching well, were open to learning, demonstrated enthusiasm to stay on track and built trusting relationships with their coaches.

The credibility of the coaches with their own senior leadership experience and global exposure enabled them to give off their best and not get discouraged with challenges that were faced.

To end, let me share the Checklist for intercultural communication presented by a dear colleague and friend, Dr Milton Bennett who co-teaches in our Global Leadership Program on the important subject of global leadership effectiveness.

Dr Milton J. Bennett, suggests five areas in which one needs to be particularly attentive to possible cultural differences. This attentiveness will pay off in improved communication and intercultural learning if you (a) recognize a cultural difference from your own 'natural' style; (b) adapt your behaviour to accommodate the difference; and/or (c) call attention to the difference to explain confusion in communication, he says.

The first area relates to language use including greeting/leave-taking rituals, compliments and apologies.

The second area relates to nonverbal behaviour including paralanguage (tone of voice), body language and time language.

The third area relates to communication style including circular or linear, indirect or direct, expressive of restraint.

The fourth area relates to cultural values including individualism or group orientation, egalitarianism or recognition of status, problem solving or adaptation.

The fifth area relates to perceptual mode including concrete or abstract, inductive or deductive, precise or speculative.

# 14

# When Indian Executives Must Measure up to Global Benchmarks

While global corporations have operated in India for many years, for a very long time the Indian operations were treated as outposts with little significance in their global scheme of things and therefore seldom on the radar of their globally mobile talent. Not any longer. For all global corporations today the stakes in India are very high from a talent and market perspective. To this end, the Indian operations are now globally integrated and fully verticalized. When it comes to staffing the leadership roles in India, the search is now truly global. Even tenured Indian executives have to measure up to global benchmarks. Fortunately, coaches with a global mindset like Rakesh Rao can help otherwise technically competent executives like Vikram to make the cut globally.

## The Case: Vikram Gets to the President's Office Successfully

The client is a Fortune listed company in multiple business domains including health care which is a dominant vertical. They wanted me to coach one of their senior leaders who had been identified for a global role. The company believes in the value of coaching as was evident from my conversation with the global lead in organization and leadership development based in the US. The vision of the international IT service division to which the executive ('coachee') is connected is to create the best information technology to drive market leadership and innovative growth for the different verticals of the firm. The role envisaged providing world class application design, development, and support services resulting in higher quality at acceptable cost and in developing new business capabilities. There were challenges in aligning international services to primary business processes, enhancing relationship management to ensure clear points of contact and accountability, and in promoting the transition to a strategic business partnership model.

## The Coachee: Personal and Professional

The coachee, Vikram is an engineer by profession; undergraduate from an Indian University; after an early stint with computer application development in a firm in India, he obtained a graduate degree from a reputed US University. Subsequent to his graduation, he began working in a global IT firm in the US in the product development space, moved on to assume senior responsibility for internal IT management application services for over eleven years; returned to India to continue to work for the same firm in an expanded role with internal clients from Middle East and South Asia. Vikram's mandate was to become responsible for enterprise services for the regions which involved delivery of projects and service management for one of the verticals. His father who retired from Government is his role model; has imbibed values of hard work, honesty and integrity. His wife is a banking professional. They have one school-going child. Vikram has built a good reputation. His journey in life is characterized by different environments both in and outside India which gave him the self-confidence to face up to new experiences and challenges. He is therefore able to view situations with multiple perspectives.

## The Story of Vikram's Issues, Needs and Aspirations

As Vikram was identified for transitioning into a global role, future challenges included confidence in networking and influencing a wide spread of stakeholders, skills required to align with all the business verticals and learn to become an effective partner; and to create a 'shared destiny mindset'. He should be able to handle organization development at an enterprise level which included adroit handling of a larger team with many members located in different parts of the globe; demonstrating more trusting, delegating and empowering styles and to provide leadership for those who were his peers earlier.

I was provided with a comprehensive set of data which included a recent 360-degree survey report (text responses when structured around great questions were very helpful), and employee engagement scores for the past two years and action taken reports on them. In addition, psychometric data, personal history record, role sheet of the proposed role, and an opportunity to discuss with the supervisor located in the US did provide useful inputs for setting the expectations. Vikram made a comprehensive presentation on the business context, challenges ahead, the organization structure including the one which was being evolved, and the profile of the team members. What did not surprise me was that Vikram needed help in making meaning out of the 360-degree data, psychometrics, etc., and this was very helpful in obtaining new insights on his current level of self-awareness. There were some 'blind spots' and we agreed to work on them during subsequent sessions. It took about three to four hours for the 'opening session' and the executive felt reasonably comfortable with the time spent which enabled me to establish the rapport with him in an informal setting.

## Arriving at Coaching Goals

This is a challenging requirement for coaching to become an effective development tool. Vikram was encouraged to prepare a version 1 of the coaching goals using a template. A couple of reminders were needed. There were scheduling challenges during the initial stage. There were a couple of iterations before we could jointly agree on the coaching goals. We also had an alignment conversation jointly with the supervisor. Here again scheduling the call took a while. However, once we overcame the initial challenges with patience, we got the traction and eventually gained momentum. To summarize, the important goals committed by the executive included:

1. to mobilize greater commitment on arriving at a broader consensus through a more inclusive strategy: increase both formal and informal interactions in meetings with global leadership on contentious issues. Share experiences and thoughts more actively with team members and significant others
2. to ensure a more balanced approach on 'task' and 'relationship': control over aggression and allow the reflective side to emerge; control the temptation to be outspoken to prevent it from being perceived as negativity; build informal connectivity with team mates; and show 'generosity of spirit'; that is, take responsibility for first time failures and pass on the credit to the followers and to 'showcase' his talent to overseas visitors appropriately
3. to become more sensitive to cultural differences as well as to the appropriateness of communication style; demonstrate respect for diversity; and manage differences and conflicts in a collaborative way
4. to deeply appreciate the nature of challenges the business verticals were experiencing at the market place thereby encouraging the team to become more strategically proactive in a spirit of inter-dependence and to become skillful to influence critical stakeholders

## Strategies and Actions

Two rounds of discussions with the global lead in leadership development and one long conference call with the supervisor who is also located in the US helped me amply understand the client expectation. In my first meeting with the executive, the strategy was to understand and explore his journey in life; the low and high points in life and the whys, lesson learnt, current challenges, future role expectations, and what meaning he wishes to attach to various feedbacks he had received. How does Vikram express himself as a leader; what are his leadership characteristics? How does he set strategy, advocate for his strategy, and mobilize resources to achieve? What are his key strengths (gifts) to leverage, any supplementary strength, important development themes, and the commitment the executive is willing to demonstrate to make the necessary changes to happen? He was encouraged to write down a statement of his aspiration. I also discussed the conditions for effective coaching, and my coaching philosophy.

I talked less and listened more actively. I held the mirror to him so often, reflecting as specifically as possible how others experienced him as a person. Building his confidence and trust early on was the key. That we were looking at this engagement as an opportunity to holistically progress as well as enable the executive to experience an overall uplifting experience in his personal and professional life was appealing to him. There were work–life balance issues which did surface during our first round of discussion.

Other strategies included an opportunity to see the executive in action; observing him and his team while doing his weekly and quarterly reviews, couple of all hands meets (and in one such meeting his supervisor who was visiting India development centre also addressed), helping him with the design of his leadership offsite which was facilitated by him, etc. Supplementary self-assessments were encouraged, especially to assess his influencing patterns, conflict management style, etc. In between the one-on-one sessions, informal conference calls were encouraged. These, Vikram subsequently shared, were also found to be timely from a development angle.

## Experiences and Emotions during the Engagement

From being 'overwhelmed' with multiple sources of feedback as well as being unsure of the consequences, it seemed that Vikram has undergone two or three stages before he commenced taking responsibility and accountability for change. Initially he felt somewhat conflicting in apparently disconnected, non-aligned insights (dots) from feedback; then slowly and steadily, by asking more than telling, by challenging as well as supporting, and by asking deeper questions (difference between a slice of potato and that of an onion) he began to see how the dots are getting connected; how a new pattern is emerging (holistic view); and how he internally realized a new sense of purpose, confidence and meaning—the beginning of experiencing 'personal transformation'. It was palpable to notice the shift from the apparent 'burden of leading' to the 'joy of leading'. There was no reluctance anymore to maintain a coaching log; or to display candour in owning up yet another area for improvement which we missed out during the early stages. And finally, when Vikram was able to articulate his vision of himself, and commenced experiencing positive changes in him, he had that 'bouncy' feeling.

## Outcomes and How They Were Evidenced or Measured

There were quite a few steps initiated by the leadership development team to assess progress—the most recent engagement score, a follow up interview-based 360-degree survey, performance metrics to measure key deliverables and internal customer feedback from businesses. A mid-term 'dipstick' of the progress made by the executive and issues yet to be addressed was carried out. The feedback from check-lists provided by global lead at the end of the engagement to assess the efficacy of coaching by the executive, supervisor and the coach independently were equally helpful. Especially evident are improvements in skills in the areas of communications, influencing others without the use of power, sensitivity to multiple cultures, listening, and overall business relatedness. Significant behaviour change was observed by the old and new supervisors as well as business customers. Three of the necessary conditions and factors which are essential to ensure lasting behaviour changes were also beginning to be evident, via more self awareness, self motivation, and readiness to practice new styles and behaviours in the real world of work.

Following his appointment as the President for the global role, at the request of the executive first, and then the new supervisor and global lead on leadership development, I provided suitable assistance in designing and supporting a 'new leader assimilation programme'. It's now over seven months since Vikram has stepped into his new shoes. While the formal coaching engagement is over, we have maintained our trusting relationship in a non-dependent way, and from the feedback so far, the engagement was termed as truly successful.

## My Personal Reflection on What I Took Away from the Engagement

I found that if the following four or five conditions are met, coaching will produce better results. First, 'self-awareness': noticing and observing thoughts, feelings, and behaviour as they happen; the capacity to form insights from connecting the dots, and see new patterns and possibilities. Second, how strong is the motivation level of the executive to bring about a change in his attitude and behaviour. Third, the executive's willingness to experiment with new habits, style and behaviour in the real world of work, and life in general. And lastly, are there meaningful consequences waiting to ensure that the changes last long.

From my side, the realization yet again that the coachee at all times 'owns' the objective, the coaching goals and action plans. He/she lives with the consequences; the explicit faith (Pygmalion) in the executive that he/she is capable of self-directed learning or diagnosing own issues and finding appropriate solutions that the person can live with. I have endeavoured, at times, strived hard to provide a psychologically 'safe space', 'reflections' (not reactions) and 'energy' to question old paradigms and create new ones; more often shifting from 'transactional' to 'transformational' agenda. Essential to success of the coach is a combination of skills like how to recognize opportunity for 'openings' like appreciative inquiry skills, active listening, etc.; building a trusting relationship (skills like empathy, warmth, respect, etc.) because essentially coaching is a 'helping relationship' to build on strengths, and to address potential improvement areas; and skills like concreteness, constructive confrontation and sometimes sharing personal experiences and insights in order to bridge the gap. Indeed, the whole engagement must turn out to be an uplifting experience to all the stakeholders.

# 15

# It Takes Innovation and Effort to Crack the Competency Code

When executives need to learn to do something that does not come to them naturally, they need to invest a lot of effort and also innovate. With innovation and effort executives can learn to develop competences in areas that just do not come to them naturally. They may still not become the best in the world at this but the beauty is that others will just not notice! When Ramila needed to develop a world view, she partnered with her coach Rohith Kapoor and came up with the extremely innovative idea of creating story boards to master the competence. The power of this idea combined with her effort helped Ramila crack the competency code.

## The Case: Ramila Develops a World View

Cracking the Competency Code

Ramila does call and keep in touch with her coach once in a while even though the formal coaching engagement ended a year ago. However, this call from Ramila was special for her coach. There was a sense of excitement in her voice as she spoke. Ramila has been invited to the London School of Economics to deliver a special lecture on the status of working women in India. Ramila considered this invitation the single biggest achievement in her life considering that till eighteen months ago she would have politely declined an invitation to speak even from the local women's club. Till that point in her life, her idea of competency was restricted to hard skills in software development and soft supervisory skills to manage a group of developers. Public speaking, especially speaking to a very distinguished and alien audience and on a subject which until recently was as alien would have caused a panic attack. Not any longer though. Ramila is charged, excited and looking forward to the event with a sense of satisfaction and optimism. But how?

The ability to reflect and the motivation to learn are qualities in a coachee that are very crucial to achieve significant outcomes. A motivated coachee can run way ahead of the coach in implementing an action agenda. Ramila was hugely motivated and deeply reflective. What of course helped her crack the competency code so quickly was her innovative learning strategy of building her own story board. The coach considers his role no more than holding the mirror in front of Ramila.

## Background

Ramila has taken over as Global Head of Human Resources of Global Tech Inc, a large publicly quoted company that employs 4,000 software engineers operates in eighteen countries. She is new to the HR role and soon after taking over the present position she went off to attend a three-month Global Managers Programme on a Chevening Scholarship in the UK. Prior to taking on this role, she has worked in software development in Pune and in the US. Considered exceptionally bright, the company's Board had identified her as a 'Fast Track Executive' who has the potential to become the Chief Executive of the company someday. As part of the plan she is being quickly rotated through many jobs. Being exceptionally reflective, she finds that some of her competencies may not be adequate to be effective in her current job. She feels somewhat inadequate and wonders whether she can apply herself to work and improve in these development areas. She already has a high degree of clarity on her developmental needs. This is when she meets the coach, through sheer serendipity.

## Growing-Up Years

Ramila describes her childhood along with her elder brother as very secure, loving and carefree. Her father being in government service she moved around many places. She recalls being physically very active, playing outdoor games with her brother and his friends. Her parents treated her exactly the way they treated her brother and she grew up (as she says) with the confidence of a 'boy'.

She constantly topped her class and studied just enough to keep a good academic record. She however had virtually no exposure to subjects outside her engineering studies. She seldom read history, literature, liberal arts or for that matter rarely read books and magazines outside her course curriculum.

She started her career with a Government defence establishment rather young. At twenty-one she met her future husband Shekar, an officer on secondment to this establishment. Ramila and Shekar went through many transfers and she learnt the value of forming new relationships. Like her father, Shekar imbibed in her the values of being upright and fearless. Ramila understood that she could cope with change quite easily. Shekar always made her feel comfortable and treated her as an equal. With two kids aged fifteen and seven, Ramila feels a wee bit guilty that by pursuing a professional career she may have somewhat neglected the kids. She has given too much to work and too little to home in the so called 'work–life' balance. Notwithstanding Shekar's support and he giving up his career prematurely to support Ramila's career, she suffers from a considerable sense of guilt. Soon Ramila settled down in Pune and moved from the government job to Global Tech Inc. hoping for a better work–life balance.

## Attitude to Work

Ramila had the privilege of working with some very nurturing bosses including some legendary ones too. From them she learnt the values of working hard, being upright and accepting failure with a sense of equanimity. She also learnt the value of constant learning to overcome ones weaknesses.

She accepts people unconditionally and is informal and easy in her social skills. She feels very stifled when people are formal with each other and even finds it difficult to cope with formal relationships. She has a fetish for dependability. If people do not keep their commitments she takes it personally and feels let down. She thinks people who are not passionate do not give their best. She is direct in her communication, bordering at times in lack of diplomacy. When angry she even ends up using intemperate language.

She was out for a year in the US and being out of home afforded her plenty of time to reflect. She returned home with a high degree of clarity on what to work on.

## Developmental Needs

Being high on intellect with a strong ability to reflect, it was not difficult for Ramila to quickly articulate her developmental needs to her coach.

1. Cross-cultural
   Her job requires her to meet people across cultures and countries. She finds her conversational skills very limiting. She finds it particularly difficult to meet strangers in a social situation. Having had limited exposure to history, culture, religion, current affairs and so on, she doesn't know how to start a conversation. Many a times she skips a formal business dinner with say prospective clients on some pretext

2. Formal communication
   She finds communication outside her areas of expertise rather taxing. She wishes she could put some humour in her communication! She has certain role models but doesn't know where to start

3. Negotiations
   She thinks that if she negotiates too hard, people might take it personally and it might result in breaking a personal relationship. So she usually gives in

4. Self-presentation
   Her upright values tell her that self-presentation is demeaning. Her belief is that other significant people, more particularly her boss should project her. She feels offended when other people brag. That reinforces her belief about the futility of projecting oneself. However, deep within her mind she resents the fact that people who project themselves tend to move ahead quickly

A recently conducted detailed 360-degree feedback exercise as well as the outcome of a psychometric tool '24 VIA Signature Strengths' was fully in consonance with the four developmental needs identified by Ramila.

While all four were strong developmental needs, the challenge for the coach and Ramila was to select one of them as their coaching goal. There was consensus that there is probably commonality between the first and the second identified areas. The coachee felt that if they can work on the theme of 'developing a world view' it might help her address the first two areas.

## Developing a World View

The coach requested Ramila to tell him why she finds it difficult to relate to and communicate with people from different cultures and different geographies. As she began to tell her story, she also began to think about it more deeply than ever before. After much discussion the Aha! moment came when Ramila realized that her lack of knowledge about history and culture of different countries and societies were the real inhibiting factors. She also felt that the best way to learn about other cultures was to encourage people talk about their own cultures.

Ramila's dilemma was this: 'How do I get other people to talk about their cultures in social situations?' The breakthrough came when Ramila realized that if she could talk about Indian culture, religion and history, then other people will share theirs. However, Ramila felt highly challenged by this thought. 'How long will it take to learn about your own culture? Where am I going to learn this from?' She was however convinced that if she could talk intelligently about Indian culture then others will talk about theirs. Thereby, over a period of time she would have learnt the nuances of many cultures and societies.

The coach felt that a good place to begin was for Ramila to read some basic literature. As a base reading about Indian history on one hand and how the world is unfolding on the other. The coach recommended four books, somewhat dated but masterpieces in their own right. They were:

1. *A History of India, Part 1* by Romila Thapar
2. *A History of India, Part 2* by Percivel Spear
3. *Future Shock* by Alvin Toffler
4. *The Third Wave* by Alvin Toffler

Three other action areas were chosen by Ramila:

1.  Could she develop coherent thoughts on ten popular subjects based on these readings? What would the ten subjects be?
2.  Would it help if she could use few of the above through well-developed story boards in social conversations with friends and colleagues?
3.  Would it help if she could observe one of her role models carrying on a conversation during social or semi-formal situations?

The coach was also secretly hoping that once initiated into the habit of reading, the coachee might feel motivated to continue the process.

Over the next eight weeks Ramila was ready to build her own conversation pieces. The first ten story boards that she decided to build are as follows:

1.  Diversity and commonality amongst Indian states
2.  Music and dances in India
3.  Christianity in India (particularly considering overseas business associates).
4.  Indian caste system
5.  Influence of Moghuls on India
6.  Influence of Britishers on India
7.  Future of out-sourcing
8.  Future of contemporary employment
9.  Women's empowerment in India and the world
10. Technology today and tomorrow

The idea of a story board was powerful. It helped her think through the subject in advance, weave it into a compelling story and through that give her the confidence to deliver it effortlessly.

She also began to observe other colleagues whom she considers very accomplished in having a world view. She particularly considers her CEO a role model in this. This process of shadowing added more story boards to her already well selected repertoire.

While her learning was quick and effortless, Ramila's confidence to deploy the learning in conversations was rather slow. Her self-limiting belief was that her colleagues might make fun of her! The coach cajoled her to identify four or five colleagues or good friends whom she could confide in and who would agree to assist her in her developmental journey. So, the story boards were first unleashed on a bunch of friendly critics! The results were exemplary.

Ramila now believes that she has shed her reticence in interacting with people from other cultures and social situations. She believes that she can now talk rather confidently about India and a variety of contemporary subjects that concern the world. Ramila had however not yet gone live with her new ability. That day soon arrived. The occasion was a dinner with a group of South African customers along with her CEO. The setting was formal but the CEO set the tone. The subject eventually was 'contribution of Indians in removing apartheid in South Africa and Gandhi's pioneering role in it'. It was Ramila's turn. Much to the surprise of the CEO, Ramila held forth. This was the first real test and Ramila feels she was still not effortless. It took many more real practices for her to feel confident and effortless.

As she began to practice her new found skills, she realized that the real payoff was not her ability to communicate better but the enormous opportunity to learn about herself and others and important things from every interaction.

And then finally as if she needed a graduation certificate, there arrived the invitation to speak at The London School of Economics.

Each one of us has our own unique ways of learning new competencies. Ramila too had her own unique way of cracking the competency code. All that the coach did was to hold a mirror for Ramila!

# SECTION F

# Managing Career Transitions

# Why Career Transitions Are Always Challenging

Aroon Joshi*

Transitions are a lifelong reality. Each one of us has been through several of them and indeed is continuously experiencing them from the moment of birth and all through life. Thus, from childhood, to teens, to adulthood, to middle age, and then old age; being single, to marriage, to parenthood, to grand parenthood; through studenthood, to working, to job changes and so on, life seems like a continuous set of transitions requiring continuous adjustments and change. There is thus always a 'gap' between where we are and where we have to be in terms of the behaviour required to meet the changed circumstances. If the behaviour is not commensurate with what is required, we have a mismatch; a 'problem' or an 'issue' as it is known in organizations. Often this requires help. It is this change which requires an outside effort to help with behaviour, not part of our normal repertoire which is painful, often because the needs are not understood well, or there is an inability to make the change happen, or a variety of other organizational reasons which bring about the need for seeking help.

We have here a set of four coaching cases describing very succinctly the gaps which the transitions have created around four persons where some facilitation from outside (Coaching) has enabled the respective persons to understand the changed behaviour required by the gap and having adopted a change in behaviour have managed to surmount the 'problem'.

*Aroon Joshi, an experienced Human Resource and Organizational Development Professional, currently offers Executive Coaching to Senior Management in several industries. Aroon is the Founder and Professional Member of the Indian Society for Applied Behavioural Sciences and a Fellow of the Coaching Foundation of India.

Ramaswamy came from humble beginnings and through dint of hard work grew with the business into a capable COO. The business grew ahead of and beyond him leaving him no time to catch up. The coach enabled him to accept the change and reconcile himself to the fast movement that the business environment demanded and at same time continue to be a useful contributor to the organization.

In the second case, Anand, a high-performing engineer, is transferred to new job quite unlike the one he is presently doing, requiring a different mindset and behaviour that left him floundering. The coach helped him get a better understanding of the change and enabled him to develop the behaviour required to deal with this change.

The third case came out of a policy of routine job rotation as followed by the company and Sumant is put into a new job which is a new experience for him. It would seem that the prevalent assumption is that any one at a senior level should be able to understand and do any job. The coach helps him to understand the ramifications of the job, with some mentoring, advising and a great deal of coaching to make the grade.

The fourth case is that of Vipin, who has been recruited at a CEO level in an organization similar to his past experience but to do a variety of things of which he has at best vicarious knowledge. The coach had to resort to making use of a senior Mentor from the organization to enable the coachee to settle into a performing individual. The stakes in this case were high as Vipin had uprooted himself from abroad to return to India into what he must have thought was a very good job. Also the organization was a critical stage and could not afford a failure by Vipin.

All the four cases referred to here seem to take place in 'Indian' organizations where a certain amount of patience with people is demonstrated to help them come up to what is required of them. A longer rope is usually given.

I was intrigued by these and similar cases that one comes across whilst working with individuals. There seem to be some assumptions operating here which are worth a thought. One such is that managers who are successful are capable of doing any job in an organization. I wonder how true this is. Experience suggests that most jobs need the possession of some specific competencies which help to perform that job better. People put into these jobs must have at least an acquaintance with the competencies required for good performance. They also need to put in the effort that is needed to acquire them and may also need some help to hand hold along the way.

Thus, Ramaswamy needed to develop different competencies for the changing times in a growth-bound organization. Anand's functional job required different capabilities from his earlier line job. Sumant needed to think and act very differently in his Sales job and Vipin was struggling to incorporate 'leadership competencies' in his Research makeup. Competencies are trainable and a little time spent getting acquainted with them in advance is time well spent.

Another worrying thought: why is there no mention anywhere of a boss/subordinate feedback session where the boss's expectations and the subordinate's anxieties are openly discussed so as to provide some feeling of support. Ramaswamy was clearly struggling to match up to the new needs and I am sure did not take kindly to the appointment of a new CEO. Could an early chat have avoided a situation? Anand was 'shocked' to be transferred to production planning, but it required the coach to explain the possible ramifications of such a transfer, a risk, if it turned out to be untrue. Why not the Boss? Sumant had to go through anxious moments due to the rotation policy of the company and Vipin would have had an easier passage had he been aware of the competencies required of him and the differences in organizational cultures and the consequences there from.

As I mentioned earlier and in fact alluded to by one of the coaches, it is a good thing that all these cases seemed to be from 'Indian' companies and not Western multinationals. With a belief that managers should be able to do anything and a 'Bell Curve' operating, what are their chances of success?

Coaching is a powerful tool to assist in enhancing performance and developing people. The role of a coach is to facilitate not direct or advise or mentor least it lead to a dependency on the coach. The behaviour change in the coachee is to be brought about by his own efforts. Sometimes the coach has to cross this line to create a movement which otherwise may not happen due to a variety of circumstances. We saw some examples of this in our cases where without some direct action such as providing a mentor there could have been a standstill in the coaching process. In each of the cases here the Coach made a conscious decision to intervene differently in the interests of the Coachee. They also consciously got back to their original role (Not easy!) as soon as the situation came back on the rails. It is very tempting for a coach to be sucked into a mentor/adviser role permanently with great harm to the coachee. The role of the coach is by its very nature short term. He comes in, does his thing and having provided the help, moves out again.

I have often wondered whether the boss can be a coach. Much has been written about it. In my mind the jury is still out on the subject although my gut feel screams a violent NO. A mentor, Yes; but a coach, No. The most useful thing that a boss can do, however, is learn to provide timely, honest and helpful feedback to provide an understanding of the changing times and the need to change. Maybe the bosses need some coaching in this regard.

# 16

# Waking Up and Smelling the Coffee

Organizations often grow to a size that is beyond the current senior leader's competence to manage. Inviting a new business leader from outside to head is often the most desirable option. Unfortunately, the incumbent leader is neither ready nor been told of his areas of development lest he decides to throw in the towel. Ramaswamy is one such senior leader who neither shares this belief nor is ready to accept the new leader from outside and begins to act in ways that are dysfunctional to himself as well as to organization. Dr Sandesh Reddy helps Ram to accept that the new reality is not only good for the organization but actually very good for him if he also embraces the change.

## The Case: Ramaswamy Learns to Succeed in the New Reality

Ramaswamy woke up in a cold sweat, looked at his bedside clock, and realized that it was just 3 am! He had been having a bad dream. Of late, the frequency of these unsettling dreams had begun to increase. As he paced around the kitchen sipping a glass of water, he began to wonder if there was any connection between these dreams and what was happening to him in his work environment. Ever since the arrival of the new CEO, the dynamics at work had changed. Ramaswamy could sense that all was not well, and the situation could spin out of control very quickly, if he did not 'do something about it'.

All through his life Ramaswamy had learnt to deal with challenges and adversity. The hard times he had endured in his childhood had toughened him, and fired him up with a strong desire to succeed against all odds. On numerous occasions in the past, when confronted with obstacles, he would somehow find a way to come out on top. This time he was not so sure … this seemed to be different.

His father had died of kidney failure when he was just nine years old, leaving his young mother and him to fend for themselves. A kindly uncle pitched in to help, and took him under his wing, and eventually he started to live with him. Growing up under such circumstances, he felt indebted to his uncle, and was driven by the need to become independent as soon as possible. After completing his 12th standard, he decided to work and simultaneously complete his graduation in Maths through a distance learning programme. From a couple of low paying jobs, initially part-time, and then full time, he managed to create an income stream, so that he was not fully dependent on his uncle.

His first break came after graduation, when he got hired by the BPO arm of a small IT company headquartered in Madurai to run the day to day operations of a twelve man team. With a strong focus on 'getting things done' Ramaswamy displayed enormous drive and energy, and soon became an indispensable and highly valued member of the company. But he was aiming for bigger things. So after a few years of paying his dues, he grabbed the opportunity to move to Chennai to join Perfection Software Solutions in 2005. The Company was a fast growing start-up of just thirty people, with an excellent reputation for doing quality work in the publishing space. He immersed himself fully into his work, running the operations and pricing teams, and soon caught the promoter, Yogesh Singhania's eye. Working under his benign sponsorship, he was able to gain exposure to different areas of the company's functions, and he grew rapidly to become the COO, a loyal and trusted member of the team, reporting directly to Yogesh. After the promoter, he was clearly the number one executive in the company, commanding the highest degree of power and influence. Ramaswamy was totally loyal to Yogesh, executing his vision and instructions without question.

Yogesh was a hard driving visionary. He was not satisfied with just growing the publishing segment of his business. He set in place several initiatives to expand the company into *an* International Knowledge Process Outsourcing (KPO) organization, providing document management services, architectural and engineering services, e-publishing, educational support and software Development. He was also keen to expand into new geographies. Not happy with catering to only the US market, he set his sights on Australia, New Zealand, and a few European countries.

That's when things started to change rapidly. With this growth of the organization and the increased sophistication of demands from these newer international clients, management bandwidth came under serious pressure, and was unable to rise to the challenge. A number of senior professionals were inducted into the company on a war footing. The new inductees came with excellent educational credentials from Ivy League institutions, higher pay packages, and a track record of having worked with some of the most respected organizations in the IT space.

For the older professionals already in the company, working with the new inductees was a source of stress and conflict, due to differences in perception, values, and approach. Reporting relationships and roles were being redefined and changed at various levels. Stress began to develop at various management levels.

A new CEO, Joseph Velmurugan, was hired, and the senior management team was now required to report to him. Ramaswamy, the COO, who had been with the organization for over five years, and who was reporting directly to the promoter, was also required to report to the new CEO. Joseph's team consisted of the new inductees, and one 'loyalist old timer', Ramaswamy.

Ramaswamy felt that the new inductees who had come into the system were seeking to make changes without understanding the reality of the business. They were challenging the way business was done in the company, trying to redefine strategy, and, what's more, had direct access to Yogesh, who seemed to welcome the opportunity to interact with the new inductees. Ramaswamy felt threatened.

Stresses developed in the working relationships of the Leadership team. Everyone was jockeying for position and access to Yogesh. The impression that was sought to be conveyed, albeit by innuendo, was that Ramaswamy was judgemental, blunt in communication, secretive, not transparent and non-cooperative. The new group was slowly isolating him from operations. Coming from a background with limited exposure, and not from an 'Ivy League' kind of educational background, he felt uncomfortable working with these new people who were being inducted into the organization. He felt threatened, and feared that a position of strength and dependency that he had created for himself through his hard work and loyalty could be jeopardized, and greatly diminished. He was filled with feelings of inadequacy.

The situation erupted one afternoon when Joseph and Ramaswamy stormed into Yogesh's office in the midst of a huge slanging match. Accusations flew thick and fast, and Yogesh was called upon to play instant jury, judge and peacemaker. Yogesh felt it was time for an intervention.

A close business colleague had used Coaching with his Senior Leadership team, with excellent results. He was tempted to give it a try. It was a Saturday morning when I got the call from Yogesh suggesting that we meet urgently. He spelt out his concerns. He needed the entire leadership team to work effectively, but he also needed Ramaswamy, whom he valued for his loyalty, dependability, and ability to make things happen. Clearly he was not willing to accept what was happening in the Company. He suggested that I 'coach Ramaswamy on how to "develop himself" and learn to work with 'well-qualified people from different backgrounds'.

I agreed to take up the assignment. I felt that this was a situation many small and medium enterprises (SMEs) in a rapid ramp-up phase would face. The promoter starts in a small way, develops one or two right hand men, grows rapidly, and then discovers that the need to hire senior professionals from outside. The trusted loyalists feel threatened. I was excited by the challenge. But first of all, I had to meet Ramaswamy and assess whether he was willing to be coached.

When I first met him he seemed eager to impress, saying the right things in a somewhat guarded fashion, and dishing out black and white responses. He was externalizing the issues, and the pain points poured out, like that of a soul in torment. What came through clearly was that here was a man who was ready and keen to be helped, and he knew it.

## The Agenda That Emerged

In our first two meetings we focussed on the coachee's story, and the problem situations that he was confronted with. Through discussion Ramaswamy identified the areas that he felt he needed to work on. In his own words, he wanted to:

1. 'Groom and prepare myself for a larger role' (important as the demands on people were growing, because of the rapid scale up of the organization)
2. 'Working with a diverse group of people' (key, because it was critical to work effectively with the new entrants at Senior levels)
3. 'Effective communication and presentation skills' (crucial for building trust and managing team dynamics)

## Selection of Approach by the Coach

Ramaswamy had a blind spot. He believed that all his issues at work were due to the new entrants, who didn't understand the industry, and were trying to mislead, and/or curry favour with Yogesh with an incomplete and superficial understanding of the business. He didn't for a moment think that he had in any way contributed to the situation at the work place. I told him to re-examine that belief. We would need to do a 360-degree feedback exercise. We chose:

1. Joseph, the CEO
2. Two subordinates, who were directly reporting to him
3. Two peers with whom he worked intensely and whose close cooperation and team work was necessary to achieve results, and ensure the successful completion of the project
4. His wife

The first sign of a breakthrough became visible after the 360-degree feedback was shared

The positive feedback received revolved around his strong 'make it happen' skills, ability to solve operational issues, total devotion to work, and the ability to put in long hours. The areas that were identified for development were eye opening. Ramaswamy's first response was one of denial. This emotion melted away as he realized that this feedback was from people that he had himself selected, with the possible exception of his boss. He then tried to rationalize why the feedback was the way it was, and who could have possibly given such feedback, and why. This opened up an interesting discussion on the behaviour Ramaswamy was exhibiting that was causing people to perceive and respond to him in the way that they did. Finally grudging acceptance emerged over two sessions, and with that the start of an action plan.

## The Work That Was Done, including Interesting Moments

While working on the root causes of the various problems, and the 360-degree feedback that emerged, Ramaswamy zeroed in on three specific areas. He believed that these high pain areas, if managed satisfactorily, would give him the greatest possible leverage towards making a visible impact within the organization. These areas were:

1. Not withholding information
2. Free access of information from his team to peers
3. Working to build working relationships with six specifically identified people of the peer group and the boss

A specific set of actions were then discussed to tackle each of these areas.

### Not Withholding information

Hitherto Ramaswamy had insisted that all information, especially pricing information, must never be shared with the Business Development team, unless it was first sent to him, after which he would decide what to share, how much to share, and whom to share it with. He believed that pricing was confidential information, and only he had the loyalty and good sense to manage it. This approach had caused serious tension in his working relationship with the Business Development team, as they needed this critical piece of information in order to develop their pricing and market penetration strategies. We decided that Ramaswamy would call his team and the Business Development team to a joint meeting. At the meeting he would share the basis on which pricing calculations were made so that the assumptions and business model were clear to all, and could be discussed on a case by case basis as and when a decision had to be made.

### Free access of information to peers

He also made a public statement authorizing his team to share information directly across levels, without clearance from him. He backed up his public statement with an e-mail confirmation.

## *Building relationships with his boss and five other key peers*

One underlying phenomenon which seemed to surface was that Ramaswamy seemed to feel that if he fixed his relationship with the CEO everything else would fall into place. It took two sessions to get him to challenge this belief and move on, and start to work on each of the other critical relationships.

An off-site company event was chosen for Ramaswamy to break the ice with two of his peers. He would spend quality and quiet time with them, try to clear the air, and form a basis for a working relationship. We chose two peers with whom he believed he could make the most headway, as a starting point, before he got to the other three. He reported considerable success.

In the next phase the coachee started to practice the desirable behaviours that he had identified in the middle of the coaching sessions. These behaviours were chosen from the part of the 360-degree that dealt with 'what Ramaswamy should START doing'. We had to keep in mind that the actions chosen were consistent with his values. He made progress, slipped occasionally, but kept going. His actions were appreciated.

The general sense of turbulence in the company resulted in exits of a few of the new inductees, including the CEO. Progressively, a new CEO and VPs were hired. The COO had to now fine tune his plans to manage his relationship with the latest set of inductees. He now seemed more confident to do so and manage the change.

The Coachee's belief was that the action plan was working, and he reported positive results after the conclusion of the coaching engagement.

## Outcomes and How These Were Measured/Assessed

There were some visible outcomes. The role of the coachee was enhanced to manage 'Transition and Strategies'. This role calls for the ability to work with a diverse group of people, and manage change; clearly recognition of Ramaswamy's enhanced ability in an area which was previously a concern.

The promoter seriously considered enrolling him in an Executive Development Programme at one of the IIMs, to strengthen his strategic perspective and, as an add-on benefit, bolster his self-confidence.

From playing a supporting role to the promoter in international presentations, Ramaswamy single-handedly made twenty-one presentations to international clients, a measure of his new found confidence and improved communication and presentation skills.

He now reports good working relationships with four of his six peers … two more to go!

His comfort with diversity within the team has improved, and he now talks about it being a 'benefit for the organization to have so many different perspectives'.

## Reflections

So why did Ramaswamy change? People are driven to change either when it comes from within, or when external circumstances are so dramatic that a change is forced upon them. In Ramaswamy's case it was the latter. The fear that he could lose favour with Yogesh if he did not adapt, the shock of the 360-degree feedback, the silent support of his wife, and his high personal stress level, provided the impetus for change. He came to the conclusion that his situation was not the outcome of, or caused by, the external environment, but that he had the power to choose his response to the external environment. 'Accept people as they really are, and learn to adapt and work with them' is how Ramaswamy summed it up, while concluding on a philosophical note. 'I never knew that differences between people can help build a new dimension in you.'

For me, the satisfaction that the coachee, Ramaswamy, and his sponsor, Yogesh, derived from the outcome of the coaching intervention was more than ample reward. Having said that I do believe that enhancing coaching competence is an on-going journey, and as I start to introspect on what I could have done differently, a few thoughts come to mind. Perhaps I could have challenged my Coachee's belief system a little more, obtained more behavioural examples from the 360-degree feedback (to make its acceptance easier, and action planning swifter), and, above all, listened more attentively to the coachee for even the smallest of nuances, as there is always a story behind the story out there.

# 17

# The Anxiety of Not Having a Position of Authority

Many of the operating roles in the corporate world are high on account-ability and are therefore accompanied by position-based authority and span of control. In the interest of long-term leader development, organizations, however, rotate these executives through roles that are high on problem solving and, therefore, call for personal authority—typically staff roles of strategic importance. Making this transition is never easy. It is one thing for senior leaders to tell such executives that they should discover their sphere of influence and it is another thing to actually to go through it. As a coach, Abhay Bhaskar helped Anand navigate this transition rather well.

## The Case: Anand Learns to Enhance His Influence

Anand Sinha, an engineer by profession, is forty-five years old and has twenty years of industrial experience behind him. He was chosen for coaching by his management because he is being groomed for the position of CXO in the near future. The coaching journey with Anand commenced after a three-way dialogue with him and his sponsor. Anand and I got together to know each other and establish rapport even before the formal engagement got under way. We began with his professional journey.

## Anand's Professional Career

Anand graduated in mechanical engineering in 1992 and was recruited up by a large automobile manufacturing company during campus selection. Amongst other product lines, this company was in the business of producing off road heavy mobile equipment. After completion of his apprenticeship as a graduate engineer trainee Anand was placed, right from the beginning of his professional career, in the assembly shop of the heavy equipment manufacturing division. With his dedication, affable and helping nature and sound engineering knowledge, he quickly rose to become the head of the assembly line within ten years, which was, in itself, a very creditable achievement. During this period this heavy equipment manufacturing division was hived off as an independent company.

In 2007, he was moved from this line function and given a strategic function as officer in-charge of production planning. Within a span of two years he was given additional responsibility for the entire supply chain and by this time he had over twenty-five engineers working with him.

When I met Anand for the first time in August 2012, for some strange reason, he seemed uncertain about his position in the company.

'I had several hundred men reporting to me in the assembly line, but I now have only twenty-five engineers working under me,' he said, with a touch of remorse in his voice.

The organization had clearly not explained the reasons for these changes in his job description, and it was far from evident to him that he was being systematically prepared for a senior management role, if that was indeed the case. Although he had found a way to rationalize these changes to himself, it was obvious that he was uncertain as to what was going on. Largely driven by his own thought process, he did not appear to be very satisfied with his present professional situation.

Anand had to spend a lot more time on the job than his scheduled work hours.

## Anand's Personal Story

In order to get to know Anand better, we spent large part of first session about his personal life. He comes from an educated, upper middle class family of Bihar. He began his life story with an emphasis on his father, who had joined the Indian Army in the short service commission immediately after finishing his education. Anand's father was a disciplined person and kept himself away from habits like smoking, alcohol and so on.

'My father left the Army because he strongly believed that drinking was essential to survive, and for career progression, and he would never be able to adapt himself to such a culture,' Anand said.

I felt that this was an irrational belief, although I kept this thought to myself.

After leaving the Army, Anand's father joined a public sector organization in their vigilance department and rose to the level of Executive Director (Vigilance). He was a gifted person. He wrote poetry, played the flute and the violin, and practiced astrology as a hobby. But he also had another side to his personality. He was a very strict person and at least in the family, he would always have the last word.

'*Bahut kadak the mere pitaji* (he was a very strict person). Even after finishing my engineering, I was uncomfortable to discuss any matter with my father,' Anand recalled.

'Ah! This sounds like a familiar story,' I said to myself. Anand's description of his father reminded me of my own father. I kept this insight to myself.

Anand's mother is a homemaker. He has an elder brother, who is an IRS officer. In 1997, he married Anita, an electrical engineer, and a colleague in the company he worked. They have two school going children, a son and a daughter.

'Anita is an extrovert,' said Anand. This musing by him was out of context at that point of time, offering a totally unsolicited piece of information at that point of time. This intrigued me. Why did Anand have to tell me about Anita being an extrovert, and that without being asked? 'Could this be a pressure point in his family life?', I wondered, but filed it away for future reference.

Upon going through his Myers-Briggs Type Indicator (MBTI) profile later I would learn that Anand is an introvert.

'I admire Anita for balancing her work and family life so well. Every evening, after work she goes to gymnasium before going home. She also finds quality time to spend with the children, despite having an equally responsible job,' Anand added.

'How would you like to describe your normal working day?' I asked.

'My normal working day finishes about three hours after the scheduled close of the day at 5.00 pm.'

'Is this your schedule every day? What keeps you at work so long?' I probed.

Anand explained that besides his own responsibility, he devoted a lot for time for many other colleagues who came to him for help. He was not only well recognized for his engineering skills, but also had a reputation of being a very approachable and helpful person. His guess was that much of this additional time at work was going into resolving issues that were not directly related to his assignment. Because of this he was left with very little time to spend with his own family, and even to look after his own health. He regretted this situation but had been unable to do anything meaningful about it for many years. At this stage I asked Anand what he felt his broad coaching agenda might be. He gave this question careful consideration and came up with three areas for consideration—improving communication, handling crisis situations, and creating a better work–life balance.

## Arriving at Coaching Goals

In early 2011, Anand had been sent for a prestigious, residential, three week, in house management development programme. At that time, he had undergone several psychometric and personality assessment tests (MBTI, RET [Rational Emotive Therapy] and 360-degree feedback amongst them), and had received valuable inputs, essential for his growth in the organization. He shared these feedbacks with me.

I critically examined his 360-degree feedback and found that it was too detailed and totally impersonal. It was also incomplete as no superior had given feedback. I therefore decided to do a second 360-degree feedback by having face to face dialogues with his superiors, peers and subordinates. The respondents were duly identified by Anand.

The 360-degree feedback was revealing as Anand's peers and seniors confirmed that communication was a problem with him. They mentioned that Anand was typically a quiet person and did not speak up in the presence of senior leadership. Their feedback was that Anand does not contribute in strategy to take the organization forward. Upon receiving his 360-degree feedback, Anand's initial reaction was to say that there was nothing new in it for him. He failed to appreciate the seriousness behind one critical element in the feedback that was provided. 'Increasingly Anand is being seen as an efficient manager but not as an effective leader' was a view expressed by his superiors in the organization.

Anand would, from time to time, talk about how he missed the authority he had exercised, and the size of activities he had controlled when he was the head of the assembly line.

'I was shocked to learn about my transfer from assembly line to production planning,' Anand had said in the first coaching session, and variants of this emotion were expressed repeatedly on a number of occasions. It was apparent that no one in the company had counselled him in 2007 about the objective of the management to shift him from assembly line to production planning. He felt somewhat reassured when he was made head of supply chain, but still harboured the feeling of being let down by the management. He should have been explained the difference between line jobs and strategic jobs.

It was now essential for me to make Anand aware of the importance of strategic jobs in any organization. I explained to him that whereas people in strategic jobs appear to have less activity compared to those in line jobs, the criticality of the outcome of strategic jobs has a far greater impact on the long term sustainability of the organization. Being exposed to both line and strategic jobs would actually help him to become eligible to stake a claim for more senior roles in the organization. Job rotation of this nature was invariably intended to prepare a person for higher order jobs that involved ambiguity and complexity. This seemed to put his anxiety to rest.

When we reviewed the three goals that had been tentatively identified it appeared that they were not likely to address the key concerns that emerged from the 360-degree feedback, and would take him only thus far and no further. He needed to work on shedding the image of being merely an efficient manager and not an efficient leader. This was the foundation on which his efforts to chart his growth in the organization would be built. After introspection and discussion Anand agreed. We finally agreed that Anand would work towards the following goals:

1. Improved communication
2. Greater work–life balance, and
3. Transformation of his image from being an efficient manager to that of an effective leader

The challenge before both of us now was to convert these into SMART (Specific, Measurable, Attainable, Relevant and Time-bound) goals and develop actionable points.

## Action Plans

Upon probing as to what he meant by improving communication, Anand mentioned that while he was quite comfortable in dealing with his suppliers and subordinates he was unable to arrange his thoughts in logical manner with his superiors and in large meetings.

'Thoughts go round and round in my head and I never find an opportune time to intervene,' was how he expressed it.

At such times, he could not articulate his thoughts and never felt confident about the acceptability of his views.

I challenged Anand to dig deeper into about the difficulty he faced in articulating his thoughts. Was he like this from childhood? Did anything happen in the past because of which he had lost confidence? Was his psyche affected because his father never let the family members speak their mind? Was he still under the shadow of his father and saw the manifestation of his father's authority in his own superiors in the organization?

As I encouraged Anand to introspect he began recognize that his father's authoritative nature had left a deep rooted impression in him. It took him several weeks to bring this subjective feeling to the surface, and to define it as an objective to act upon. The cause was now apparent to him. He agreed to work on himself and leave this irrational fear behind.

The second agenda dealt with his work–life balance. Anand's 360-degree feedback had revealed that he was very helpful and knowledgeable, but was too quick to take upon himself the load of his subordinates and other colleagues. He even helped unrelated people in the organization and would spend a lot of time in resolving their technical problems. It was not unusual for a person of his nature to respond to others' needs in this manner, but he did not realize that this helpful nature was eating into his private time. He needed to appreciate that he need not actually get down to doing other people's jobs, and he could also help them by merely providing guidance and thereby reducing his personal involvement. Anand appreciated this intervention and decided to work towards reducing time that he spent with the people by being more focussed in the inputs that he provided, helping to identify directions that these people needed to pursue, and encouraging them to work on it for themselves.

'Was this in reality the only factor?' I challenged Anand.

'Truly not' was his realization. In his position, he was responsible for the outcome of several tasks. He had not assigned many tasks to any of his subordinates, even though several of them were not of great importance or significance. He was spending his quality time to personally engage in and execute such tasks. On being asked if he had ever worked with his HR team to augment the capabilities of his team, both through training, outplacement and recruitment, his answer was in the negative.

Anand had discovered the road map to work–life balance now.

We were now on to the third, final and, arguably, most critical goal. How was he going to transform his image from one of being an efficient manager to that of being an effective leader? This required careful thought. How does one draw a clear road map to become an effective leader? There are any numbers of books on leadership but do these tell you how to change yourself meaningfully? Helping Anand to transform was challenge for me.

I shared with Anand an article, 'Making Yourself Indispensable' by Zender, Folkman and Edinger, published in the *Harvard Business Review*, October 2011. The article's hypothesis was that to be recognized as an effective leader in an organization, one must be known to be a master of many skills, and the higher this number was, the better were one's chances to become a CEO. These skills encompassed character, personal skills and capabilities, the ability to get results, interpersonal effectiveness and the willingness to define and lead a process of change. The authors suggest that executives should identify their strengths and then work on these so that they begin to be personally identified with these skills.

Anand studied his 360-degree feedback, introspected, correlated the outputs to his recent learnings and came up with four strengths that he would aim to leverage in his efforts to be seen as an effective leader:

1. Display of honesty and integrity
2. Exhibition of technical and professional expertise
3. Building relationships
4. Collaborating and fostering team work

## Work Plan and the Results

To improve his communication skills, Anand took two fold steps for changing his mental make-up:

1. Grow out of the shadow of his father's authority
2. Make a determined effort to shed his unfounded fear of superiors from his sub-conscious mind

Anand realized that just change in the mental makeup was not going to be enough. To exhibit credible and convincing change in performance, preparation before the meetings was the key. At a tactical level, he invested time and effort in preparation for the meetings ahead of time. He recognized that not speaking out his thoughts was worse than creating the wrong impression that he did not have any views on the subject being discussed. Backed by preparation, he now began to state his views. At a strategic level, he started to think on his feet and attempted to portray the image of a confident speaker. This strategy started working for him. He developed a matrix to record his perception of his own performance in the meetings, and his self-assessment revealed that more often than not it improved, even though it occasionally dipped, the overall trend was positive and one of continuous improvement.

To create time and space for himself and bring in work–life balance, Anand took following steps:

1. On scrutinizing roles and responsibilities of subordinates reporting him, he discovered that certain tasks were not assigned by him to anyone and he ended up doing those on his own. He ensured that no task remained un-assigned.
2. He changed the job allocation of people according to their capacity and capabilities.
3. He began working on right-sizing the department in consultation with his HR department.
4. Finally, he started drawing a line between being helpful and doing work for others. He began giving only guidance and his expert opinion to others.

Anand kept log of his satisfaction with the outcome of delegation and the results were very similar to those that he experienced in the area of communication.

Anand was now beginning to be perceived by his superiors, peers and subordinates to possess these skills that he was actively working to enhance. Improved communication and superior work–life balance led to a surge in his personal feel good factor, and resulted in enhancing his level of self-esteem. This, in turn, rubbed off on the confidence with which he was now relating to his superiors, and set him on the road to be perceived as a becoming an effective leader, in addition to being an efficient manager.

Transforming perceptions in organization on more than one such competency is naturally a process that will takes time, and Anand certainly has his task cut out. As a coach, I left Anand in a state where he felt equal to the challenge, and convinced that he had it in him to work successfully on these dimensions and make the transition from a manager to a leader.

# 18

# Revisiting Functional Leadership

It is not often that leaders who have spent significant time in business leadership roles return to functional leadership. When they do return, it is not the lack of deep functional skills but their inability to appreciate some of the nuances in their functional role that can derail them. Omkar, the coach, realized that making such a transition was tough for Sumant, the coachee. Staying sensitive to the culture of the sponsor organization which had initiated such a transition was crucial for Omkar Parel to navigate his way through the engagement and help Sumant succeed.

## The Case: Sumant's Unusual Transition

The growth trajectory of Premium Conglomerate Inc. (PCI) is legendary. Founded three generations ago, PCI has grown into one of the largest family-managed conglomerate businesses in this part of the world. The nimbleness and risk-taking ability of the promoters combined with the high-quality strategic execution capabilities of its professional managers is universally admired by its peers. It is this terrific combination that has helped it register enviable growth. PCI's human resources strategies have played a key role in this great growth story.

As a part of their leader development process, they rotate their executives across roles, some of which might be unconventional rotations.

PCI uses both internal and external coaches for their leader development process. Most executives in senior levels are familiar with the process and benefits of executive coaching.

Soon after the coach was invited to coach Sumant, a comprehensive dossier about him arrived at my desk. The dossier consisted of the performance appraisal reports for the past five years, a report from a development centre he had attended, two 360-degree assessment reports and numerous psychometric reports such as MBTI (Myers-Briggs Type Indicator), DISC (Dominance, Inducement, Submission and Compliance) profiling and FIRO-B (Fundamental Interpersonal Relations Orientation-B). This was accompanied by a report on his developmental needs prepared by the Head of Group HR of PCI and ratified by Sumant's boss. Finally, a note on the specific skills and competency requirements of Sumant's current assignment was also enclosed. The coach was overwhelmed to see the quality of the document the likes of which he had never seem in his experience as an executive coach. So even before the coach met Sumant he knew that he is getting into an organization which had very mature processes to support coaching. There was however an unanswered question in his mind—Sumant had been on his new job for a year.

Typically coaching for such a job transition should have happened either before the incumbent moved into the new job or soon thereafter. What explains such a delay in an organization otherwise evolved in its developmental processes, thought the coach.

## The First Meeting

Sumant received the coach in his office with great courtesy. In his early fifties Sumant came through as a very affable man of few words, speaking in a measured and purposeful manner. He also came through as someone with great executive presence. The coach knew that Sumant had moved into this role after having handled a series of responsible and successful leadership level assignments. There was an aura of seriousness around the coaching table. The coach intuitively felt that the coaching relationship would be characterized by a high degree mutual professional respect. As time lapsed, this respect did grow into trust.

Sumant told his story with candour and intricate details. As was not uncommon thirty years ago, he chanced upon meeting a Director on the Board of PCI in a family wedding just when he was completing his professional course. The Director offered him a job then and there, and mentored him over the next decade. This made Sumant believe that PCI is really his 'home'. Sumant never ever had the occasion to regret his decision. Very early in his career Sumant was made Commercial Head of a commercial entity within PCI. Soon he became Head of this relatively smaller enterprise. Twenty out of his thirty years of experience was spent heading one enterprise or the other within PCI. His last job was as CEO of a manufacturing company within the group which PCI decided to exit profitably. Sumant was elevated to his current leadership position as Director Sales and Marketing of a multibillion dollar PCI subsidiary company. Being in the commodity business, there were huge fluctuations in its fortunes and unfortunately Sumant's entry coincided with a downward cycle. This was at a time when PCI had extremely ambitious plans to become a global leader in this business and had committed several billion dollars in new investments. PCI understood the cyclical nature of business and had long relied on its able executives to fight it out like warriors. Clearly one of Sumant's critical roles was to be the General who would lead the war on the frontlines during times like these.

The coach was beginning to assess the degree of burden on the shoulders of Sumant—a new man on a job, in an unchartered territory, in an extremely difficult time, having to lead a team of leaders hugely experienced in the line of business, perhaps even rightfully aspiring to get his job.

Given that it is not very often that someone with long years of general management experience mostly as the Head of a business is called upon to return to lead a function, the coach asked Sumant two tentative questions—When did you last head Sales and Marketing in an organization? Why were you specifically chosen for this rather high profile but audacious assignment?

Sumant answered stoically. First, he had never ever worked in Sales and Marketing in his entire career, but for twenty years he had overseen the function as the Business Head. Sumant politely avoided answering the second question by saying that he had the confidence to be on the top of the job. In a philosophical way he said 'those who took the decision surely would have had their own reasons'.

Sumant was most supporting of the Coach's wish to have 360-degree conversations with his boss, peers and subordinates. What emerged from these conversations was that people all around him had a huge sense of respect for him as a person of commendable integrity and as an exceptional performer. Many however wondered if his lack of specific industry experience would be a deterrent.

Here is what emerged as potential watch outs for Sumant:

1. The industry was in a state of volatility. Every morning pricing decisions needed to be made. A rupee of price reduction would amount to several million dollars in loss. Not taking the decision might mean losing a couple of percent points of market share for the day. It was like being between the devil and the deep blue sea. An informed call needs to be taken every morning. Sumant on the other hand was a man who needed a significant amount of hard data for making a decision. He was uncomfortable making decisions on the basis of inadequate information. As a result, his direct reports managed to reach out to Sumant's boss, the CEO who fortunately for them (and not so fortunately for Sumant) had been the Head of Sales and Marketing before Sumant came in. So effectively, a critical part of Sumant's job was being performed by his boss.

2. The boss saw the decision making delays as a sign of procrastination. He was under pressure to make sure that company's performance did not slide down while Sumant was still learning the ropes. That expectation gave his boss the legitimacy to intervene.

3. Long years of being a CEO in a known and stable business had allowed Sumant to run his previous business without much travel. On the other hand, for a Sales and Marketing head, being present on the ground almost everywhere every week is seen as a necessity in a dynamic business environment such as this. Sumant is however wondering what is the need to constantly travel when he could achieve the same outcome by speaking on the phone?

4. In terms of style, Sumant seemed to prefer long one-on-one meetings to formal team or group reviews. This style of long unscheduled meetings combined with an open door policy was leading to huge schedule slippages for him. Talk about his being very late for critical meetings constantly appeared in the 360-degree conversations.

5. All in all, notwithstanding the respect for Sumant many had become cynical about his ability to succeed.

While the coach became anxious seeing the situation on the ground, the coachee was surprisingly quite calm. It was clear to the coach that Sumant must appreciate and adapt to the hurly-burly life of a sales leader. Speed of decisions and actions based on inadequate data was critical.

It was also apparent that till he learns the rope he must constantly be in touch with his boss and build a sense of consensus in the decision making process till he built the confidence to do it himself. So, constant communication with the boss was also critical. It was equally important that his boss blessed the process of slow but sure transition of decision making from him to Sumant.

Finally Sumant needed to be very regularly in staying in constant touch with his one downs and holding structured monthly reviews.

Above all, the key to success in this assignment was the commitment and support from his boss.

## Getting a Buy-In

It was not as important for the Coach to have this view. It was important that Sumant discovered it himself. This was not too difficult given that Sumant was a seasoned executive. He agreed with the critical areas that were identified.

The first three-way meeting between Sumant, his boss and the Coach was critical. The good news was that the boss not only fully endorsed the action plans but also assured to fully back him in the transition process.

The coach figured that it was important to arrive at action plans that would be simple, habit forming and help Sumant enhance his action orientation.

For example, in somewhat of a simplistic, but hopefully effective way, it was decided that first thing every morning say around 12 noon Sumant would either meet the boss or have a long telephonic conversation. By then Sumant needed to have complete market data as of the very morning collected from all Regional Heads. Jointly both would take the critical pricing decisions that would then be communicated by Sumant to all concerned. The boss agreed to two more steps namely, he will not encourage Sumant's Regional Managers to talk to him directly. He would also accompany Sumant to the regions for a few months for the monthly review meetings. It was of course understood and agreed that Sumant will receive fixed time calls between 10:30 and 11 am from all his direct reports and be fully briefed about the market situation. And finally, the coach and Sumant will jointly work towards developing the process and a format for a robust monthly review meeting.

At this stage, at least on paper, it appeared that everything was set for a very successful outcome in this coaching assignment.

## Motivation to Change

Over the next several months, every time the Coach met Sumant, he would religiously follow up on the actions plans already made. Notwithstanding all commitments, the coach found that the progress on implementing these highly structured and disciplined steps was rather slow.

For example, Sumant was unable to make the morning call to his team and therefore unable to touch base with his boss. Given his seniority and stature, it appeared that the boss was not monitoring him on his promises on a daily basis. The coach observed other unusual behaviours. It became clear that many people seemed to be fully aware of Sumant's coaching need and context. But it did not stop there. They were quite unabashed in directly asking the Coach how Sumant was progressing thereby almost intending that progress was not as good. While the bright side of this was that the Coach had a barometer of progress, the dark side of it was the lack of respect for the boundaries of confidentiality. The coach decided to be somewhat charitable about it and assume that there are many who are keen to see Sumant succeed.

As weeks sent by, the Coach had to dig deeper to find ways to help Sumant stay accountable to his commitments. For example, the coach found that one of his productivity derailers was his unwillingness to use his Blackberry for e-mailing! The coach convinced Sumant that every e-mail that he received from important people around him needed to be responded to; even though the response may say 'will get back by 3 pm'. He had to convince him that while modern day technologies may intrude into one's life, they have a huge role to play in performance enhancement! A small step of this nature yielded huge results!

A second such derailer was his inability to get in touch with this boss irrespective of whether he was in town or not—a product of the old school thought that one should not intrude into his boss's privacy while he is travelling. It took some doing for Sumant to change this belief and start calling his boss.

There were of course times in the coaching engagement when Sumant would present himself as a victim to the coach and blame others for his plight. During these times, the coach had to step sideways and play the role of a mentor and share some wisdom, give some tips and even prevail upon him to try and do things differently.

The most difficult step of all was his inability to get into a system of formal reviews. With every passing session, the coach started working with Sumant's secretary to see if she could help matters. The good news is that by towards the end of the coaching assignment Sumant had gotten down to formal full day reviews by regions though he was yet to start a formal country wide review. That was still work in progress.

The great thing about Sumant was that none of the pushing and prodding by the coach upset him. He was quite welcoming of it. It is just that these were not things that came to him naturally and age was not on his side.

## In Hindsight

So, after many months, Sumant did indeed move forward quite definitively. His Manager admitted it even though with some caveats and some sympathy. He now had a working relationship with his boss. He was now falling into a rhythm of action orientation. He was now reviewing his team and holding them accountable.

As the coach looks back on Sumant's situation, he recognizes that growing up from a functional role to a CEO's role is challenging but in an inspiring way. The challenge here is to recognize that as the CEO he needs to transcend functional boundaries and provide organizational leadership. However, when a reverse transition is called for, there is need to move from breadth to depth and this called for a far greater degree of discipline, rigour and proactiveness.

It is not as if intellectually Sumant doesn't understand it. But regaining the long lost motivation and attitude to get back to doing 'the routine of the day' was the key.

Sumant was making a doubly difficult transition. Things should have been easier for him if his boss was an old seasoned CEO. Alas, his boss was also making transition from a Functional head to a CEO and had great comfort in constantly re-entering his earlier functional job, thereby, hampering Sumant's empowerment. The good news is that Sumant succeeded. He succeeded because of the huge credibility that he brought into his new job. He also succeeded because in a family business when senior people get anointed to a new position they are seriously thought through decisions that are not so easily questioned. Finally, Sumant's pace of implementing the key actions during coaching journey may have been somewhat slow but there was a sure footedness about the implementation.

In the meanwhile the industry began to look up. The company returned to robust profitability, significantly reducing the volatility in the market. Sumant can now take a breather and do the job as a thinking man looking for detailed data rather than having to take decisions based on inadequate data.

The last question in the mind of the coach was this: 'would Sumant have succeeded if had he worked for a multinational corporation?' The answer is probably a no. It is the ability of family businesses to see life beyond quarterly reporting that breeds loyal, wisdom and a team of executives who are ready to weather storms and not quit at the onset of the storm! It is this difference that a coach needs to factor in and display that cultural sensitivity while dealing with coachees from both sides of the fence.

# 19

# The Need for a Coach–Mentor Partnership to Facilitate Radical Career Shift

Executives are constantly making transitions of one kind or the other throughout their careers. They are changing jobs, changing career tracks and even geographical locations. However, when you have to do all of them together it can become hugely complex and onerous as it was for Vipin who was transitioning from being a senior research scientist to taking profit-centre responsibility for a large R&D business across continents.

When the demands for change parameters are this complex, efficacy of coaching alone as an intervention begins to show strains. Anikat Murali discovered how coaching when combined with mentoring can cook up a healthy sandwich for the client.

## The Case: Vipin's Healthy Sandwich

The drive from Mumbai airport to the R&D facility in the interiors of Navi Mumbai was not particularly enjoyable despite the Innova. The road was damaged in some places and nonexistent in others. I was imagining the plight of the employees of the R&D facility who had to do this every day. I was especially sympathizing with my new coachee whom I was about to meet in a short while because the ride through the dusty interiors of Navi Mumbai must have been a far cry from the lovely roads in California and Connecticut where he had spent the last twenty-five years. The decision to make the shift could not have been an easy one. The prospect of having to travel all the way from Chennai to Mumbai and then to this place for a coaching engagement over the next several months was not exciting, but I knew the coaching engagement itself would compensate for the physical discomfort. I brushed these thoughts aside and focused on the task on hand—getting the best out of my first three way meeting with Dr Vipin Agarwal, President Biotech division, Syngeta Laboratories, and Anand Gupta, MD Syngeta Laboratories. Vipin and Anand were waiting for me as I arrived at the Biotech facility. For the next two hours, energized by dry fruits, biscuits, coffee and juices, we had some very high quality discussions about why Vipin needed coaching support and what the nature of that support might be.

As the sponsor, Anand Gupta did the initial talking. While he had given me a brief outline about the context and about Vipin in our telephone conversation three weeks ago he now went into these aspects in greater detail. Syngeta entered the biotech space in 2005 with a small team of about six or seven people. Their first five years were spent in building the team and its capabilities, and in investing in some early research efforts. Anand had been directly leading these efforts during these formative years.

In 2010 the Board decided to induct a full time President to leader the business. A global search was launched to find a leader who would be able to provide both technical and business leadership and build a respectable business. Their search led them to Vipin, who had completed his Masters from Bombay University and then a PhD from a reputed University in the United States. He then completed his Post-Doctoral Fellowship and worked in various biotech firms in the US.

Vipin belonged to Mumbai and had always dreamt of coming back to India to spend time with his father who lived in Mumbai. The Syngeta opportunity with a promise of a business role was hard to resist. He was about four months old in the organization, which had about hundred employees and two products about to enter the clinical trial phase. Having built the team and found the leader the Board now wanted to see the business deliver results. Anand mentioned that he was beginning to see certain settling down issues with Vipin in the early days and felt that it was best to reach out for help immediately given the high stakes involved. He then outlined some of these settling down issues. For one, there was a change of guard—from working with the MD directly the team members had to now work with a new person. As a result, some of them seemed to be putting the new man to test.

Having worked in the US for over twenty years it appeared that Vipin was not comfortable with some of the style differences from a cultural perspective. Some hand holding seemed necessary as was apparent from some of his recent interactions.

Most importantly, in his role as the President of the bio-tech business, he was responsible for its profit and loss (P&L). He also had to learn to work with the group's corporate resources which supported all group businesses, and had to win their commitment and support to achieve his goals. Having to shoulder complete P&L responsibility in a large group seemed a big transition. His preference for a collegial and participative style may not work with 'typical Indian Managers', he felt. He was also not comfortable suddenly dealing with so many inter personal conflicts.

Vipin was of the view that the cultural issues were affecting him the most and this was the aspect we should devote our energies on. I closed the meeting after explaining the coaching process. I also clarified that on the cultural aspects I might choose to play the role of a mentor and share certain information and ideas that might help Vipin quickly readjust himself. As I left the meeting two thoughts came to my mind.

1. The success of the business depended on Vipin's success and that was certainly driving this engagement, and to that extent Anand Gupta's involvement and concern was understandable. In fact, I could sense this.
2. I had an early hunch that it may not just be an issue of cultural adjustment. I decided to file this away in my mind.

Vipin and I agreed that in addition to a 360-degree feedback process I would also send him some self-completion tools to assess areas where he had cultural difficulties. I spent the next few days completing Vipin's 360-degree feedback interviews while he spent the next few days completing the cultural assessment tools.

What emerged from these two sources of information further reinforced the hunch that I had about what the real coaching need was.

Vipin was perceived by his respondents to be technically very competent and sound, interpersonally very approachable and accessible, and managerially quite effective in terms of planning, setting expectations, reviewing, delegating, making decisions and so on. He was seen as an effective communicator and, above all, as someone with a very strong 'values orientation'. His respondents however pointed out that he was having difficulty dealing with conflicting situations and tended to avoid them rather than face them squarely. They also perceived him to be somewhat withdrawn and task oriented and to that extent had not built a relationship with them. These two areas were understandable because he was somewhat new and still trying to find his bearings.

Three areas in the 360-degree feedback concerned me.

1. One was to do with his tendency to be somewhat innocently open in his communication style. It appeared that in moments of frustration he would share his frustrations with his direct reports with a level of candour that they could not handle. While Vipin saw it as his openness and transparency, his team members read too much into it. It appeared that Vipin was not managing perceptions well.
2. The second was his habit of using the limited time he had with his boss, Anand, to ventilate all his problems and challenges rather than discuss his plans for the future. His managers wanted him to be a lot more self-assured and less anxious.
3. The third challenge was his inability to read and manage some of the organizational processes. Vipin was all along used to working in small research organizations where he had to deal with only one manager. However, at Syngeta, Vipin needed the support of many of his peers who were managing corporate functions in order to accomplish his objectives. He also had to engage with the Board and the Promoters, and evangelize the biotech business. Vipin had just not factored any of this into his overall strategy.

Interestingly, on the cultural front, other than communication style and time orientation, not many areas emerged as different and difficult for Vipin. Cultural diversity seemed to be a red herring.

Having completed the 360 it was clear that team related concerns were also not of great significance. Many of Vipin's challenges were to do with his inability to manage upwards and sideward.

My next task was to share these 360 findings and arrive at the coaching goals. Finding time was not easy, and six weeks after the first meeting managed to meet Vipin once again. While I was trying to share my findings, Vipin wanted to talk more about his challenges with his team and the fact that he needed to spend a lot of time to get them to deliver on their commitments. His narration over the next fifteen minutes helped me to understand him as much as the 360-degree feedback had. Here was a person hired as a President of the business, mandated to come up with a new vision and take the organization forward, but was completely overwhelmed by operational and team issues.

Eventually, we spoke about his need to manage perception, organizational processes, to rally his team around the vision for the business, and so on. After a lot of discussion Vipin began to recognize that he had *to become a lot more mindful and deliberate in his leadership style and approach, and pay attention to the larger leadership demands.* This in many ways emerged as the tentative coaching goal.

As we discussed this further we were able to identify three dimensions to this tentative goal.

First, he had to display a persona or image that was befitting his stature as a leader. He could not afford to say what he wanted to. Second, he had to rally his team around a compelling business agenda. Third, he needed to become a lot more politically astute to get his peers and seniors as well as his manager and the promoters to support his business plan.

Vipin agreed quite readily that his habit of ventilating with his manager was actually counter-productive because it was presenting him as someone who was not in charge and he agreed to stop this immediately. He promised to think about this, refine the goal, discuss it with his manager, and get back to me.

I spent the next eight weeks trying to find out if Vipin had spoken to Anand about his goals. There was no word from him. He was perhaps continuing to be overwhelmed by the operational challenges in front of him.

Meanwhile, Anand's office sent me a brief reminder asking if the engagement was going well. I took the opportunity to speak to Anand and informed him that I was waiting to hear from Vipin. Anand sounded more anxious now than he was three months ago. I used the opportunity to ask him what he thought would be a goal that would give leverage to Vipin. His first expectation was that Vipin should stop transmitting his anxiety all round including to him. His second expectation was that he should define his business plan along with his team, present it to the management committee, obtain their approval and then sell it to others. He also had to build his organization.

Listening to all this I got the sense that the situation was far more serious than what Vipin realized. Being aware of what Anand thought of him, on one hand, and seeing what Vipin was struggling with, on the other, was quite disconcerting. Vipin seemed to be busy with many things which, in his view, were high priority areas, but his MD clearly felt differently. It was important for Vipin to talk to Anand about his coaching goals and plans. I decided it was time to send him a blunt and strongly worded communication:

*Dear Vipin,*

*How are you? I have not heard from you for a long time. I was wondering if among the huge number of things that are fighting for your attention, our coaching engagement is finding a place or not. I might be wrong and you could well be working on things that we had discussed and agreed, but I have no means of knowing if this is true.*

*I would like to hear from you your thoughts on what the next steps should be, and when you would like to action them.*

*Warm regards*

This mail got Vipin acting and he mailed me back saying he had managed to speak to Anand about the coaching goals and that he would soon organize for a three way call. This call took place a few days later. In the call Anand confirmed that the broad coaching goal was in the right direction. He went on to re-emphasize the two areas he wanted Vipin to pay attention to.

He wanted Vipin to define the business objectives, sell it to people through discussions and deliberations, and use that as a basis for individual goals. He also wanted Vipin to carry all stakeholders with him. At a personal level he wanted Vipin to present a more confident persona. He concluded by emphasizing that he would now like to start seeing results.

At the end of the call, I was quite certain that Vipin would have been somewhat taken aback by Anand's candour and blunt talk about what needed to be done. My only hope was that he would sense the urgency and start to engage with me more regularly. Unfortunately, that was not to be. For the next two months, there was no news from Vipin. He did, of course, mention that he was travelling a great deal. What could be going on, I wondered.

Two months later, I managed to meet Vipin. I decided to be somewhat direct and confront him in this meeting. I also decided that I might need to break some rules and give him some direction and mentoring oriented inputs if required.

It did not take much for Vipin to start telling me how he had been in the past two months. He was taken aback by Anand's feedback, especially the bit about his transmitting his anxiety. He then confessed that he was not aware of the situation on the ground when he took charge and that the efforts needed to set things right was far higher. He went on to talk at great length about all these issues. Of course, he reported that the two team members who were non-cooperative had left and he now felt better.

I then shared some feedback with Vipin. I asked him if he was paying attention to the big picture or was lost in all the details and daily issues. I reminded him that this was Anand's expectation too. I also asked him where he was spending his time. He said it was on technology, operations and people. He was not spending time on stakeholder management and business.

As far as the business plan was concerned, Vipin told me that he had mailed the plan to Anand. Why would he mail him such an important document, I asked him. Why would he not push for a face to face meeting?

I brought to Vipin's attention the possibility of having created the image of being helpless, and of someone who is not really in charge. I told him that most MDs wanted their leaders to act in a manner that suggested that they were in charge. After a long discussion, Vipin agreed that he needed to act now.

He agreed to visit corporate headquarters every week to meet the key stakeholders and build relationships. He agreed to get his plans signed off by all key leaders. He also agreed to negotiate his role, especially where he felt he needed some empowerment. Finally, he agreed to act more confidently and stop taking up issues to his boss. He seemed confident of doing these things.

Vipin seemed really committed to what he promised. It appeared clear to him that he had to act. I left the meeting very hopeful that Vipin would be able to move forward.

Unfortunately, it did not quite turn out that way. There was no news from Vipin once again for many weeks. It was now close to six months since our three way call with the sponsor and over nine months since we started our engagement. I had a sense that Vipin was struggling with something that was beyond him but finding it difficult to ask for help.

I genuinely believed that Vipin was sincere and committed and had so much at stake. My guess was that he was struggling with the competencies needed to get the business plan in place. He was also struggling with the competencies to sell it internally for lack of political savvy. Unfortunately, these were not needs that I as an external coach could fulfil. It needed to be an insider job and it had to be done very fast. Helping Vipin was now well beyond just my own efforts.

I decided to call Anand and share my perceptions with him. I started by telling him that I was now about to cross one of the boundaries of my role as a coach—the boundary of confidentiality, in the interest of helping Vipin. Anand appreciated this and asked me to go on.

I told him that in my opinion, the gap between what was expected of the head of the biotech business and what Vipin was currently capable of delivering was very wide and it was important to intensity the nature of help to bridge that gap. Anand agreed. He however, reconfirmed that he was committed to helping Vipin because it was so critical for the business. I suggested that he should find an internal mentor—someone senior, someone who had been there and done that, someone who could work closely with Vipin for a few months. I said I would work with the mentor as a team. Anand was excited about the idea and promised to look at a few possibilities.

Meanwhile, we put together a list of things that the mentor could help with. This included imparting skills and support in coming up with a business plan, the wisdom and perspective in selling the plan internally, coming up with implementation strategies and above all helping him in shaping his role and time as a President.

Anand acted swiftly. In two weeks he identified Mr Dilip Shah as the mentor for Vipin. Dilip has led many businesses within Syngeta. He was also one of the stakeholders Vipin had to work with to market his products. He was of course much more senior and a Syngeta veteran.

Soon a meeting was organized at corporate headquarters for Vipin and me, as well as a three way meeting between Vipin, Anand and me. I first met Anand to agree on the terms of reference for Dilip. We then met Dilip and briefed him about his role. Dilip was a man of great wisdom and poise. He readily offered to help.

I then met Vipin and took stock of where we were. I then brought up the subject of the skill gap and how it might be affecting him in getting things done and the mentoring idea. Vipin's face lit up. He readily accepted the opportunity to work with Dilip whom he knew very well.

I reiterated the agenda ahead and the company's expectations from him. We then walked across to meet Anand, who officially told him about providing him with mentoring support and outlined his expectations. Vipin agreed and thanked Anand. He seemed genuinely happy to see that the organization was doing a lot to help him to succeed.

He agreed to meet Dilip right away and get started. Anand thanked me for suggesting this option. I heaved a sigh of relief. I was now not walking alone.

In the next several weeks, I allowed the mentoring process to take shape and did nothing. Exactly three months later, I arranged for a three way call with Dilip and Vipin.

Some great progress had taken place. Vipin had met Dilip at least five times. He had prepared his business plan and even sold it to Anand and other key members of the Board. Dilip's knowledge of the organization had helped Vipin to learn whom he should sell it to, and how he should go about selling it. Dilip's own team was now extending great support to Vipin.

By now, Vipin had also hired his new team. His confidence was high, and he sounded extremely positive. I asked about his style of engagement with Anand, and he reported that he was a lot more brief and focused, and avoided burdening him with his issues.

It was now a year since I had started work with Vipin and only now was I beginning to see results on the ground. I was, of course, in no hurry to close the engagement. Keeping it open offered me the opportunity to sustain the pressure on Vipin to learn and change.

Three months later, I visited him in his office, travelling all the way on the same muddy road!

I met a much more confident and cheerful Vipin. I asked him to summarize what his takeaways were and he listed the following:

1. Greater tact while communicating with his team
2. A lot more precise and business like communication with Anand
3. A lot of time being spent aligning his team to the vision of the business
4. Having built a new team
5. A business plan in place, a plan that was now accepted by the Board and all stakeholders

Since we were nearing the close of the engagement, I asked if Vipin would like to receive some feed forward from me for his on-going development. He said he would appreciate that.

I told him that he had to be the biggest evangelist of the business internally and externally. To that extent, he had to radiate hope and optimism to all those who looked up to him. He agreed.

I suggested that he always have an elevator pitch ready to use whenever he visited headquarters. He had to have an agenda for discussion on each visit, and be purposeful in his lobbying efforts. I also requested that he continue to leverage the mentorship support. He agreed.

I finally asked him one hard question. 'How much time do you have, to prove yourself?'

'Two years,' he said.

What are the shorter milestones that you need to achieve during this period I asked and he outlined a few.

Vipin thanked me for my support over these months.

We agreed to meet in a month's time for our closing meeting in Chennai. This was a light celebratory meeting. We recollected all that we had been through, the things that had helped and the things that he was richer by. Vipin agreed to sustain his efforts in the coming months. The next day I sent off a closing report to bring the fifteen month engagement to a close.

As I wrote this report, I was able to see many progressive changes.

Vipin was now feeling at home in the company. He had found his place and built a good working relationship with his manager and others. His communication style had changed. He had become a lot more self-reliant and was now able to engage with his stakeholders. He had developed certain critical business skills. He had a team in place. He also had a business plan in place.

I also realized that there was a lot more he had to do. He had to strengthen his business acumen. He has to demonstrate greater confidence in his style and presence. He had to stay networked inside and outside.

I am happy that we had come this far. Could I have done something to get here faster, I wonder? Or was it that the seeds I sowed in Vipin took time to germinate? I would never know!

# SECTION G

# Grappling with Emerging Executive and Entrepreneurial Agendas

# How Do Executives and Entrepreneurs Grapple with Their Compelling Agendas

R. Ramaraj*

## Leadership Challenges for Entrepreneurs

So who is an entrepreneur?

John Q. Adams said, 'If your actions inspire you to dream more, learn more, do more and become more, then you are entrepreneur.'

Entrepreneurship begins with a dream, a vision to do something usually very different from your peers. This can be exhilarating, inspiring, admirable but often lonely and off the beaten path.

In pursuing this dream entrepreneurs are willing to take many risks and face uncertainties, but in some critical areas fall into the trap of staying within their comfort zone or living with some blind spots.

Unlike corporate executives, most entrepreneurs are often alone in what they do and may not have access to support systems or safe spaces to dialogue, discuss or reflect about themselves and what they are going through. This can make the problem look even bigger and the consequences much more catastrophic than it actually is.

Entrepreneurs face and solve numerous business challenges. It is often the human challenges that trouble them the most and this is where coaching help can be most beneficial as is evident from the cases under review. There are two such human challenges that I would like to talk about.

*R. Ramaraj is the Senior Advisor at Sequoia Capital and is a member of the global Board of Trustees of TiE (The Indus Entrepreneurs).

1. Hiring the wrong team member, especially early on in the journey
2. Fear of failure, more often after some initial success

Many first time entrepreneurs make regretful hiring decisions, especially early on. Instead of hiring people with complementary skills they often end up choosing people too much like themselves. Here they tend to work on familiar grounds and hire friends and classmates as early employees or even as co-founders. In doing so, many entrepreneurs take leadership skills for granted or underestimate its criticality, in themselves and in these friendly hires. They are not objective in this really critical hiring process.

While there could be some advantages, like trust, when you hire a friend as a co-founder, this needs to be backed up with an objective assessment of passion, drive and most importantly of complementarity of skills. Many unfortunately hire clones. As a result, all of them have the same blind spots and make the same mistakes.

Having decided to hire a friend, many do not invest in ensuring that there is role clarity and a clear definition of expectations of outcomes, just as one would or should do with any other hire. Stressing on relationships leads to poor or wrong assessment of people. From wrong assessment come misplaced hopes and unrealistic expectations. Why can't the lily be more like an oak? You hire a lily and expect it to stand up strong like an oak!

In summary, in any partnership or in an early core team it becomes the entrepreneur's prime responsibility to assess the skills of his team members, hire people with complementary skills, provide role clarity and set clear expectations of performances or outcomes.

It is a tough ask, but most partnerships fail because of the lack of just this. Assess, set expectations measure. Remember, Peter F. Drucker said 'Effective leadership is not about being liked, leadership is defined by results.'

The second challenge faced by entrepreneurs is the 'fear of failure.' This happens more often, after some initial success. Forbes recently stated that it is not failure that holds people back but the fear of failure. The wonderful thing about failure is that it is entirely up to us to decide how to look at it. Successful people don't see failure as catastrophic, they see it as a good data point to guide their next attempts.

In India the ability to cope with failure seems tougher. From early childhood one is compared with classmates and peers and success seems to be relative to someone else's marks or job or status or salary. Fear of failure is closely linked to the fear of rejection and criticism from others. Shakespeare put it really well 'our doubts are traitors, and make us lose the good we oft might win by fearing to attempt'.

By choosing to become an entrepreneur, one has already taken the first step, has moved away from the normal. Now he has had his first little success. Now he has to push on aggressively, scale, build on his success. Here is where he hesitates not wanting to lose out what he has got, however tiny!

How then does one try and overcome this fear. The first step is to remember the dream with which one started this journey. Define what success means for you not as measured by other people's expectations of you, but what it really means to you. For example, to one, success may not mean only the acquisition of wealth but to have a sense of meaning and purpose in whatever is done.

Fear of failure is also a sense of insecurity, the fear of losing what one has got. Been there done that once, reaffirm to yourself that it can be done again, maybe more easily. Being bold is not to be mistaken for being stupid. Assess the risk and then be bold and take action. Finally sometimes, initial success creates a complex - in some inferiority, in some superiority. This often becomes a barrier to success. A poem by R.W. Emerson handles this beautifully. It seems a mountain and a squirrel had a quarrel, the mountain called the squirrel 'a squirt' a tiny useless thing. The squirrel response 'Talents differ all is well and wisely put; If I cannot carry forests on my back, neither can you crack a nut.'

In all this, if entrepreneurs can engage in a trust based relationship with individuals or groups to discuss, dialogue and reflect about their fears and their blind spots, they can certainly achieve their dreams.

Needless to say, what I have written about entrepreneurs applies to corporate executives too, albeit in different forms.

# 20

# When a Young Entrepreneur Has to Make a Life-Altering Decision

First-generation entrepreneurs are often highly motivated and hungry to learn and surge ahead. In their quest for learning and moving ahead they leave no stone unturned. Second-generation entrepreneurs, on the other hand, may live in self-doubt, given the prospect of having to step into the larger-than-life shoes of their father who founded the business and may even hesitate to ask for help.

Karthik and Ganesh, young first-generation entrepreneurs realized that they were in a partnership that didn't work and desperately needed help in thinking through the situation and making decisions. MK, on the other hand, was wondering how he could find a way to break free from his father's shadow and prove his worth to himself. Karthik and Ganesh were fortunate to find Rajan Prakash and MK was fortunate to find Sateesh Dubey as their coach. With their help, Karthik, Ganesh and MK took some important calls.

# The Case: Karthik Takes a Call

## The Curious Case of Karthik and the Mythological Mango

### *Meeting the sons of Lord Shiva—An introductory phase*

I was stepping down from the podium after a presentation on 'How Entrepreneurs should spend time in Sales to grow their business', when I spotted the two young men aged about thirty years, a little far away from the crowd that gathered around me hungrily for my business card. These young men slowly walked up to me as the crowd was dispersing and asked me a direct question, 'Sir, can you coach us on how to grow our business—we are struggling with our business for the last five years?' After my usual volley of questions about their business, I told them that we needed to meet first and understand how I could add value to their business.

Karthik and Ganesh had co-founded AXE, a small sized multi services IT/BPO with clients in India and Europe. They had been running this company for five years. They were struggling to grow the company and Karthik, the CEO was unclear whether the problem laid externally, that is, the wrong strategy or whether it was centred on poor execution styles of himself and his co-founder. I asked them whether it was all right for me to meet them one on one and draw out data. Karthik had no issues, while Ganesh whined a little about how they were like brothers and how they went about everything together, no secrets and how every decision was based on a consensus. Ganesh was clearly not keen to do one-on-one sessions. After some information sharing about why people tend to be more open to the coach while doing a one on one, Ganesh reluctantly agreed. While my preliminary diagnosis was that AXE had both problems, external (strategy and approach to market) and internal (poor execution styles by and between the co-founders), I let the coach in me prevail and held back my diagnosis until I had gathered enough data through the one on one meetings. The meeting ended, somewhat fruitfully with a realization that I was willing to provide skilled help and that AXE needed my value add. However, I had to do this pro-bono.

## Face-to-Face with Karthik and Ganesh

I embarked into my first of a series of one-on-one sessions with the brothers in arms. Unlike the mythological sons of Shiva—Karthik was the elder one, the CEO and Ganesh was the younger one, the CTO. Karthik was a post graduate in Computer Applications and an MBA with over seven years of track record, working as a professional in the IT Infrastructure Management space. He considered himself good in his ability to position the company well with customers, do good client management and get orders. Ganesh with an MCA degree and programming experience claimed to be good in technology and back end operations. These sessions revealed a stark difference in the mind sets of Karthik and Ganesh. Karthik felt that there were at least three big areas that needed to be worked on—a clear strategy and market positioning, geographical focus in the European markets and a more well-defined offerings portfolio. Ganesh felt that everything was fine, AXE simply needed to add more sales people and whip them into performance. My probes on the roles that each of them played and what they were accountable for, revealed, that all was not well in their professional relationship, although they were good family friends and classmates in their college life.

I had been in this situation myself before with my own co-founders and I was gearing myself to face the reactions that Karthik and Ganesh would spew forth when I revealed to them that there were key differences not only in their approach to the business but also in the perception of their roles and what was expected of them. As I had guessed, it was a revelation to them that they had run a business for five years without having deep conversations on what is wrong, what could they have done to redeem the situation. I saw Ganesh whisper something to Karthik and then Karthik spoke 'Sir, It looks like we need to discuss this between us and we will come back to you when we are ready.' I thought to myself that perhaps I did a poor job of sharing sensitive issues and walked out telling myself that here was an organization with potential but the co-founders felt that the need to be with each other is more important than running the business professionally. At this stage, I knew, one of two things would happen—they could simply carry on struggling through this or one of them would realize that the truth was staring them in the face and call me. The call would come only in case I had managed to establish enough empathy.

## Cappuccino Ablutions with Karthik—Establishing the Coaching Flavour

The wait was a bit longer than expected but well worth it. One month later Karthik called me and wanted to desperately meet me at a Coffee Day nearby. He said he had reached the end of the road with Ganesh and he needed my help. I promised to meet him the very same day. This session was perhaps the most emotionally tiring and intellectually stimulating session that lasted four hours and six coffees. A series of incidents had happened over the last one month. This had led Karthik to arrive at the following conclusion. He was struggling to scale the company, despite huge market potential and happy customers. He believed that he was working extremely hard but was unable to motivate/make accountable his co-founder, Ganesh, who was in charge of technology and delivery. He needed help to determine whether he was performing his core function well and also help him establish whether the problem of growth was being retarded by his co-founder and if so, help him take necessary action. I requested that he keep this conversation confidential even with Ganesh and in turn I promised to do so.

To ensure that both of us were not suddenly painting Ganesh as the source of all the ills at AXE, I asked for a 360-degree assessment to be done on Karthik with Ganesh would be a peer respondent. Four of Karthik's reportees also participated. Karthik readily agreed. I was silently hoping that Ganesh in a competitive mood will also ask that his 360-degree also be done so that he would know where he stood. But that was not to be. In any case, all Karthik's subordinates rated him very high on most leadership attributes, except his ability to be assertive (especially when it came to Ganesh and his activities) and his ability to clearly articulate a vision and create a strategy around the vision. Ganesh's response was predictable; he rated Karthik high on all parameters. I also administered the SOP questionnaire to Karthik and this clearly pointed that his big source of pressure was his peer, Ganesh and his own inability to borrow more money when required. He had already reached his wits end by mortgaging his father's house to raise the last bit of money. It was time that we set ourselves a set of coaching goals. It was now clear that Ganesh was not going to be part of these powerful conversations that were happening between me and Karthik.

## Placing the Arrow, Drawing the Bow and Sighting the Target

Over the next few conversations, this time in serious locales (not coffee shops), Karthik decided it was time to set goals for himself. These were to test himself on how he was performing his job and to also test whether Ganesh was hampering his growth plans. I had suggested some recommended reading of two books co-authored by Ram Charan to both the co-founders.

1. Every business is a growth business
2. Execution

While Karthik lapped it up; Ganesh apparently felt these were not relevant readings for him. Karthik summarized his learnings from the books as follows:

1. Growth requires a constant outside in view of the business
2. Growth will not be accomplished without a change of DNA in the organization

Based on what he had read and how our sessions transpired, Karthik set himself a clear role definition and was determined to rate himself on his performance through a Key Performance Indicator (KPI) document with clearly listed task lists. Based on this document he discussed with Ganesh and had him put down a list of supporting activities that Ganesh had to fulfil over the next thirty to sixty days.

Karthik then requested me to meet with him every fortnight where he would present his progress on his KPIs. Karthik was clear that he had to get all operating issues out of the way before embarking on a strategic shift in thinking. He had also wanted me to sit through his review session with Ganesh just so that facts were clearly available for him to take a final call on his relationship with Ganesh. He wanted some mediation help from me during these reviews. However, I ensured that each review was a presentation of each one's self-appraisal and I did not perform the role of a reviewer, lest Ganesh feel that this was all a drama to ease him out.

The next five sessions, mainly centred around reviews and on scoring each one's performance against metrics that were pre-set. It was emerging very clearly that Ganesh was simply not serious about the business and would not even complete 30–40 per cent of activities that he had agreed to do before the session. Karthik was progressing with great confidence and he told me at the end of the fifth session 'Sir, if I need to prosper, it looks like I cannot hang onto Ganesh who is now looking more like a stone around my neck,' I asked him 'So, given this conclusion, what are you going to do about it.' He replied 'I know I need to grow and that the only option is to do this without him—let me think this through.' The target to split with Ganesh was now well set in his mind.

## The Battle for the Mango

The stage was now set for the battle for controlling AXE (much like the mythological fight for the Mango) Karthik spent one whole session discussing and rehearsing various options that would crop up when the bad news was conveyed to Ganesh. He laid down the following parameters:

1.   Karthik will make an offer to buy Ganesh out at a price that is higher than what he would get in the market
2.   If Ganesh made Karthik the same offer, he would be happy to leave the company to Ganesh and walk out
3.   Whoever takes the money and walks out will not compete with AXE for a period of one year
4.   Given the cash situation in the company and their personal selves the pay-out had to be done within the next six months

Karthik wanted me to endorse the ethics of the stance which I readily did because I felt it was more than fair given the poor track record of the company.

In the mythological fight for the mango the parents Shiva and Parvati had not bargained for an extended emotional battle that led to Karthik getting extremely angry and running away to Palani, a small hillock near Madurai. Similarly, given that the founders of AXE had families that were close friends, Karthik called me one day and gave me a briefing, saying, Ganesh's parents are sitting in his house and pleading with his parents to somehow accommodate Ganesh. I asked him how he was dealing with the situation. He simply said 'Sir, I have gone through 4–5 sessions with you before clearly deciding to split with him. My mind has been clear ever since then. I will go through with this no matter what, because, his presence is detrimental to AXE and I don't want to live through this problem of working with him again.' I said 'I am happy that you are clear. Fine then, let me know when we need to meet on our next objective.'

After a few more weeks of posturing, pushing and shoving, Ganesh agreed to sign a separation agreement in line with what Karthik had proposed and the mango (AXE) was now Karthik's baby. The action arrow on the first goal was now complete.

## Ripening the Mango

However, the mango had to be ripened before the juice or the fruit could be consumed. The time for the second developmental area had arrived— Creating a Vision and strategy and translating this into action. We spent two sessions or more where Karthik articulated several vision statements and strategies. I was constantly probing him on which ones he felt were likely to yield short term, medium term and long term results. This was basically meant to help him focus on a set of offerings that his current organization could tackle without being audacious. He drew up an offerings road map and this helped him whittle down his vision to a set of strategic focus areas. I established through a short dialogue that he was indeed inspired and happy to pursue the road map. I also took a short session and helped him delineate what could be pitfalls in his approach. This was to ensure that he was pursuing a strategy with his eyes wide open to all the positive and negative implications that would ensue.

Karthik plunged enthusiastically into this exercise, and came out with an inspirational strategy to focus on mid-size logistics companies in Europe and provide them with a bouquet of services (outsourcing and technology). Part of the action items was to induct a few good mid-level managers who would replace Ganesh and to constantly tour Europe and grow the business. We decided that we would meet once every fortnight and review how the execution was going, discuss bottlenecks and brainstorm potential solutions to removing these bottlenecks. Over three months, Karthik was so passionate that I could feel his contagious enthusiasm was influencing my thoughts as well. Nevertheless, I put this down as necessary positive energy needed to grow the business and went ahead with a sense of attached detachment. The numbers were beginning to show—good growth in revenue and profitability.

## Plucking the Fruit and Drinking the Juice

It was a Sunday and Karthik gave me a call saying 'Sir, I am back from Brussels and I am in your area, can I drop into your house?' I was just finishing a leisurely lunch, I quickly checked with my wife and called him back and said '2:30 pm is fine, come over to my home'.

Karthik thrust a sheet of papers into my hand and said 'Sir, I want you to read these and tell me your thoughts.' It was his annual report it showed a twelve fold increase in sales revenue and a huge profit that was more than his revenues of the previous year. I told him how proud I was about the way things had turned around for him. I then called on my wife to serve him some mango juice to sweeten the great situation that Karthik had worked through with me. The twist in the tale is obvious isn't it, Karthik ended up with the mango here while in the fable, it was Ganesh who had got it. Any which way, Karthik changed and is clearly now ready for a bigger corner office.

My takeaways centred around two critical aspects of the importance of neutrality and being non-prescriptive.

I was extremely mindful, at all times, to be completely fair and neutral to both Ganesh and Karthik. I ensured that whatever questions I posed or bibliotherapy I administered should be relevant and appear fair to both.

Several times when Karthik wanted an immediate fix, I restrained myself from giving a solution, just to ensure that he owned the problem and definitely, therefore, the solution had to come from him. Over time and with practice, refraining from playing a mentoring role started coming to me naturally.

Nevertheless it left me wondering if there was an invisible force of destiny that was driving the results in a particular way. Otherwise, why would Karthik have got the proverbial 'mango'. Perhaps, he deserved it more? I guessed Lord Shiva must have gone through this as well when he handed over the mango to Ganesh in the mythological story, knowing fully well that all this would result in the creating a wiser Karthik at the end of the day.

## The Case: MK Decides to Believe in Himself

It was sometime in May this year. I had got up early to work on one of my assignments for a client. I heard the faint sound of an e-mail arriving in my inbox.

It was from MK, a young man who I had worked with a couple of months earlier. I was a bit surprised to hear from him. The content of mail was something that would delight every coach.

> Stepping into a small but successful business as a second generation entrepreneur, I had many self-doubts. Did I have the confidence, the ability to lead the business, make it grow, inspire the team to take new challenges and, most importantly, fill some very big shoes of my father?
>
> You helped me first realize what I was really good at, my natural strengths which I could use to overcome most challenges or obstacles that I had imagined even dreaded! It helped me put together a vision for me and my company in the near future. It taught me that I necessarily don't have to be the best at everything.
>
> Suddenly self-doubt became self-confidence and I have today started taking baby steps in helping our business diversify and grow. I feel good about myself and thank you for helping materialize a certain important change within myself.

## I Want to Retire and Hand Over My Business

My mind went into a flashback mode. I began to think about my coaching engagement with MK which was nothing but a series of crucial conversations over a period of time in which my role was really to ask him the right questions and through that help him get more and more clear about what he really wanted to do. Of course it was also about helping MK believe in himself.

My mind actually flashed back to the very first meeting I had with MK. I remember it was a Sunday morning. MK and his father arrived around 11:00 am. MK's father was introduced to me by a mutual friend.

We sat around the dining table, as my wife served 'filter' coffee. As she discreetly excused herself, the father asked me about what I do. I told him briefly about my work, and ended up with a question 'So how I can be of help?'

I watched the two of them as the father spoke. MK was quiet, did not look me in the eye. I was not sure if he was listening to his father but kept an intense expression. I wondered about what might be going through his mind.

The father talked about his rags to riches story (an 8th standard pass who owns and runs a multi-crore business today) and how he had come up through hard work. The business was good and he was considering handing over charge to his son. However he was not sure about what his son wanted to do. As I was listening to him I got the feeling that he *did not have* the confidence that his son could fill his shoes.

MK did not speak a word right through the two hours we spent. We concluded the meeting with a decision that I would meet MK alone at a place and time mutually convenient.

## Meeting the Cub in the Lion's Den

MK called the very next day. He was polite but matter of fact. He asked for a meeting in his factory in one of the industrial estates, in the suburbs. I could not make out whether he was doing this to please his father.

I arrived at his factory on the appointed day and time. MK met me with a not so firm handshake but with a warm and welcoming smile. He led me to the office, which seemed well appointed.

'Nice office,' I observed. 'My father's office; he fixed a meeting for himself so we could talk here without any disturbance.'

He was still somewhat matter of fact, keeping me at arm's length. His answers were non-committal. It dawned on me that he was just being an obedient son, going through this.

'MK today's meeting was for us to get to know each other, and see if it will make sense for us to work with each other. On my part I would like to work with you.'

I saw him react differently for the first time. 'Why?' The tone was more challenging than curious.

'Because you remind me of my younger days. For a long time I also did things, because my father told me to.' I saw MK laugh for the first time in the two hours we spent.

'I would like to give this a try,' he said as he extended his hand. This time he held my hand firmly and sealed it with his left hand too.

## Meeting the Man Inside the Obedient Son

As I started preparing for the meeting, I realized that it was not going to be easy to get MK to speak. I saw that he had worked out a way of giving 'correct, but short answers' and closing the door. It was evident that regular conversations with MK will get me nowhere. I had to 'design' the session in a way that would let him express himself better.

Given my creative background, that was not easy. In fact, I normally use interesting questions, visuals and movies as stimuli for my coaching discussions and find it helpful.

We met again in his father's office. MK was at his polite best. He was ready to 'give this a try' as he had said. He put his mobile on the silent mode and instructed the operator to hold calls.

As we began to talk, MK slowly began to thaw. The man inside the obedient son was a talented, articulate person, who tried hard to gain his father's confidence. MK was an average student with varied interests. He wanted to become a journalist but his father wanted him to become and engineer which he could not.

He loved the F&B business, obtained a Hotel Management diploma and loved wines. He however ended up working in his dad's business which he felt was boring. He was not sure what his father wants to do, is overwhelmed by the routine and sees his father's shoes as larger than life.

While he was close to his mother, he grew up believing that he could not be the son that his father wanted him to be.

It was obvious that MK was feeling like a misfit in his current work. Yet he did not want to leave this because his father would feel let down once again by him.

I asked him what he wanted to do and what would make him and his Dad happy. He said he was not sure and felt trapped. 'There must be a way out but I am unable see it,' he said.

Having covered so much ground, we decided to give ourselves time to reflect about all this and reconvene. MK liked that respite.

## 'Leaving My Father Is Not an Option'

MK's father's expectation from the coaching engagement was to see if MK could be helped to decide what he wanted to do. Implicit in that expectation was the question, 'Will MK take over my business and run it or would he want to do something else on his own?'

We, therefore, really started talking about what MK wanted to do. MK's views surprised me. He was clear that he did not want to leave his father's business! It was true that he found the business as it currently existed quite boring. At the same time he was keen to inject some excitement into the business. Leaving his father and starting something on his own was not an option.

I asked him why and he explained quite lucidly. 'This business matters a lot to my father. He wants me to look after it and be successful in doing it. I do not want to do anything that will hurt him. I have already done enough of that. Maybe we must change the way we run this. I do not know. I am determined to do what pleases my dad, but on my terms.'

I could see where he was coming from. Earning his father's trust and affection was his priority. The challenge was to do this in a way that MK found enjoyable. A broad coaching goal emerged from this discussion: 'Earn the trust and respect of his father, yet do it in a way that was in line with MK's style.'

The first thing that struck me was MK's willingness to look at the issue through his father's eyes. He was not doing this grudgingly but with sincerity. At the same time there was a sense of searching for his own identity in the process. That was very touching and inspiring.

## Be a Detective of Good Things

It was evident to me that while MK was clear about what he wanted he was quite unsure. So, I really had to start helping him to discover his strengths, own them and display them with confidence. I had to be that detective of good things and that is what I did going forward. This was the next big agenda.

MK had a range of talents and many strong points. However his reticence in his father's presence concealed most of them.

MK started to slowly, but surely articulate what he stood for. He saw himself standing for excellence, imagination and elegance in whatever he does. He also asserted that he would never compromise on ethics, quality and respect for others—no matter what.

According to him, what made him special was his ability to learn and try new things, his ability to persuade others convincingly and the ability to combine sensitivity and objectivity even in business.

When asked what he could do better than most others he said he could take on new challenges, learn new things, master them and teach others.

## Flight to the Future

Having honoured himself in some ways, MK was now ready to take a flight into the future. This I thought would un-hinge him from today's realities and logic, and imagine a future that excited him. This was especially important because the current goal seemed to have come out of a certain level of compulsion.

In my next interaction with MK, I guided him through a process of dreaming—of taking a flight into the future with me. His dreams were truly fascinating.

In his dream this is the way he felt about himself and his work: *Work doesn't feel like work, I am confident of what I do, I am an authority on my subject and I take the company to new heights.*

This is how he dreamt about his company: *ABC United, a company with Pan India presence.*

*It has expanded into several new areas of business building on its core strengths.*

This is how he saw his role in this growth: *Business assessment, Strategic Marketing,*
*Training and HR, Liaison.*

## Preparing for the Pitch

Having clarified what he wanted to do, having become more assured about his strength and having dreamt of what he wanted his future to be, MK was now ready to convert his dreams into designs. Clearly his designs had to be grounded and had to be defendable.

I suggested to MK that he should prepare a pitch as though he was pitching to his bankers to get funding. That helped him become more focused and objective.

Over the next several days, MK had done his home work and was ready to validate his thinking with numbers. We spent time together where I challenged him with some sharp questions and some naive ones, to ensure that he did not come through as if he was flying kites.

Finally MK put his plan to the 'Daddy test' as he called it. He imagined the questions his father might ask. He modified some sections based on practical issues his father might raise.

## Final Presentation

When MK was ready to present to his father, I asked him two questions: 'Do you want me in the meeting?'; 'Do you want me to speak to him first?'

'No, I will handle it myself. That will be best.'

The mail I received from MK came nearly six months after the presentation he made to his father. His father had accepted one of his ideas and they have invested in the business.

MK says that the best thing that has happened is that his father's doubt about MK's commitment to the business is settled. This has eased the relationship and has helped in better conversations.

'Suddenly self-doubt became self-confidence and I have today started taking baby steps in helping our business diversify and grow. I feel good about myself and thank you for helping materialize a certain important change within myself.'

Look at the wonders that can happen when someone decides to believe in himself, I thought!

# 21

# Coaching Principles Applied to Peer to Peer Business Mentoring

The need to maintain secrecy of their business ideas and the absence of a supportive group of like-minded peers prevent many successful first-generation small- and medium-sized business owners from freely opening up and speaking about their problems and dilemmas and through that finding meaningful solutions. Unfortunately, it is this group of entrepreneurs who need the most help because they form the backbone of the Indian entrepreneurial community. Understanding this need, a leading industry association partnered with a leading coaching institution to create an innovative platform of support for such entrepreneurs called Business Mentoring Forum (BMF). Each forum has a group of 8–10 members from non-competing businesses and meets every month. The BMF is based on the principle of peer to peer mentoring facilitated by a business coach. Dr Krishan is an early beneficiary of such a forum. With the support of the peers and the facilitation of the forum's coach Aryan Ahuja, he is able to resolve a crucial dilemma.

# The Case: Dr Krishnan Resolves His Dilemmas

## Dr Krishnan's Background

On successful completion of his postgraduate studies and few years of practice as a consulting surgeon Dr Krishnan evinced serious interest in getting back to his home, a million population strong old city, in southern India, and offer affordable but high end healthcare by setting up of a hospital. His elder brother, two cousins and a friend of the family all of whom are in the medical profession joined hands to set up a hospital that became the largest in the city. Over seven years of initial struggle the business grew enough to acquire two other hospitals in the same city to become the undisputed leader of healthcare delivery in Dr Krishnan's home town. Soon the five partners felt that the time had come for them to take their quality services and brand to a metro city. A large multi-speciality hospital setup from grass root was about to be inaugurated. Quite an accomplishment by any standards. Each of the partners including Dr Krishnan while practicing in their own area of medical expertise was also asked to manage one functional area of the health care business.

Over a period of time, Dr Krishnan's functional expertize and experience gave him insights into a potential business opportunity. He began to delve deep into the area and research it further and soon discovered a great business idea and go to market model.

These were also hard days financially for the new fledgling hospital chain of theirs. He had time on his hands. He thought he could spare some of his time to cut out his idea. The first launch effort of the idea was hugely successful both in terms of customer satisfaction as well as on financial parameters. Dr Krishnan got enthused to now scale this business to several cities in India and also to several countries in India's neighbourhood. Dr Krishnan's success caught the eye of other players overseas who even expressed an interest in taking a small equity stake in his venture. The valuation as per Dr Krishnan was 'mind boggling'. And there lay a tale!

In the early days of this new enterprise, his hospital partners were very encouraging. Increasingly, with its growth and success they began to be somewhat cold. And in recent months Dr Krishnan senses almost open hostility! The kind of question that he hears through whispers (not necessarily confronted) include; why does he use the hospital brand name for his new venture, being a partner in the hospital isn't he expected to devote full time to the hospital?

Dr Krishnan is increasingly angry. In his view the new enterprise is entirely his venture; no other partner has contributed to it. He has spent minimal time, never neglecting his responsibility at the hospital. The use of brand name may have actually helped the hospital rather than his new enterprise. Above all, he fails to decipher the reason for hostility. Is it jealousy? The more he reflects the more he thinks that the hostility from the partners is unfair and misplaced. The fact that they do not talk to him directly angers him all the more. He thinks that if this state of affairs were to continue for some more time the harmonious relationship between the five partners, four of whom are his family members, may begin to disrupt.

## Dr Krishnan's Dilemma

There are several feelings and resultant actions originating from his mind as outcome of his deep reflection:

1.  Should he confront his partners and bring this subject to a head so that a solution is found?
2.  The venture is entirely the outcome of his blood and sweat. Why should his partners in hospital enterprise have any say?
3.  The way it's going, the valuation of the new enterprise could well surpass the health care enterprise. Why should he do something to disrupt a good thing happening?
4.  The partners are being frivolous, it is none of their business to interfere and he is been wronged for absolutely no fault of his

Dr Krishnan is stressed. The only person he speaks about it is his spouse who is also a medical professional in the same hospital. His spouse is as stressed and cannot bear the thought of any disruption within the family. There is no one else that Dr Krishnan is comfortable to talk to.

## Peer Mentoring

The power of first generation successful entrepreneurs is often the power of an idea and a business model, built around it to make the venture profitable. It is therefore not surprising that the first generation entrepreneurs are paranoid about the confidentiality of their business models.

This inhibits many of them to open up and speak about their challenges or dilemmas to anyone they perceive to be an outsider. It also means not opening up transparently enough with their own trusted employees. This causes serious challenges for the entrepreneurs to gain from the power of mentoring or coaching.

It was in this frame of mind that Dr Krishnan, who is one of the members of the BMF, came to the forum and poured out his dilemma to seven of his peers and the coach–mentor at the BMF.

## Peer Views

The first meeting …

Peers listen to Dr Krishnan intently and patiently. The coach–mentor facilitated an orderly question–answer session. The skills were to force a discipline that the peers don't become judgemental, personal or give out their views before weighing the pros and cons. Also, the peer language of communication needed to be non-directive, somewhat tentative and transacted with respect that an equal peer deserves. Each mentor had an opportunity to summarize the situation and speak as to what he would do if he was in a similar situation.

The recommendations that emerged were very synonymous. In essence:

1.  It is Dr Krishnan and not his partners in the hospital who need to carry the burden of consequence. They felt Dr Krishnan in effect is the cause of disaffection. They felt that while he may have received early encouragement, the ethicality of growing the business without communication with the partners could be legitimately questioned. The onus of keeping partners informed on the status of the new business rested on his shoulders.
2.  Going for a solution; they felt that one choice Dr Krishnan could exercise is to divorce himself from an operating role in the hospital and remain as a shareholder and a Director. That is if he feels that his new enterprise has possibility of larger wealth creation.
3.  Dr Krishnan could offer part of the equity of the hospital enterprise to the other four partners for a nominal sum or even free of cost. This would be in the spirit of togetherness of all shareholders in words and in deeds.

4. Dr Krishnan could hire an operating Chief Executive to take care of his new enterprise and spend very limited time for this enterprise. Even in such an event he could offer token shareholding to his other partners.

Dr Krishnan became more inflexible as more advice of similar kind came from one peer to other. At the end he was almost exasperated defending his personal thesis on the ethicality of his thinking. The coach–mentor closed the session without resolution of the strong views held by both sides. He requested Dr Krishnan to think and reflect on all the suggestions made over the next thirty days till the next BMF session takes place.

## Dr Krishnan Reflects

It is perfectly imaginable that thirty days was too long; surely for the disturbed mind of Dr Krishnan. Dr Krishnan reacted in three days. He sent a mail to all his peers by profusely thanking them for all the suggestions made. He apologized in case he appeared too stubborn during the session. He said that the answer surely lies in one of the suggestion made by the peers. He promised to come back to the next meeting with his preferred action plan.

As thirty days came to close, Dr Krishnan was ready to brief his peers. He said that he recognizes that if he has to live in both the boats he has to extend his hand of equity to his partners. Not resolving the crisis would surely rupture the relationships between the partners, which has been built over a decade through thick and thin. And finally he has great respect and affection for his partners and he would not be the person to disrupt the relationship. His decision was to offer 10 per cent equity to each for free to four of his partners so that he keeps the majority 60 per cent. He would hire a full time CEO to manage his new enterprise and devote full time to the hospital as a Partner, Director and Operating Surgeon.

This was hugely applauded by the peers. Alas, this was not the end.

## Further Reflection

Dr Krishnan returned to the next session another thirty days later. It was now his turn to brief the peers as to how well he has implemented his decision. He said, 'I have actually solved the problem without parting with the equity.' Peers were curious to know how such a miracle could happen! Dr Krishnan elaborated:

> I spoke to my elder brother. Apologized to him for my entire mistaken notion and said that I am fully committed to work together in the hospital venture. As a token of my honest intentions to share the enterprise I have set up I will offer him and other partners 10 per cent equity each free of cost. My brother nearly came to tears. He held my hand and said Krishnan I really respect your feelings. That you have been so magnanimous as to offer free equity to all of us is good enough. You do not have to actually do that. I accept your good intent and welcome you back to a harmonious partnership in the hospital. I am sure you will not do anything that strains our partnership. He offered to speak to other partners. I thanked him for his large heartedness.

This was far from an acceptable solution to the peers. All the peers almost unanimously felt that Dr Krishnan jumped at what can be called as a 'convenient solution'. They cajoled him to reflect again as to whether this is a really permanent solution? Would other partners accept the proposition as magnanimously (or as emotionally) as an elder brother has done?

Dr Krishnan quietly heard through the suggestions made by peers. He was quiet probably with a hint of remorse. The peers were keen to see that Dr Krishnan is helped to reach a more permanent solution. The genuineness in their feelings was expressed very well by their peers individually and collectively. The genuineness helped Dr Krishnan to think through the suggestions all over again.

## Another 30 Days Go

Dr Krishnan returned with a smile this time! The peer felt comforted that some good news is coming! Not what they thought but probably something more. Dr Krishnan decided to have the conversation with all the partners together in the same meeting giving each one an opportunity to air their views as openly as they could. This led to first expression of emotions bottled up for so many years to lighten their hearts. Then came wide appreciation of Dr Krishnan's gesture almost as if it is the return of the prodigal son home! They all felt that they would not like to take away part of the fruits from the tree that Dr Krishnan has planted. They decline to take his equity for free and left the entire equity in hands of Dr Krishnan.

They encouraged this thought to hire a Chief Executive so that he could devote almost entirely to his work in the health care business.

Something more important emerged. Somewhat akin to the concept of a Family Council, the partners decided that they must all meet together in an informal atmosphere with some regularity, say, once in couple of months. All important partnership decisions needed to be discussed in this forum and be divorced from more formal discussions that take place in the board meetings. A general broad principle was agreed for similar entrepreneurial ventures in the future. Namely, each partner can raise the idea of any new venture in the family forum. Once the project is approved each member will be allotted certain shares in the new venture and in some cases the company might decide to fund the new venture partly or fully. In the event of limited appetite of other partners for the new venture, whether one partner can own and manage the venture will be discussed on a case to case basis with an approach of consensus building.

The achievement was more than what Dr Krishnan would have expected. Surely more than what the peers expected. The unity among the partners was reinforced. Dr Krishnan found a way to continue to oversee his new venture without devoting too much of time. And most importantly, a family council is in place as the ultimate decision making body for disputes and dilemmas in the future.

Dr Krishnan now has appointed a CEO for his new enterprise. He reminisces,

> When I began to speak to the peers it was enormous cautiousness. I knew I was opening my heart to people who I don't even know. At the end their genuineness made me feel that whatever they are saying is always keeping my interest at heart. Nobody had any other angle. The coach–mentor made sure that the best came out of everybody. I am back to work with a new vigour and with no guilt in my heart. I also know that I now have a forum to informally communicate with my partners without letting things drift.

## Learning for the Future

To force an atmosphere of trust is a significant key to the success of peer mentoring. Quite apart from the fact that every member is sworn to confidentiality; repeating that at the beginning and the end of each session creates certain tangibility. The peer members may or may not have exposure to the formal process of mentoring. That puts a challenge on the coach–mentor to gradually and almost through osmosis lay down the basic rules of mentoring; to listen empathically, not to be judgemental, be non-directive, think what one would do in the other person's shoes. The coach–mentor needs to play the role of keeping the discussion focused and affording scope to bring his own experience to bear while chairing the sessions.

In days to come, peer mentoring forums can become an extremely cost effective means of mentoring in a group by one experienced coach–mentor.

# 22

# The Importance of a Thinking Partner

The work life of CEOs with large global corporations is filled with anxiety, ambiguity, change, performance pressures and, not to mention, public scrutiny and evaluation. It is in this setting that executives need to make meaning, solve problems and take crucial decisions that impact the fortune of the business and the life of the people. In the course of doing all this, they have their emotional side to take care of too and they have to do all this alone. Well, they don't really have to do it alone. At least Bharath realized that he could partner with his coach Rohit Kapoor even as he grappled with his complex executive agendas, and use him as a sounding board.

## The Case: Bharath Is Not Alone

As Coaches we are most familiar and comfortable with engagements where we are able to quickly zero in on a specific set of needs, confirm that through an assessment process using tools like 360, use that data to arrive at specific goals and then work with the coachee to implement actions that help achieve the goal.

Now, what is convenient for a coach may not be of value to a coachee. Coachees needs do not fall into clear and simple structures. Especially when you are working with a CEO of a large global corporation who has so much of complexity, ambiguity, change and of course performance pressures in his job, what he is looking for is help to grapple with the many agendas that are competing for his attention and a sounding board to make sensible decisions. Beyond all this, he will use coaching as a safe space to ventilate, to just have a trust based conversation with and through that feel lighter and clearer. After all, even the toughest of CEOs are fallible, vulnerable and emotional.

As a coach it takes a lot to be open to this possibility and be available to offer that space to the coachee even though he might not articulate this need in clear terms when you get started.

This is exactly what happened in the course of my coaching engagement with Bharath.

I have known Bharath professionally for many years and during this period have had many opportunities to meet and exchange professional views and ideas. I have always respected his deep desire for self-development. Similarly, Bharath has always valued me as a professional and generously acknowledged my work. So when Bharath wanted to talk to me about coaching, I was very pleased and readily agreed to meet him at short notice. Given our familiarity, we got down to talking about the subject at hand very quickly.

Bharath had recently taken over as CEO and MD of this very large engineering services firm where he had worked for over twenty years right after completing his Masters in Management. His first and only Manager and founder of this business had recently sold the business to this European multinational in the same engineering services space. Having completed the transaction, his founder moved on. Bharath was the natural choice for the MD and CEO position and the new owners were quite happy granting him the job. While Bharath has been in a business head role for some time and of course knew the business and the organization so well, becoming MD and CEO was quite another thing. Being an efficient manager and a trusted follower to the founder for many years was one thing and donning a hat of a leader of a 1,000 employee organization was quite another thing, Bharath realized. Having worked with a single manager for such a long time, building a relationship with his new manager would take time, he felt. As CEO he now had to provide leadership to a set of team members who were until now his colleagues. It was for these reasons that Bharath was seeking coaching help. While Bharath did not seem daunted about this task he knew it would be uphill.

The fact that he chose to work with someone he knew and trusted was the first sign that he was looking to leverage coaching to address his executive agendas and not merely acquire skills.

With a challenging coaching context and a highly motivated coachee I obviously said yes immediately. Bharath had spoken to his manager who sits in Sweden and told him that he would like coaching help. His manager readily agreed to support this and requested Bharath to find someone he was comfortable working with and that's how Bharath got in touch with me. Over the next few days Bharath spoke to his manager and got his approval. I requested Bharath to organize for a three way meeting. Since his manager was in Sweden he joined this meeting via conference call.

After exchanging pleasantries I requested Mark to share his thoughts on the context. Mark spoke about the management changes and Bharath's choice as the MD and CEO. He spoke specifically about the ease with which he was able to establish a close relationship with Bharath during the course of his interactions during the transition process. Mark was generous to acknowledge the contributions made by Bharath during the transition period especially in terms of completing a host of time bound tasks as well as some rationalization and right sizing of the business. As a career employee of the organization the Board has reposed faith in him as the MD and CEO and was fully behind him, he clarified.

Given that he was sitting far away and had multiple countries to oversee he saw the need for someone close to Bharath to support him and serve as a sounding board for reflection, feedback and development he felt. This was the second indication that Bharath and his manager were clearly expecting the coach to serve as a sounding board to address his emerging agendas.

Having outlined the context, Mark went on to share his expectations from Bharath as a leader. He wanted Bharath to bring about significant cultural changes in the organization. He wanted Bharath to prepare the organization for big changes and come out of its sense of complacency. He also wanted Bharath to re-engineer the business model including the business mix, enhance organizational capabilities and through all that achieve improved margins. He wanted Bharath to lead this initiative by coming up with a sound approach and a clear strategic agenda. He also wanted Bharath to take a hard look at his leadership team and feel free to make changes if he felt there were competency gaps. Finally, he wanted Bharath to develop greater self-confidence and feel a lot more self-assured. Mark clarified that he was happy to stay engaged and involved in the coaching engagement as much as Bharath desired.

I took advantage of the time I had with Mark to continue a one-on-one conversation and obtain his personal feedback on Bharath as a part of my 360 efforts. Mark happily shared his feedback. Over the next few days I completed my next 360-degree feedback with ten other respondents named by Bharath.

As I undertook my 360-degree interviews it emerged that resolving conflicts seemed an area of significant challenge for Bharath. So I requested Bharath to take the Thomas Kilmann Conflict Mode Instrument.

Bharath's 360 respondents saw him as a leader with a very sound value orientation. They also saw him as a very result-oriented person with high energy and a strong number focused. He was also seen as an accessible, responsive and humble person. They also felt that he maintained grace under fire. In terms of their wishes for him they wanted Bharath to take a big picture strategic view of things and bring that big picture orientation into all his discussions. They wanted Bharath to pick on a few strategic agendas and put his weight behind them so that they do not fall by the way side. They wanted Bharath to be the public face of the organization. Finally they also wanted him to manage conflicts and deal with inconvenient issues with courage.

I met Bharath in a few days and shared the 360-degree feedback as well as the conflict style tool results with him. Bharath spent time understanding the results. He said he found it very insightful. However, it was not the 360 results that Bharath wanted to discuss that day. He wanted to talk about a more pressing issue that seemed to be pre-occupying his mind.

As Bharath and I spoke at length, we were able to identify that there were at least three questions weighing in his mind:

1. Does my manager believe in me and support me? Am I really the chosen one to drive this agenda or am I really an interim CEO?
2. Will my team support me in this journey of making big changes or will they seek stability? Will I be caught in the middle, between corporate headquarters and my team?
3. How do I work on a business plan that I had no part in creating? How I wish I had negotiated the boundaries of my role better instead of walking into it cold?

I could see the pressures of the new role and the newness and complexities of the context weighing on Bharath. Given his natural style and preference, it did not seem easy dealing with all these changes and conflicts.

We spent a lot of time talking about these questions. The fact that Bharath was able to share all that was going on in his mind made him feel lighter. As a result, he was able to start reflecting more deeply about his own position.

After a lot of exploration, Bharath was ready to think about what he could do about all these concerns. He pointed out that his annual performance review was coming up in a few weeks. This review was normally done over a call. Bharath decided that this time around he would fly down to Sweden and do it face-to-face. This he felt would make it easier to establish a good relationship, raise key issues with his Manager directly and also help him set clear expectations. I eagerly encouraged Bharath to do this.

Within a few days Bharath called to tell me that he now had Mark's approval for a face to face meeting and he was very excited about what was in store. We met very soon and spent a lot of time brainstorming about how Bharath would handle this meeting.

As we discussed this further it was becoming clear that his relationship with his manager was somewhat fragile and even transactional. As a result there was little trust and confidence to deal with conflicts or have difficult conversations. As we discussed this further, it emerged that this was the case not just with his manager but also his direct reports and many others in his life. In all these cases having authentic and difficult conversations was not his strength. As a result he was constantly wondering where he stood without taking the courage to find out. Bharath agreed to experiment with some new behaviour. He agreed to have a discussion with his team members to jointly arrive at his plans and goals before meeting Mark. In fact he even decided to share his 360-degree feedback with them. Bharath also agreed to come back from Sweden and spend a couple of days with his team in a retreat to share the outcome of his meeting.

At the end of this meeting it appeared that Bharath was until now using the coaching relationship to deal with and address some of his emerging agendas rather than work on the issues that emerged in his 360. Since it seemed to benefit him, I went along with the flow.

In about a month's time I met Bharath. He looked quite self-assured and happy. He was happy with his meeting with Mark. He also spoke to about his offsite with his team and about the high quality discussions they had. It appeared that Bharath was now in the right frame of mind to take the coaching agenda forward and craft good goals and action plans since some his executive concerns had been addressed. Bharath and I therefore spoke at length about his 360-degree feedback and his own situation and on that basis arrived at a broad coaching goal. Bharath's coaching goal was to develop the emotional ability to be more decisive and be able to deal with conflicts that might arise out of being decisive. Bharath pointed out that his organization was due for pay increases and that certainly seemed like a good place to start practicing some of the skills of being decisive and dealing with conflicts. It looked like we were now moving forward.

About six weeks later, Bharath wanted to meet me. He said he wanted to share with me certain developments. It appeared that his Corporate Headquarters had initiated an audit to examine certain accounting irregularities of the past years that had been brought to their attention. The manner in which the whole audit was launched seemed to have rattled Bharath quite a bit. He spoke with a lot of pain and sadness about some of the unpleasant details of how the entire exercise was launched and was being executed. Despite being a career employee of nineteen years standing and now serving as the CEO, is this the way one should be treated, Bharath asked. The lack of grace and respect was causing him a lot of pain and hurt. As a leader he was also concerned about the impact of all this on the organization and the potential it had to distract the team from focusing on delivering results.

This was not all. Bharath also informed me that he was instructed to ask his CFO to leave. Bharath was personally very disappointed but had to take the decision. He was sad that he had to do it and spoke at length about what it meant to him.

Having worked with a Founder who handled all boundary issues all these years, Bharath seemed completely unprepared to deal with this situation. At a personal level, he was deeply hurt with the way things were going. We discussed the many dimensions to this issue and about all the things that Bharath could do. Bharath decided to talk to his Manager about how he felt and register his concerns.

Over the next few days Bharath informed me about his Manager Mark's visit to India and requested that I make time for a three-way meeting. Bharath, Mark and I finally managed to meet face to face. Mark acknowledged that Bharath was now a lot more expressive and direct in his communication. This was making it easier for others to understand him and for him to get their support. He also found that Bharath was now more comfortable dealing with issues directly and having difficult conversations. I thought we had a good meeting. Bharath too confirmed that Mark was happy with the progress we were making.

In the next two months I did not hear from Bharath. I called him to find out how things were going and he immediately responded and asked for a meeting. From my meeting it appeared that the audit and investigations were prolonging and while nothing material seemed to have emanated it had taken a heavy toll on Bharath and the organization. There was too much uncertainty, anxiety and even a sense of losing dignity. As we spoke, it appeared that Bharath was slowly recognizing the inevitable challenges of working in a global corporation, the risks that accompanied a CEO's position and his role in insulating the organization from such events and still deliver results. Having dealt with his emotions and found the time to reflect and gather his thoughts, Bharath seemed a lot more prepared to do what he needed to do as a leader in this situation.

Over the next few weeks, Bharath took some big steps. He was able to take some tough decisions to reorganize the work of one of his team members to address certain competency gaps. Bharath was also preparing to receive his new CFO who was seconded from headquarters. He was keen to help him settle down and learn to work with him. His manager appreciated him for both these decisions and saw it as being very professional. His strengths of being resilient and holding grace under fire were coming in very handy now. His deep loyalty towards the organization and his relationship with his manager had helped him come to terms with the realities and face it squarely. A few weeks later Bharath and I met to bring the engagement to a formal close. We reflected at length about the progress we had made but more significantly about all the emerging agendas that he had to grapple with.

While we were closing the engagement formally, I did have a sense of incompleteness, a sense of walking away while my coachee was still struggling. I therefore offered Bharath continued support for a few more months at no extra cost. Bharath jumped at the idea and accepted it.

A few months later, we did meet. Bharath reported with a sense of pride that the audit was now closed and there was nothing significant that came up, nothing at all. He and his team were feeling happy. The business situation was also improving and he now seemed all set to move forward.

A few weeks later, Bharath called me again and asked for a meeting. Well, it looked like it was not over and settled yet. Bharath reported that Mark, his immediate manager had left the company and he would now report to a new manager and would have to start building his relationship all over again. We had a long chat about this, but this time around Bharath seemed eminently prepared to deal with it and was taking a rather objective view to the situation. Well, he is a new manager and I am sure he will have a new agenda and I will work with him. I will invest all the time I need to, to build a relationship with him, he said.

What is mostly visible to the outside world is the tough and demanding exterior of a corporate executive. What I got in touch with was the huge vulnerability, the anxiety arising from the uncertainty and above all the need for proving one's legitimacy all the time. And to do all this all by oneself is really the biggest challenge. So, it is not just lonely at the top. It is lonely, cold and anxious at the top.

It was clear that all the hardship that he had experienced had ended up shaping him as a better and stronger leader. He was now a lot more mindful about what it took to be the CEO of a global company. Bharath seemed to recognize that the future was bright but not easy and seemed to be quite prepared to face it.

In all this, I had perhaps done very little except being a sounding board, a listening post and at best a thinking partner.

Of course, as always I continue to feel that I could have done more.

# SECTION H

# Enhancing Coaching Effectiveness

# What Contributes to Coaching Effectiveness

## R. R. Nair*

The subject of evaluating coaching effectiveness is neither new nor unique. In the advertising world, from Ogilvy's time, the debate regarding the effectiveness of advertising has been continuing. Training effectiveness is another non-stop discussion topic among HR professionals since the 1970s.

In today's competitive world, leaders at senior levels have to work with and through people. Technical knowledge and domain skills alone are not enough. Leaders like Mayur, Ram and Deeraj seemed to progressively realize the need to leverage coaching to improve their ability to lead inspiringly, influence others effectively, sharpen team development skills including lateral team working, enhance their capability to adroitly balance both task orientation and relationship orientation, and learn, unlearn and relearn to manage one's emotions intelligently.

However, before embracing coaching, leaders like Mayur, Ram and Deeraj are keen to know how formal executive coaching will add to their leadership development.

Coaches and coaching institutions too have been addressing the need to sharpen the measurement of coaching effectiveness. Coaches are aware of the importance of improving the quality of coaching outcomes. Clients have been asking for a more structured process before a formal coaching engagement commences.

*R. R. Nair serves as an Independent Director, CEO Coach and leadership development facilitator for leading global and Indian corporations. He had an illustrious career spanning over three decades with Unilever where he served as HR Director for its subsidiary companies.

The key to evaluating coaching effectiveness starts with very clearly defining the coaching goals. What is the goal? Why is the goal important? What is the current reality? What is happening now? What choices do they have? What is the way forward? Goals must be specific, measureable, offer stretch and be time bound. There is evidence in the case studies to confirm in varying measures some of the key steps in the goal setting and evaluation processes which include:

1. Matching the coachee-coach profile, followed by meeting between the two: A comprehensive dialogue with the coachee to explain the coaching process and to obtain background information appears vital. A variation would be that the coachee is given an opportunity to choose a coach from a shortlist of two or three coaches sponsored by HR. Chemistry is important. I place high importance on building a trusting relationship. Because, essentially coaching is a helping process. HR must ensure that the coach is provided with relevant information including but not limited to career history, job profile, key performance indicators, relevant improvement areas from appraisal data, organization's leadership competency and values, industry challenges and so on.

2. Conduct interviews and carry out assessments: The coach holds discussions with the manager, peers, direct reports and a few significant stakeholders. Concurrent with these dialogues, the coachee completes a series of diagnostics that assess the gifts or strengths, development areas, and leadership competencies. 360-degree survey feedback is an important supplement. Data from the assessments and interviews are integrated into a summary report that is now used for the 'alignment conversation'. In the alignment conversation with the boss, HR Leader who often is the 'sponsor' and is responsible for the leadership development agenda, the coachee and the coach jointly discuss and agree on critical development areas. This would help in setting a clearer expectation besides clarifying the nature of support required from the stakeholders. The frequency of reviews on the progress being made is also established. Post this meeting the coach and coachee will preferably co-create a customized development action plan. The coachee is expected to share the plan with the boss and the HR leader.

3. Implementation plan: The coaching process continues with the implementation of the action plan. Regular meetings are held between the coach and the coachee to review progress toward specific coaching goals. If required, these monthly coaching sessions would involve working with the coachee together with the team and assist in improving team dynamics. Observation of the coachee in real time business events and off-sites would generate rich data about styles and behaviours. This will enable the coach to provide specific feedback or illustrate with evidences on the progress being made.

4. Completion of coaching: Additional sessions if required are held to continue the coaching process including informal phone coaching in between 1:1 sessions. The coaching process is completed by having a review with all the four as in the 'alignment conversation'. A final action plan for on-going development of leadership competencies and the changes needed for the coachee to help continue to reinforce and develop is also created.

Very often, I have seen coaches taking the voluntary step by offering a follow-up contact at 30, 90, 180 days to review progress and to determine any additional needs on a pro bono basis. Care must be ensured that we should not create a 'dependency' syndrome because ultimately the coachee must become self-reliant of one's own actions.

While, the case studies have highlighted the importance of a structured approach to coaching, I believe that coaching is also a personal process in which by dynamically interacting with the coachee, the coach endeavours to tailor coaching to the person's needs. Probably, we should not rely on tests; and pre and post 360-degree surveys only to assess coaching effectiveness. Study the behaviours, actions and decisions of coachees, and link these to actual business outcome. The coach's observations must be rigorous, specific and nuanced. The coachees at all times should 'own' the coaching goals, the agenda and the action plan; in fact the 'content' is owned by them while the coach owns the 'context'. The coachee must be capable of self-directed learning, of finding and diagnosing own issues and the solutions, and rising to take actions based on the new paradigms, and learn again. Successful coaches enjoy watching others grow in a 'self-actualization' sense, provide positive reinforcement, and use the 'Pygmalion factor'.

The case studies also encourage us to raise the question whether all or most of the following conditions for effective coaching process are present:

1.  'insight' is the first one … do the coachees know what they want to better at. Coaching is a self-realization process for the person
2.  second is motivation. Are they willing to invest time and energy to accomplish the results?
3.  third, do they experiment with what they know in real business setting in order to break down old styles and habits and build new ones
4.  do they take accountability to stick with it and are there meaningful consequences for making the change
5.  and finally, does the coachee experience a sense of accomplishment; positive reinforcement, and 'Pygmalion Effect' from the boss

Coaching has been gaining favour as an element of succession planning. Where, when and how do successful leaders get their life-changing coaching? What kind of coaching influences senior business leaders as they make their way to the corner office and then as they sit in it? How specifically have they used the coaching inputs on the job? Settings and ways in which messages have been delivered and insights and reflections are absorbed makes a difference. When a business situation seems dire and desperate, leaders often get scared, more like a deer in the headlight. They focus on the crisis itself rather than on what needs to get done. Coach's crunch time comment tend to stick with the coachees, creating a new way of looking at and thinking about different situations and how one want to tackle them.

I believe feedback both on the coaching experience and on the coach *per se* are integral part of enhancing coaching effectiveness. Would Mayur, Ram and Deeraj have found the following questions on the 'coaching experience' challenging to answer? Following are illustrations only:

1.  What learning really stood out for you over the past months? Where can you apply these learning to your current role, career, and your life as you move ahead?
2.  What has changed for you in your professional and personal life as a consequence to the coaching process?

3.  What did you do that surprised you during the coaching process? Have you unlearned and relearned anything about you as a person?
4.  What was the greatest block or breakthrough of the series? Were there any significant turning points you have identified?
5.  What new habits or styles impacting performance have you taken up as a result of coaching?
6.  What support systems do you have in place to sustain and develop further those new habits?
7.  Did you experience a shift from the 'burden of leading' to 'joy of leading'? How do you intend to celebrate the completion of the coaching journey?

And finally, how about some feedback on the coach? Think of coachees as the 'arbiters' of benefits of coaching experiences presented in the case studies. What would they be saying? Probably the following illustrative set of questions may elicit some insightful feedback:

1.  What were your expectations of coaching? To what extent these have been met by your coach? Not met?
2.  What were the three major contributions you feel the coach has made?
3.  Did you honestly receive value for money for the coaching? How much was the coaching worth?

# 23

# The Power of Public Accountability in Influencing Change

Business Leaders and CEOs have for long leveraged the power of holding themselves and their teams publically accountable for their grand visions and audacious goals. These leaders realize that by making public their vision statements and long-term goals, they are, in many ways, putting themselves in positions they cannot retract from. They also use their public proclamations as constant reminders of the promises they have made. Through this, they perhaps have a far better chance of getting there than if their plans and dreams were top secrets. This time-tested principle applies equally to the world of coaching or counselling or any behavioural change for that matter.

When clients make public their resolve to change, they are not just holding themselves accountable publically. They are also tacitly enlisting the support of their well-wishers to remind them about their promise and nudge them when they falter. As a seasoned business leader, this approach came very naturally and easily to Mayur when it came to changing a few behaviours of his which others found dysfunctional. With such a strong accountability system in place, working with him was a delight for his Coach, Tarun Jacob.

## The Case: Mayur Sets Himself Up, Intentionally

Imagine the scene of a loving mother waiting for her child to come home and show her school report card. The child walks up to her, keeps a straight face and hands over the score card giving the mother a few anxious moments. Then as a palliative she says 'Don't worry mom, I've stood first.' This is exactly the way the Coach felt when Mayur's call finally arrived from London after a couple of days of waiting.

While Mayur was ostensibly invited to London for a long-term strategy review with the Global Head of Operations Mayur very well knew that the real objective was an interview for the position of CEO of the EMEA Region (Europe, the Middle East and Africa) of Das Capital. The new job meant going significantly up Das Capital's Global hierarchy from being the CEO of one country to becoming the boss of seventeen CEOs in the EMEA Region. 'Will Mayur make it?' was the question in the mind of the Coach. There was also another question on the coach's mind—one worse 'Can Mayur cope with the disappointment if he doesn't make it?' This subject had of course come up for discussion between the Coach and Mayur and he had expressed the view that he did not see the prospects being very high. Why was an otherwise optimistic Mayur not sure?

When Mayur's coaching sessions were almost drawing to a close; he received a call from John. Mayur was hardly ready to listen to and accept what John had to say. John has managed to get an excellent job opportunity in his home country and has decided to put in his papers. This came as a big blow to Mayur. Mayur always knew that he was first in the potential list of natural successors to John whenever he moved to another role. He expected such a move to happen a year from now. He also knew that John would have a significant role to play in the choice of his successor. Alas, with John moving our prematurely, the role had opened up at least a year early and John would have no role to play in it. While most decision makers knew Mayur's coaching agenda which was a prerequisite for his elevation, Mayur wasn't sure whether they were ready to accept Mayur in the new job which was opening up a rather out of turn.

Fortunately, Mayur's reflective abilities helped him remain calm. He told the coach 'What's meant for me, will come to me; what doesn't come to me, is not ordained.' Much to the unhappiness of the coach, Mayur even began to plan his life around remaining in India and started planning for his daughter's higher education in India given the changed circumstances. His spouse was happy for the family, but wasn't sure whether it was good for Mayur.

Life was to move on till the call arrived from the Global Operations Head in London. Mayur knew from experience that this would be an important meeting. He made it!

So when Mayur called the Coach, he was listening not just to his words but his tone, the enthusiasm and so on. The coach felt that Mayur was rather sombre, probably more tentative than he normally is. Was it like that little child, he thought? Finally, Mayur said, 'My new boss has now asked me to take your help in preparing my "first 100-day agenda" in Dubai in my new assignment.' The Coach's sigh of relief was interrupted by Mayur's affectionate order 'Please come to Mumbai next week for sure'. Such moments of victory, albeit private are the true source of happiness for many coaches. Mayur's Coach was in seventh heaven!

## Background

Some twenty years ago Das Capital one of the largest Global services companies in the world had set up their representative office in India with the intent of starting a full-fledged operation here. The CEO was looking for students at the Indian Institute of Management with some prior relevant experience. Mayur didn't make the grade till the CEO realized that none of the toppers at the school was interested in joining a new entity with rather uncertain plans. Then it was the CEOs turn to do a hard sell to Mayur to accept the job.

In the next twenty years, Mayur has never looked back. From one desk to the other and from one service vertical to the other he came out of every job with flying colours. Six years ago he was made CEO of Das Capitals largest vertical that contributes to some 70 per cent of India's business. His business has grown several tens of times during these years. Das Capital's worldwide Chairman has several times referred to Mayur's name in his dispatches to hundred odd countries where the company operates. During these twenty years Mayur also spent a couple of years in an international location to get familiar with its global operations.

While Mayur's peers and supervisors recognized and appreciated him, they also clearly knew what the reason for his undoing might be but never got down to giving him that feedback lest they end up demotivating Mayur and thereby inadvertently slowing down his voracious growth engine. His undoing was to do with his style and some of the accompanying behavioural traits. As far as Mayur is concerned, given his performance track record, he believes that his future in the organization will be as meteoric as the past. John and Linda sitting in regional headquarters wanted to find a way out.

John had serious concerns about Mayur's style and behaviour with his team as well as his peers. He felt that Mayur's rather feudal style may have been hugely successful and even appropriate for the Indian geography but may be dysfunctional in an international location. John's greatest fear was that word about Mayur's elevation may even trigger many voluntary resignations at the geographic head levels. Linda on the other hand felt that given Mayur's significant self-awareness and propensity to reinvent himself and given the time at hand Mayur might benefit from an experienced coach. When the coach was selected and briefed by Linda, his recollection about the brief was 'Here is a wonderful copy book coaching case on preparing for transition.' Well-planned in advance, significant developmental areas very well delineated with the promise of high levels of engagement by the sponsor. Now the coach was ready to have the first meeting with Mayur.

There were several surprises in store for the Coach right from the start. Mayur wanted the meeting to be held in his office—which is not always the case with many other coachees. When the coach arrived, Mayur's secretary received him at the reception and asked if he is Mayur's coach—a second surprise. Mayur was sitting with a clean table and buzzed his secretary not to be disturbed for the next two hours or so. The final surprise for the day—Mayur walked the coach to the coffee vending machine and introduced him to a couple of colleagues near the vending machine as 'My executive coach.' The coach merely filed away these unusual attributes—to be revisited many months later!

## Mayur, the Person

The Coach's first observation was that Mayur was rather affable, very self-assured and very welcoming. He wasn't the one to waste time transacting inane courtesies. He was ready, well briefed and waiting to start.

Mayur came from a rather well-to-do business family. His father was sent to Europe to study engineering, but unfortunately returned without completing the course. This fact weighed so heavy on his head that he neglected work, drifted away from his family and fell into financial distress. It would appear later to the coach that part of Mayur's single minded motivation to succeed may have been triggered by his father's economic neglect! It is almost as if Mayur knew in his bones the outcome of financial decline. He didn't want to bring himself and his family anywhere close to this situation! Failure in anything that he picked up was unacceptable and non-negotiable. Life is full of battles to be fought and won one at a time! Sterner stuff and deeply held!

Mayur's wife, a medical professional has a deep understanding of her husband and is full of respect and empathy for him. It would appear that she is the sheet anchor who holds the family deeply bonded and probably acts as a 'sink' for any of the personal or professional frustrations of her husband. It is rare to see a spouse coming from a very different professional background to have such deep understanding. On this count, it would be appropriate to think that Mayur has been as lucky in his personal life as he has been in his professional life. On the balance Mayur is humble and almost reclusively private. From his hectic day he returns to his nest to recuperate. Socializing and more particularly socializing for climbing the corporate ladder is not his cup of tea. There lies a tale. His professional career could well need a more than reasonable degree of socializing which he so meticulously avoids.

## View from Many Mirrors

Unlike some reticent coachees, Mayur enthusiastically accepted his coach's request to speak to some significant people around him who may have deep insights into him as a person and as a professional. Before the ink dried Mayur had already written to twelve of his peers, superiors, direct reports, friends and his spouse indicating that his coach will speak to them. He cajoled them to be frank, truthful and not hold back anything in the conversation. The result was some delightful insights into many aspects of Mayur's life that was not so apparent during the first long conversation. They were large unanimity in the insights shared with the coach. Broadly classified, these would fall under four or five themes:

1.  Seen as a hugely successful person who has created great value for the company through hard work, dedication, commitment and an acute sense of focus.

2.  He shares an extremely high level of commitment to his team. Is willing to go the extra mile and if necessary even fight with his peers and superiors about rewards and furthering the career of his team mates. Thanks to this, many members of his team are now in key positions in many geographies.

3.  Peers seem to have respect for him but not admiration. They felt that Mayur had a need to win every battle that was fought across the table. He forgets the sense of materiality and is unwilling to ever concede a single point to anyone with a contrary view, they felt. This leaves many of his peers bruised, leading to a certain sense of resignation while dealing with Mayur.

4.  One of his direct reports commented 'Come Sunday lunch time and all of Mayur's direct reports are beginning to get anxious. What will be Mayur's mood on Monday morning?' This is a feeling that was shared by many. Mayur could be very direct in his views bordering on being brutal. He would be unconscious or maybe unconcerned about other people being present. His language can become intemperate. When he is angry or in a bad mood it was considered a good idea to stay out of his way. And this comment is made by people who are deeply respectful of him and may have been great beneficiaries of his coaching and sponsorship.

Over Chinese soup in one of the famous clubs, Mayur was reflective while listening to the feedback. It was difficult to say whether he agreed. For once he was reticent. The thought in his mind was about 'moving forward'. Mayur never wastes time on the past; what is important is what can be done with the piece of data. Mayur was clear that he wants to pay attention to changing his behaviour with his peers and direct reports. He was conscious of the fact that it might mean significant change in his day to day style of dealing with them. By the end of the lunch an action agenda was in place.

1.  Criticism in private and praise in public. Simple words, but difficult to practice. Mayur agreed that he will maintain a log about his losing his temper and the use of intemperate language. When

it happens he will also keep a record of what could have been appropriate behaviour under that circumstance.

2.  While dealing with peers, particularly on issues with divergent points of views Mayur will consider 'materiality of the case' before he wages the battle. As a recovery mechanism, if he thinks he may have bruised the feelings of a colleague he will walk into his room after the meeting and apologize. In an extreme case, he may invite the bruised peer for a glass of beer in the pub! (It may be noted that in the current situation, it does not even occur to Mayur that it is his duty to smoothen the ruffled feathers. He thinks that all these are in nature of duties and *nobody* should take it personally.) He was now willing to accept that 'nobody should take it personally' is a self-limiting belief which he must overcome.

## More Surprises

As is customary the coach sent a detailed feedback report named 'Gift of Truth' to Mayur summarizing the spirit of feedback received from all the twelve important others. To the coach's surprise, he found two sets of mails sent out by Mayur the same day. The first one was to the feedback givers, thanking them profusely for the time given and for their candidness. He also committed to them that he was going to work towards changing his behaviour in light of the feedback. The second mail with the report attached was sent to his line boss, two of his matrix bosses in two different geographies and to the Head of HR, Linda. Given the personal nature of the report, one would have expected Mayur like other coachees to put away their 360-degree feedback report somewhere safe. Time hadn't come for the Coach to ask Mayur to explain this rather unusual. He would soon find the answer.

Over the next four months Mayur's log keeping was meticulous. In every situation where he kept bordering on displaying anger, he recorded it in his computer. Every time he couldn't control himself, he logged it in with an appropriate explanation. Every meeting that followed with the coach, typically every month, Mayur would bring in a printout of the log. The recurrence would have been usually statistically measured month and month and analyzed. There was a sharp downward trend but there were times where the situation also got out of hand.

With his peers, his mental discipline to remain conscious about the materiality of the subject of debate that he was about to engage in was adequate to display restrain. For the next several months there was no occasion for Mayur to apologize or to smoothen the ruffled feathers after a stormy meeting. It was simply not necessary any longer. This part of his changed behaviour got easily noticed and most easily appreciated by his peers. Life is not always smooth though. One fine day one of his confidants walked up to him and said, 'Boss, you heard what people are saying? They think you are not as involved in peer meetings as you were in the past. You don't seem to be fighting any longer. I hope everything is alright.' Mayur had to explain to this direct report the fundamental nature of change that he has consciously decided to adopt!

## All the Surprises

Months later, the Coach is now having lunch with Mayur to discuss his first 100 days agenda in his new job. The Coach asked Mayur the inevitable question. Why on earth was Mayur so transparent in sending out his 360-degree feedback report and even his session reports to all his supervisors? Why on earth was Mayur so pleased to present his coach to his colleagues at the work place? What Mayur said was simple yet startling.

## Mayur Reminisces

> Over eighteen years, I have developed a reputation at Das Capital. If Mayur puts his teeth into something everyone knows that he shall not stop short of achieving it. At the same time my style of dealing with people is equally well known. I knew that I can drive change in myself but I wasn't sure what it takes to change the perception of other people. I didn't know how long it will take. I wanted to make sure that everyone knew that Mayur was committing to change his style and behaviour and that that he has a coach who is helping him in this. The fact that I am making a public commitment will help me live up to it and achieve it.

The idea of public accountability certainly paid off for Mayur. In fact it happened much faster that even what John had expected. Eighteen months after assuming his new role in the corner office, Mayur is recounting his experience to another coach who is his coach's colleague.

I had a great experience with the coach. He made me wise to the fact that I must be sensitive to and pick up the feelings outside my cabin. I didn't think feelings are important at the work place. Now I know that emotional regulation is not only important at home. Having said this, do I occasionally blow my top? The answer is yes I do. But when I do that I instantly know that I have crossed the boundaries and I have some undoing to do!

As the Coach thinks about this engagement, he realizes that often times, the coachees are smarter and wiser and are capable of taking complete charge of the engagement and therefore their destiny even if it means that they will set themselves up intentionally. In times like this all that the coach has to do is to follow the coachee's instincts and not question them!

# 24

# It Takes Trust, Time and Team Work to Succeed

The sponsor organizations often have well-identified developmental needs for the nominated coachee. The coachee in turn, more often than not, sees merit in both agreeing and pursuing with the identified needs. Notwithstanding levels of motivation change can take inordinately a longer time than what is planned for and the delta of change is not discernible. Experienced coaches often find it beneficial in putting the early identified goals to question and recommend a mid-course change. They often find it beneficial to put the coaching case to peer review with another experienced coach to delineate the next course of action. As a part of ethical practices of the helping profession, many coaches choose to invest significantly higher amount of time without seeking commensurate compensation. Vishal Nekkanti encounters such a coaching proposition in case of his coachee Ram.

## The Case: Ram Finally Shows That He Can

### Prologue

I was pleasantly surprised to receive a text message one morning from the HR Head of one of my clients—a very large multinational in India. He wanted to share with me some positive changes in Ram who I had coached a year ago. He said, 'Ram has made major strides both in form and content' and went on to explain what he meant by this. The previous day there was a meeting involving Ram's immediate manager, the expat Country Head and the HR Head to discuss his next career move. The next move was not necessarily a move up but a lateral move to another role—not necessarily a come down but definitely not something he had expected. What was most heartening was the way Ram handled the entire conversation with the senior management team. The HR Head added that during the meeting Ram was observed to be assertive in his body language, asked all the right questions in a complete manner and made suggestions in closing and forwarding actions that would help him make the transition smoothly. The HR Head, who had known Ram for a long time and also the one managing talent at leadership levels, was amazed by the changed behaviours demonstrated by Ram. He labelled this as a 'huge change'.

## The Context

The client company is a well-respected large multinational having deep roots in India. They have been around for over fifty years in India and have learnt over time to successfully manage their business and people. In fact in many respects they have come to be identified as one of the most-preferred Indian brands!

The coachee has been a 'one company man' since the start of his career in 1979 as an engineer trainee. Over the years he had built strong technical expertise for which he was well respected by his peers and superiors. Ram aged about fifty-five years old leads the technical, engineering and plant maintenance function for two of the large manufacturing units in South India.

We started with a pre-engagement discussion with the coachee's manager and the coachee to understand the context and the sponsor's expectations. The discussions were cordial and open and the sponsor had great clarity about his expectations from the coaching engagement. This was followed by a 360-degree feedback survey with the peers and colleagues of the coachee. The qualitative 360-degree feedback process was rich and valuable and there was close corroboration between what emerged from the 360-degree feedback and the sponsor's identification of the coaching needs.

We jointly reviewed all the available information, including the annual performance dialogue process of the organization and finally arrived at a list of goals that the coachee believed as crucial for his development.

1. Transition from Managing technology to Leading and inspiring people
2. Ability to assertively communicate his ideas to a peer/superior/cross-functional group
3. To show confidence and inspire enthusiasm in a group (body language)
4. To take tough decisions (for example, differentiation)
5. Task orientation—establishing stretch targets and be more demanding with the internal group

This was quite a daunting list I thought.

Apart from the coaching goals it was important to understand the coachee's issues, needs and aspirations that would influence the coaching journey. While the coachee brings strong technical expertize, he is currently in a role which spans across multiple and diverse areas from technology, to maintenance to shop floor incentives, to maintaining a pollution-free work environment and contributing in a team role in CSR. This multitude of work does pose challenges in effectively managing and delegating.

Ram is at the onset of the next important career move. From being part of the 'Country Leadership group' he is to move to become part of the 'Global Leadership group'.

He would therefore be benchmarked with fellow global leaders.

This will probably be the last career opportunity that the coachee will have before his retirement.

## Strategies and Actions Implemented to Achieve the Goal

The initial coaching sessions focused on the 'story behind the story' and some interesting facts emerged from the conversations.

A good part of Ram's career was spent in technology—machine building, etc., and overtime he had gained high level of expertize in these areas. The organization also recognized and progressed Ram based on the expertize that he had built. So it was more about the depth of technology and engineering rather than the breadth of managing business. The growth of the business in the past in India was also slow and cyclical and did not place undue pressures of managing and leading teams.

The post liberalization era necessitated aggressive growth. The organization got more globally aligned and the Indian organization started receiving more and more global attention, involvement and investment. *Inter alia* connecting and establishing networks globally within the large organization, working in a matrix across and influencing rather than using authority became an important way of working. All of this called for a different type of behaviour which did not come naturally to Ram.

Ram was comfortable handling discussions in groups and management team meetings on matters involving technology as part of his domain expertize. It also helped Ram when he was given the time to prepare and talk or present rather than having to do the same extempore. In matters requiring his contribution beyond his domain and on larger issues facing the manufacturing organization, Ram would either be a silent observer in team meetings or wait for his turn to come to contribute. On most of the occasions his participation in meetings came late by which time the group or team would have moved on to another topic. Hence his contributions in group discussions had minimal impact.

Ram hailed from a humble middle class Indian family and therefore he sometimes came across as being diffident. This was not so much of an issue in the past when there was more of the Indian culture prevailing in the organization. However, in the new order he needed to have the executive presence and stature which meant that he needed to possess the poise, stature and personal skills commensurate with the ability to represent the company in various forms at national and international levels. He needed to display the stature and skills to be the role model for his employees and win the attention of an audience by showcasing the depth of his expertize. He was also expected to be comfortable in diverse and unknown environments, possess cross cultural intelligence and be able to think on his feet.

While Ram had many challenges and many coaching needs it was important to identify the one that would be key or give leverage to Ram in multiple ways and would yield immediate returns. After further probing and dialogue it was clear to Ram that he needed to become more assertive to be able to achieve many of the identified goals effectively. With the assistance of the Coach, Ram was able to articulate his action agenda to be more assertive. They are:

1.  Communicate effectively and completely.
2.  Have a more confident body language.
3.  Effectively participate in group discussions and management meetings.
4.  Be more task oriented with his staff.
5.  Become more performance oriented rather than forgiving and be able to differentiate talent in a more incisive manner.

Using this Ram then created his detailed Individual development plan for the next six months with specific learning actions and reviews. This included a variety of learning experiences such as:

1.  Role plays during coaching sessions on preparing for meetings and participating actively.
2.  Seeking a buddy at work to provide feedback after group and management meetings so that he could further improve his participation.
3.  Reading books on having powerful and crucial conversations and trying to apply the concepts at work.
4.  Viewing web resources on YouTube and other publicly available training videos on communication and leadership.
5.  Seeking opportunities at the workplace to practice task orientation, holding difficult conversations with his people and being more decisive, for example while deploying goals for his staff, conducting performance appraisal of his staff and differentiating talent.

## Coaching at Crossroads

Notwithstanding his high level of self-awareness and motivation and enormous time invested by Ram and me over the next several months, I sensed somewhat slow progress being made by Ram. Now came the dilemma. We had completed the contracted six coaching sessions. From my assessment, while Ram had achieved a high level of self-awareness and had made some improvements in being assertive, there was no recognizable change in him to say that the coaching intervention had made a significant difference. The learning was slow and I was left with this nagging fear of failure at the end of the six sessions. The HR Head during an informal discussion did raise concerns about not seeing any major change in Ram's behaviour and therefore wondered whether it was time to close the coaching engagement There was also this concern raised about Ram's readiness for the next career move and hints that he would not 'make the cut' for the global assessment process that he will have to go through in order to be considered for the higher responsibility. All this added to my sense of responsibility and angst.

It is at this stage that I decided to brief my peer guide. The peer guide, usually an experienced coach often brings completely different points of views from his experiences, being not so immersed in the actual coaching processes.

An objective external view becomes critical and helpful in testing assumptions and approaches since the coach could become subjective during the coaching journey.

The system of peer guidance provides insurance for the client. In a helping profession more help is always comforting and gives a lot of confidence to the coach.

The discussion with my guide gave me clarity on the way forward.

I now decided to understand what's at stake and therefore what are the consequences of failure from the coachee's perspective, as this is a coachee centric development initiative and the coachee's interests are uppermost. Having understood this, the next step would be to help Ram (through coaching) to see the realities and make the transition (whatever might be in Ram's best interest). It also became clear to me that I will have to be more directive with Ram in getting him to go through a quick communication skills training (as there was reluctance on Ram's part about this for whatever reason).

This called for a meeting with the sponsors to understand the consequences of Ram not changing and to seek permission from all parties to give time for three more coaching sessions. I went about doing exactly this.

My meeting with the sponsors helped 'clear the air'. *Prima facie* Ram was still high up in the order in the eyes of the sponsors as far as his technical expertise was concerned. This was very comforting to hear. The consequences of failure were that Ram would not get the next higher responsibility that he was being considered or aspiring for. But then being an Indian organization at heart and given Ram's strengths and his long standing career and contributions he will either stay on in his current role or side step into another role till his retirement. It emerged that there would not be any dramatic change in Ram's life that he would have to deal with. This again was very comforting to hear. I then sought agreement for the three additional coaching sessions.

## The Journey Continues...

I explained the benefits of an external communication coach at this juncture to Ram and received his acceptance to bring in the expert. We had two sessions with the expert where Ram did many role plays on effective communication and received some tips on preparing and actively participating in meetings. In the third session we discussed about the coaching outcomes. Ram made a self-assessment and was quite objective about many of the areas that he still needed to continue to focus on. This self-assessment helped in gaining a better understanding of where Ram stood at the end of the coaching journey. It was also clear that making it to the next career could be a challenge for Ram and that he could look at other opportunities available that could complement his strengths. He was therefore able to develop a more balanced and realistic outlook on what he could do and what he could look forward to.

Having invested the additional effort (of course pro bono) and having provided for specific skill training and having helped him develop a more balanced career goal, I continued to feel that the coaching engagement did not meet the expected outcomes until I received the call from the HR Head.

## Some Reflections...

I found Ram extremely open and sincere in receiving feedback and eager to work on the same for his betterment. This as a result had given him a heightened level of self-awareness of his needs.

With this heightened self-awareness Ram continued to learn and sustain momentum and the change for the better became visible. Ram has started communicating assertively—loud, clear and complete. I have had many discussions over phone and have observed positive changes. He has started to demonstrate positive body language and the feedback from the HR Head about transformation in 'form and content' in the recent senior management meeting involving his next career move is definite evidence. During the coaching assignment Ram did practice task orientation while deploying goals in teams and being decisive in appraising and differentiating and rewarding his people. The transition to the new role seems to be a win-win situation both for Ram and the organization. In the next role he will probably be more comfortable where he will put to use more of his technical strengths. Most importantly, Ram has taken charge of his development.

I could, however, strongly sense the struggle that Ram was going through in making the change of behaviour that the globally aligned organization called for. Given his prior 'strong and in-depth technology silo' experience which was very strongly ingrained in him; making the transition to a more diverse role, mired with networking and upwardly managing was a challenge.

The coaching was timed 'to make him ready' for the next move. Though this was unintended it did cause anxiety in Ram, whether he would 'make the grade' at the end of the coaching engagement and what would happen if coaching failed. Ram was reluctant to go beyond the organization boundaries to learn when required or try out new learning opportunities. For example he did not seek an external resource for improving his communication skills and I had to in a directive manner bring in the communication coach. I also made the effort to understand the consequences for Ram.

On the other hand, I am happy that I engaged with the sponsor and also sought peer guidance.

I am happy that I gave more time and brought in a communications expert.

Having said all this, I believe that lack of early and challenging development experiences can lead to slow learning and personal change. Just imagine—if only Ram had the opportunity early in his career to work more on a front end job or a sales and marketing job. He would probably have been better prepared to take on a variety of roles with confidence.

While it is important to spot opportunities and make them available for the coachee, it is equally important to spot limitations and set expectations with the sponsor and the coachee as required. Finally I recognize that in a helping profession, the coach is also a human being and has his own personal dilemmas and situations. Nothing like having another helper help and give relief in today's stress-filled world.

# 25

# The Pygmalion Effect in Coaching

The effectiveness of coaching depends as much on a supportive boss and an encouraging environment, as it does on the nature of the relationship between the coach and the coachee and the tools and techniques used. To that extent, the so-called self-fulfilling prophecy (a term coined to describe the relationship between Elisa Doolittle and Professor Higgins in the movie *My Fair Lady*) very often plays out in a coaching engagement.

The self-fulfilling prophecy as applied in a coaching context answers the interesting question: 'Should coachees be appreciated by their managers only when they see significant change or do coachees change significantly because they are appreciated by their managers even for their small first steps?'

Unfortunately in Deeraj's case, his manager missed the opportunity of appreciating his small and initial efforts to change and, therefore, in his eyes he continued to be seen as flawed despite his and his Coach Gaurav Mittal's efforts.

## The Case: Was Deeraj a Victim of His Manager's Self-Fulfilling Prophecy?

*Dear Mr. Pritam Kulkarni*

*I had a coaching session with Deeraj Kumar on Tuesday the 6th of December 2011 in Chennai.*

*This was my sixth face-to-face meeting with Deeraj. I have in addition had three sponsor review meetings with you. I have also done an initial 360 and a follow-up 360.*

*Commenced in December 2010, this engagement has gone on for a year. It now appears to be logical for us to close the engagement and give Deeraj the time and space to reflect deeply and act decisively on the commitments that he has made to himself. As Deeraj's coach, I have no doubt in my mind about his intention and ability to do so.*

*Deeraj and I are, however, acutely aware that there are varied perceptions about the level of success we have achieved so far. In my last meeting with Deeraj we discussed this and he has identified one or two additional areas that he will address in this regard. I am confident that there will be greater convergence in perceptions in the coming months.*

*While I am formally proposing to close this engagement at this stage, I have offered to meet Deeraj sometime in January 2012 to know how he is progressing. I am also available to you at any time should you wish to discuss any further about Deeraj's development journey.*

*I thank you for your invitation to work with Deeraj. I thoroughly enjoyed working with him. I especially liked his congruence, his integrity and, of course, his warmth.*

*I enjoyed working with you too. You were warm, understanding and yet rightfully challenging in the interest of bringing the best out of Deeraj. Deeraj fully recognizes and greatly appreciates this support that he has from you.*

*I also wish to thank Veena and Rajeev for their support and efforts in keeping this engagement on track.*

*I wish Deeraj the very best in his efforts in the coming months.*

This is how my coaching engagement with Deeraj Kumar, which extended over a one-year period, finally ended.

I believed that Deeraj had made progress. Deeraj believed that he had made progress too. The follow-up 360 survey also indicated many improvements. However, Deeraj's Manager felt that perceivable change was not evident. The HR Head was also not convinced that there was visible progress. I realized, that having invested the time and effort that Deeraj and I had and having developed a very strong trust-based relationship, I was somewhat disappointed that his Manager was not acknowledging the progress.

I spent several hours discussing this engagement with my peer guide. The rhetorical question that stayed in our mind was this: 'Should coachees be appreciated by their Managers because they change significantly or do coachees change because they are appreciated by their Managers even for small efforts. Can coachees benefit from the self-fulfilling prophecies of their managers?' At least in our minds, the answer was very clear.

So how did the Pygmalion Effect play out in the case of Deeraj? Read on.

Deeraj is the Executive President of a large integrated fertilizer unit belonging to a very large Indian conglomerate. As the Executive President he is responsible for all aspects of manufacturing, projects, associated units and facilities and all that goes with maintaining and effectively running a very large township with thousands of employees in a remote location.

Deeraj is an engineer with over twenty five years of experience. He has always been in the same business his entire career. This business was acquired by the conglomerate from another company a few years ago and as a result of this Deeraj moved to this group. Deeraj was one of the senior executives handpicked by the Group for being groomed for succession based on potential and stellar performance displayed by him. As a part of this potential assessment process the group had identified in Deeraj many strengths and of course some development needs. He was recognized as a very strong results person, functionally and technically very sound, operationally efficient and very fact based in his decision making. He was considered very task oriented and demanding. From the assessment it emerged that in the interest of his future career he needed to adopt a more inclusive style of decision making. It was also felt necessary for him to be inspirational and a lot more sensitive in his relationship with the team paying special attention to his listening abilities.

While the group had very well evolved HR processes it appeared that they were embarking on formal coaching as an intervention for the first time and in that sense they were designing processes on the fly. My initial interactions were with Veena from the Corporate HR function, who was responsible for executive coaching. After my initial discussions I was introduced to the HR Head of the business to which Deeraj belonged so he could help me make the first meeting with Deeraj happen.

In the early interactions with HR, I was alerted that the coachee was not fully convinced about coaching and why he needed to undergo the same but had agreed to meet me. With some effort our first meeting took place in one of their manufacturing facilities. Deeraj was warm, respectful and of course very gracious. From the efficiency with which Security received me at the gate and the way lunch was served it was clear to me that Deeraj ran an efficient ship. From my first meeting it emerged that Deeraj had a set of strong values and beliefs. Loyalty to his organization and therefore having a strong performance ethic was certainly one of them. Being candid emerged as another value for him. In fact, Deeraj seemed to believe that it was dishonest to feel a certain way and say something else.

Deeraj also seemed to believe that workmen and others who were socially marginalized needed to be cared for and protected. Deeraj pointed out that there were certain cultural differences between the organization that he grew up in and the current group and he was still to come to terms with these differences.

Deeraj acknowledged straight away that he was aware of some of the interpersonal style issues that had been pointed out to him and expressed his willingness to work on them. He specifically said that he was keen to find more effective ways to communicate difficult messages and especially try not to hurt people. At the end of the meeting Deeraj confirmed his willingness to work with me. He also expressed his willingness to organize a three way meeting with his Manager so that we could have a common agreement on his coaching agenda.

Having met Deeraj, Veena from Group HR requested that I have a face to face meeting with his manager and the sponsor of this engagement Mr Pritam Kulkarni. This seemed necessary because the sponsor had not met me. She also requested that I meet the Business HR Head while I am there. So I made a visit to Mumbai to meet his manager and sponsor. From this meeting it emerged that his manager's relationship with him was only about eighteen months old and he had met Deeraj perhaps only once face-to-face during this period. Mr Kulkarni acknowledged Deeraj's strengths and spoke about his specific development need which was very similar to what was identified in the potential assessment process. He added that Deeraj had to encourage healthy dissent and moderate his strong likes and dislikes. The meeting was certainly useful but I regretted that the three of us namely, Deeraj, Pritam Kulkarni and I hadn't had a common meeting. I also met the Business HR Head and obtained his views on the engagement. In about four week's time this common meeting did happen albeit via phone. This meeting was more procedural than anything else and we ended up summarizing what we had spoken separately. We were now ready to actually commence our formal coaching engagement.

A month later I went to Deeraj's plant location and spent a couple of days completing his 360 and presenting the feedback to him and discussing potential goals. Deeraj's 360 which covered five of his direct reports threw up no major surprises. He was seen as a very principled leader and effective manager and strong decision maker. He was seen as someone who cared for his employees, who communicated very well and someone with very sound technical knowledge. The one area that came up very strongly in Deeraj's 360 was to do with his emotional regulation. His respondents felt that whenever there was a failure or mistake, Deeraj's reaction was extremely strong and often disproportionate to the situation. His words as well as body language came across as very strong. This seemed to result in people having a huge sense of fear and hesitation in trying anything. It also seemed to make the team climate somewhat tense. His team members also felt that he was sometimes very rigid in his opinions and did not modify his stance and urged that he listened more carefully.

Deeraj accepted the feedback and confirmed that it was in line with his own self-perception and what he had heard from others. He agreed to work on this. He specifically agreed to pay attention to regulating his emotions by controlling his impulse to react immediately.

We agreed to several action ideas and Deeraj agreed to begin practicing them. At the end of this meeting I felt that while his sincerity was not in question he would need some handholding in terms of action ideas given the very behavioural nature of the goal. I therefore did not hesitate to send him some prescriptive tools and techniques to implement these actions. One of the tools that he responded to was an emotional intelligence questionnaire. This questionnaire clearly pointed out that he was overly emotional and not so rational in his approach to solving problems contrary to his own perception and this was somewhat of a surprise to Deeraj because he always believed that he was a rational person.

A few days later Deeraj and I spoke with Mr Pritam Kulkarni to communicate the goals and action plans to him and obtain his endorsement. This call went quite well. Over the next few months we met a couple of times to sustain the momentum of change and incorporate additional ideas.

Deeraj reported that the frequency of his emotional outburst had come down but he was committed to sustaining his efforts. Based on my interactions with him, I was convinced about his commitment to change and his efforts in this direction. While this was going on I was beginning to sense a certain level of anxiety in Veena of Corporate HR about how the engagement was going. From the couple of conversations we had, it emerged that part of the anxiety was driven by her need to be seen as doing the right thing. Part of the anxiety was from some data points being brought to the notice of the Business HR Head, suggesting that there wasn't enough progress. While I was not privy to these data points and was not aware of what was actually going on among the various people involved, it was evident that some form of pressure was mounting and opinions getting formed that Deeraj was not showing change. I was not happy bringing this to Deeraj's attention.

Instead, in my next meeting with Deeraj I asked him how we could validate the progress and suggested the idea of a follow-up 360. Deeraj accepted this idea immediately. I gently asked him how he would like to keep his manager informed about the progress he was making. He immediately offered that I could share this 360 data with his manager. In the course of the conversation it emerged that but for the three way conversation that I had facilitated, Deeraj and his manager has not had any conversation among themselves on this subject. Meanwhile Veena from corporate HR suggested that I have a word with the business HR Head. Not knowing why, I spoke to him. He pointed out that the HR Head in the plant had not been included in the original respondent group of 360 and to that extent the 360 data was incomplete. I tried to explain to him that there was no paucity of data and his exclusion was not material at least from a data point of view. From this conversation, it was clear that he too was not convinced about progress. The number of discordant notes surrounding the engagement was slowly growing and I was certainly not enjoying it. I scheduled another visit to the plant location for my follow-up 360. I met the original respondents once again. This time of course Deeraj asked me to meet his HR Head too. All the respondents confirmed that there was visible evidence of better emotional moderation and expression. They saw him being a lot more sensitive and a lot more respectful. He was certainly beginning to listen more and confirmed that the frequency of outbursts had come down. However, they cautioned that while the frequency had come down the intensity was high when it did occur. They also suggested that he should practice active listening a lot more and sustain the efforts.

Clearly Deeraj had made an earnest effort and it was evident from the follow-up 360. Deeraj was glad to see this and again committed to continue his efforts. With Deeraj's permission I sent the 360 report to the sponsors including Veena, the business HR Head and Mr Pritam Kulkarni. For over a month I did not hear from them. After some follow-up, I was invited to Mumbai for a review meeting. I met the sponsor one-on-one first. He mentioned to me that he had seen my report but said that his impressions were to the contrary. According to him things had deteriorated and quoted one specific incidence to me. I got the sense that he was seeing the glass as half empty and I was seeing it as half full. A short while later Veena from Group HR, the business HR Head Mr Kulkarni and I had a meeting. Deeraj joined via video conference.

I opened the meeting and set the context and shared the follow-up 360 data. Deeraj shared his views as well as his commitment. In this meeting the sponsors including the HR Head said nothing to Deeraj. Clearly I did not want to raise an issue on behalf of the sponsors when they were choosing not to. The meeting ended with my suggesting a few efforts to sustain the momentum.

I had one more meeting left with Deeraj which I had a couple of months later. In this meeting I brought to Deeraj's attention the fact that our perception of change was not shared by his manager. I went on to share the specific incident his manager shared with me. Deeraj was very calm and composed and listened to me and gave me his version of the incidence and why he acted in that manner. After hearing him out, I was convinced that Deeraj was right. Deeraj and I spoke at length about the way large organizations work and the multiple factors that influence decisions about individual careers and the need to be diplomatic and manage perceptions. Deeraj told me that he understood what I was saying but said that he was governed by his internal value systems and while he was willing to change his behaviour he would not try hard to please people beyond doing his job. We of course spoke about these and other organizational realities and closed our engagement. For the next three months I did stay in touch off and on with Deeraj.

I have thought a lot about Deeraj and this engagement. Clearly, emotional intelligence is not Deeraj's greatest strength and I had told Mr Kulkarni this. But he has certainly made a sincere and earnest attempt. Unfortunately, for reasons not known to me he did not enjoy the relationship enough with his manager for him to appreciate him for the modest progress and sincere efforts. The business HR Head seemed to have been influenced perhaps by what his team member was saying about Deeraj. Corporate HR was overtaken by the anxiety of making coaching a grand success through their first and maiden endeavour. Caught in this crossfire Deeraj had little chance of being seen as a success. Maybe someone more political savvy would have handled it differently but not Deeraj. Of course he was too strong to allow any of this to affect him and I was deeply committed to the coachee to see the situation any differently.

What is certainly clear is that a coaching engagement cannot succeed or be perceived to have succeeded unless the immediate manager is willing to acknowledge progress, however little it might be. Coachees often fulfil the prophecy set by their managers.

# An Introduction to Typical Coaching Processes and Some of the Frequently Used Terms

Seasoned coaches normally follow reasonably transparent coaching processes in their coaching engagements. They are also committed to adhering to certain commonly understood ethical standards. They are also trained in a certain uniform and scientific application of skills. In addition coaches are trained to use a range of tools to understand their coachees better.

In the interest of presenting the coaching stories in a crisp and lucid style, we have removed excessive references to these processes, tools and other explanations about the technical aspects of the coaching engagement including the way coaching engagements are set up and the way they unfold, the way tools are deployed and so on. We have instead outlined in this chapter an overview of how coaches typically approach a coaching engagement as well as explained some of key terms in Coaching. Readers may refer to this chapter should they have questions about some of the technical aspects of a coaching engagement as outlined in the cases.

## Coach, Coachee, Sponsor, Peer Guide

The *Coach* is the professional who is delivering the coaching solution.

The *Coachee* is the executive who is participating in the engagement.

*Sponsors* are those within an organization who engage the coach to provide services to the coachee. Usually the coachee's manager and/or the human resources head might be sponsors. They are the ones who pay for the engagement and evaluate its effectiveness.

A *Peer Guide* is another qualified Coach who is available to a Coach for discussion, review, supervision and guidance in a coaching engagement.

## How Coaches Typically Approach a Coaching Engagement

While coaching is a very personal process and therefore does not follow a single universal flow or sequence, and different individuals and organizations have their own unique needs and contexts, there still are certain universal principles that if adopted can help establish robust coaching relationships that work and deliver sound returns.

A typical coaching engagements include three distinct phases—the pre-engagement phase, the engagement phase and the closing phase.

## The Intake Meeting

The intake meeting (also called the pre-engagement meeting) is the first formal meeting where the coach meets the coachee and the sponsor. It is in this meeting that the broad outcomes expected from coaching are discussed and agreed upon. It is in this meeting that the coach and coachee also meet each other and affirm their comfort in working with one another. In this meeting the coaching process is clarified and confidentiality boundaries are reiterated. It is quite likely that some part of the intake meeting will be three way (and sometimes the HR leader may also be present) and some part might be only between the coach and the coachee. It must be clarified that the intake meeting must not be used to assess the credentials of the coach. This should happen prior to the intake meeting. At the end of the intake meeting the coach and coachee must be ready to sign off or agree to start work.

## The Coaching Contract and Boundary Considerations

Coaches typically ensure that there is reasonable clarity in terms of all the boundary considerations in the coaching engagement. This includes things like the broad agenda for coaching, the overall duration, the number of sessions, the data requirements, confidentiality conditions, reporting requirements with the sponsors, commercial terms and review arrangements. Typically these are laid out in a formal coaching agreement or contract.

## Assessment and Feedback

Coaches often require access to high quality assessment data about their coachees and to this end most commonly undertake a 360-degree assessment. Sometimes, coaches may ask for psychometric assessment if they see the need to understand the causes behind behaviours in the interest of helping clients see themselves more completely. Large organizations might also be able to give coaches access to relevant portions of past potential assessment records or development centre reports.

## Agenda, Goals, Strategies and Action Plans

The coaching agenda is the initial hypothesis that the coach forms about the coachee and why he is seeking help and the kind of help he needs. This initial hypothesis is also validated through the expectations statements made by the sponsor of the engagement.

The coaching goal is a specific change objective or a SMART goal that the coach and coachee agree upon. Typically there are only one or two such goals in an engagement.

Strategies are broad decisions on how the coachee will deploy his energies and resources to best achieve the goals. Strategies are often based on what will work best for the coachee.

Action plans are specific time bound steps that the coachee will undertake on a daily basis to achieve his or her goals.

## Confidentiality

While coaches and coachees are firmly committed to maintaining confidentiality, it must be understood in an executive coaching context that there is a sponsor whose involvement and support is very critical in helping the client make changes or learn new skills. Therefore confidentiality must be interpreted keeping in mind the extent of support that clients require to implement their action plans. For example, clients must be actively encouraged to share not only their coaching goals but also their action strategies with their immediate managers. This will ensure back home integration of some of the action plans and also align the coachee's actions with expectations from his immediate environment. Coaching is indeed a very personal helping relationship with a huge emphasis on confidentiality. However in the name of confidentiality, we should not treat coaching as a secretive art where the coach cannot involve and partner with the sponsor in making the relationship a success or encourage the coachee to engage his manager to obtain his support. Of course, all this must be done even while upholding professional standards and the respect and dignity of the coachee.

## Coaching Skills, Process and Tools

Coaches rely quite significantly on the quality of their skills to establish a trust based relationship that helps them understand, empathize and of course challenge their coachees. They also rely on certain psychometric and other tools for diagnosis and facilitating learning and change. They also adopt a well-structured process which serves as a road map to navigate their way through the engagement.

## Spontaneous Support, Referral and Accountability

Quite often, clients might experience the need for a sounding board on a set of issues outside of the stated coaching need. Coaches must demonstrate the flexibility to be available to their clients to address such needs without in any way creating a sense of dependency.

Coaches must also be able to refer their clients to other sources of help to replace or augment their own work. For example, the coach might see the need for the client to seek counselling support to deal with a certain psychologically distressing situation or might see the need for certain structured inputs in a few functional areas that are outside the purview of the coach's competence. All of these would call for referral.

Once the goals and action plans have been made, the coach has to focus on ensuring accountability. Coaches constantly look for ways to ensure that their coachees are held accountable for the plans that they commit themselves to. This can happen through regular reporting of progress by the client or by the coach observing the client at work or through sponsor reviews or follow up 360-degree feedback processes. The efforts of the coach to hold the client accountable ensures that action plans are implemented and end up becoming an integral part of the way the client works.

Coaching engagements are time bound interventions meant to empower clients. They must therefore end in a transparent and mutually agreed manner at a specific point of time. Coaches must focus on bringing the relationship to a clear and sound closure after ensuring that the goals that they set out to achieve have been accomplished in the best possible manner. Sometimes, coaches undertake a follow up 360-degree feedback assessment to capture improvements and changes that the client has made and present it back to him as reinforcement.

In some cases, clients might come back for continued support on a new set of goals and coaches and clients and sponsors need to carefully consider such requests to ensure that the agenda is indeed new and is justified and is not a sign of dependence.

Of course, the coaching engagement is not complete without the coach reflecting on his work and also receiving feedback from the client and sponsor about the perceived benefits.

# Brief Profile of Our Case Contributors

### V. D. Augustine

Augustine is an accredited CEO Coach from Coaching Foundation India. He is able to use his deep knowledge of psychology and his long professional experience as HR resource person to quickly enable clients to unearth their blind spots, develop insights which urges them to move beyond their current dilemmas and issues with ease.

### Oscar Braganza

Oscar is an experienced Strategic Leader, Executive Coach and Consultant with a strong accent towards the Service Industry and the Incubation of fast growing start-ups. He is Advisor to the Marg Group.

### Sharada Chandrasekar

Sharada is an Executive/Business Coach, Consultant and Enabler, focused on building visionary leadership and change management through personal transformation. As an independent, full-time coach, she has worked with senior executives of several organizations in India.

## Ganesh Chella

Ganesh is a practitioner, consultant, coach and thought leader in the field of Organization Development, Human Resources Management and Executive Coaching. He is the founder of totus consulting and totus HR School, Co-founder and Vice Chairman of CFI. He authored the book *Creating a Helping Organization* which was published in 2011.

## Saroja Kannan

Saroja is a marketing professional with over two decades of experience. Among other things, she has spent considerable time training, mentoring and developing people to their full potential and helping them align their developmental goals with organizational objectives and rates these among her significant achievements. She is a practising Executive Coach and is Chief Marketing officer at CFI.

## Anand Kasturi

Anand Kasturi is a Consultant Trainer and an Executive Coach. As a Consultant Trainer, his focus is on 'Services Management' and offers workshops around the globe. He offers his Executive Coaching services to top MNCs in India. He is CEO and Consultant at Anand Kasturi Consulting.

## Savita Mathai

Savita is an Executive Coach with expertise in Talent Acquisition, Learning & Development, Performance Management, and Organization Development. She currently heads HR at the DraftFcb Ulka Group and has had many years of line experience before moving to HR.

## Pradeep Kumar Menon

Pradeep is an Executive Coach and a Consultant specialized in Business Execution Excellence, and in helping companies solve complex problems aligned to strategic goals. He is the founder of Beyond Z Consulting LLP.

## Pradipta K. Mohapatra

With long years of business supervisory experience, Pradipta has the distinction of having coached and mentored over 30 first-time CEOs and large number of senior executives. He is the Co-founder and Chairman of CFI and Chennai Business School Ltd. Pradipta has co-authored the book *India's Global Powerhouses* (2009).

## R. R. Nair

Over the years, through his global corporate management experience and deep commitment in people success, 'RR' has developed a 'coaching mindset'. And the skill sets that enable leaders to identify solution opportunities, set goals, develop an action agenda and achieve their growth plans. He also believes that these skills are not just tools but creative ways of uplifting them in their efforts to improve the quality of their lives.

## Sundar Parthasarathy

Sundar is a coach and a consultant who helps executives and organizations move to higher levels. He was in CEO/MD roles in entities belonging to Cummins and United Technologies Corporation.

## N. Raghunandan

Raghu is a Serial Entrepreneur turned Executive Coach focusing on business transformation through Executive Coaching, Business Coaching and Strategy Implementation. He is Founder and CEO of Disha Strategic Foundation.

## Pradip Shroff

Pradip is an Executive Coach and a Consultant with a CEO level experience of leading Medical devices, diagnostic and highly innovative engineering businesses for a multi-national company and for an Indian company. He is a full-time CEO Coach offering his coaching services to top MNCs and global Indian companies.

## R. Sridhar

Sridhar is an Innovation Coach, Consultant, partner IDEAS-RS. His mission is to help people who want to do things better, do things differently. He has recently launched TickleMeThink—an iOS app for iPhones & iPads to help people get out of their habitual ways of thinking.

## P. S. Srinivasan

Srini is a Consultant and an Executive Coach with expertise in the field of Human Resources Management. He is a full-time Coach working with organizations in developing a culture of coaching through effective leadership styles.

### Kalpana Tatavarti

Kalpana is a Consultant, Trainer and Executive Coach specializing in the field of Leadership Development. Her key focus areas are Women's Leadership Development and Diversity Training, especially in the corporate sector. She is a partner at Interweave Consulting Pvt. Ltd.

### Suresh Thawani

Suresh is a highly accomplished executive and currently Managing Director of Tata Sponge Limited. His thorough understanding of human behaviour combined with practical experience of work-place challenges makes him adept at connecting with the professional situation of his coachees and enables him to add value to their professional life and accelerate their career progression.

### Srinivas Uppaluri

Srini is a Consultant and an Executive Coach with expertize in the field of Strategy, Marketing, Brand and Leadership building. He is a full-time Coach and Advisor for select small- and medium-sized companies.

# About the Authors

**Pradipta K. Mohapatra**

 Pradipta is a business leader with over three decades of experience in managing large Indian businesses as well as British, American, and Japanese Joint Venture companies in India. He pioneered India's foray into modern organized retailing as well as early digital media and e-commerce.

He has experience in managing businesses in IT, Telecom, Entertainment, Pharmaceuticals and Biotech Businesses. He sits in the board of 20 publicly listed as well as private companies in India, Sri Lanka, Japan, China, UK and USA.

Pradipta has led Industry and Businesses of Southern India by Chairing Confederation of Indian Industries (CII). The CII members represent about 50 per cent of India's businesses and industries (www.cii.in). At the national level, Pradipta significantly contributes to assisting industries and government in policy formulation by being members of CII's National Committees on affirmative action, ethics and governance and corporate social responsibility.

Pradipta co-founded Coaching Foundation India Limited (www.cfi.co.in) that pioneers coaching of entrepreneurs and business leaders, as well as Chennai Business School Limited (www.cbs.org.in) that assists young professionals to study management post-graduation in important industry verticals. Pradipta also assists and coaches a large number of first-time CEOs and young entrepreneurs to succeed in their businesses.

He co-authored *India's Global Power Houses* (2009). He did his under-graduation in Chemical Engineering and Management at Bombay University and Harvard Business School. He was invited to be a Fellow of Chartered Management Institute, UK, and was president of Madras Management Association. Pradipta travels extensively around the world and represents India in many global forums and conferences.